Miriam Hoyle Higgins.

KT-583-849

THIS PLOT OF EARTH

A Gardener's Chronicle

By the same Author—

DOWNLAND MAN
SHEPHERD'S COUNTRY
REMEMBRANCE
THE ENGLISH COUNTRYMAN
THE TREE OF LIFE
MEN OF EARTH
ETC. ETC.

THIS
PLOT OF EARTH

A Gardener's Chronicle

BY

H. J. MASSINGHAM

LABORARE EST ORARE
Stephen Harding

Collins
48 PALL MALL LONDON
1944

DEDICATED TO PENELOPE
without whose craftsmanship in the
kitchen my labours in the kitchen-
garden would have been wasted.

COPYRIGHT
PRINTED IN GREAT BRITAIN
COLLINS CLEAR-TYPE PRESS : LONDON AND GLASGOW
1944

CONTENTS

Part One

Part Two

Part Three

PREFACE

THE ICKNIELD WAY on its journey south-west over the Thames into Wiltshire crosses that wild garden on the borders of Norfolk and Suffolk called the Brecks. For some years large areas of them have been in the hands of the Forestry Commission. It has regarded them as a kind of barracks yard for raising regiments of spruces, perpetually standing at attention and presenting arms. Accordingly, the Icknield Way that traverses their gloomy ranks has been re-christened Queen Mary's Avenue. We speak of things and persons, now only "a handful of grey ashes", as "dead as Queen Anne." But the Icknield Way is older even than Queen Boadicea. Its present name therefore might have been better chosen.

But it is characteristic of this century's attitude to the land of England, the attitude of an urban civilization severed from its own roots. It regards its own country with either a melting or a calculating eye, and the one takes frequent advantage of the other. This double view is perfectly represented by the Forestry Commission's actual dealings with the Brecks on the one hand and its renaming of the old road that crosses them on the other. It is in fact a degeneration of the once universal principle of use-and-beauty which governed the conduct and feeling towards the land of the pre-industrial Englishman who still lives in the post-industrial one. But the use has become commercial exploitation and the beauty sentiment. There were many ill doings in our old country-side, but this general principle was as a matter of fact rarely if ever violated, though the beginnings of heresy are to be traced in the Enclosures and grandiose pleasure-parks of the 18th century.

What has this to do with a book about my own garden? In a sense everything. My record as a gardener has recapitulated this aspect of the national history with this difference; that mine has been the other way round. The earlier Englishman looked upon the land of England as a garden for both use and beauty; the later Englishman looks upon it either as an investment or a show. I began with the last and have ended up with the first. Not out of wisdom but hard experience. Perhaps it is the curious like-ness with a difference between my individual and the national

7

history that has made me unable to keep the land of England apart from my own speck of it in this chronicle of a gardener.

Just after I had finished writing it, I was sitting in a hotel in the south-west of England with two men, one a buyer of flax who will look at none but the best, the other a great husbandman who is often to figure as such in these pages. This man was talking to us about soils and ploughing. In his view, the "liveness" of our soils had been reduced by 75% since the days of husbandry had passed away. One of the reasons was modern ploughing. For one thing, we plough too fast; the old ploughman fell into a natural pace and rhythm which did not unduly disturb the structure of the broken clod. The gyro-tiller, for instance, merely stirred up the soil, not cultivated it. Nor is harrowing cultivation, as its name betrays. We do not to-day begin to understand the meaning of cultivation. Except in our gardens. Digging was the most perfect ploughmanship of all because it handled the soil in the correct manner and left the weather and the elements to do the work of disintegration at the proper time. That was probably why the most fertile and productive place in the world is a garden, which at the same time returns all its residues to be converted back into soil. The words of this man, one of the best and most experienced farmers I have ever known, are, I think, a proper heading to this book.

A small portion of it appeared under a different form and wording in *The Field* and *The Geographical Magazine*. I thank the editors for my drawing upon it. I also have to thank Mr. Montague Fordham for an extract from the Tudor Garden Prayer quoted on p. 93. I am deeply indebted to my friend, Mr. Arthur Bryant, who read the manuscript. His editorial comments, witty, severe, encouraging, sagacious and penetrating, have been of the utmost service to me. It is almost entirely due to him that this present book is more simply expressed than any of my former ones. I also have to express an equal obligation to Mr. Milton Waldman of Messrs. Collins whose advice as to the structure of the book I adopted to its great consequent improvement upon the original plan. It consists of three parts. The first and longest describes the garden itself and my interpretation of what a garden should be; the second part brings my conclusions, based on practice and experiment, in relation to the world without, and the third looks away from that depressing spectacle towards hopes for a more harmonious future. These hopes have also sprung from my own experience and are organically linked with the garden. Lastly I have to thank Mr. W. A. R. Collins for his unfailing and friendly encouragements and suggestions during the writing of the book. It has taken me longer to write (two years in all) than any others in a period of authorship covering thirty years, and it is full to capacity with a great many facts. I have, therefore, thought it good to supplement certain parts with illustrative footnotes.

The principle behind the book, one that has never yet been properly ventilated and hardly even suggested, can be stated in a sentence. It is that the fertility of the earth, on which the existence of mankind depends, cannot be achieved without a self-sufficient economy. This I regard as the very first issue, far above all others, that confronts the nation.

H. J. M.

September, 1943.

Part One

CHAPTER ONE

GARDENER'S FOLLY

I. A Gardener Looks Back.

"God gives all men all earth to love,
But since man's heart is small,
Ordains for each one spot shall prove
Beloved over all."

SINCE I have been more or less of a gardener for about fifteen years, this lapidary stanza comes home to me. It might well be a substitute on a sundial for the customary "Horas non Numero . . ." I began with what our forefathers called a "grass plat" in the Cotswolds. It was a duodecimo lawn ramped by dry-stone walls, bordered by a trout stream with a slab bridge and growing in profusion little more than wild strawberries. I thought more then of the wild garden of the Wolds than of anything domesticated. But I still possess the pair of Irish yews I grew on that green pocket handkerchief, and I still grow Alpine strawberries.

I then went on to a proper cottage garden, about twice the size of the plat, on which I toiled and moiled instead of strolled and reclined. But it was in an acquisitive frenzy entirely foreign to the tradition of the cottage garden. In this, of course, beauty is a by-product of utility just as it is in country craftsmanship. But my proceedings were distinguished only in degree from those of the jackdaw who makes a hoard of "glittering prizes" just for the pleasure of seeing them sparkle. I look back upon this horticultural phase with hardly a suspicion of pride. There was something decidedly barbarian about it, a love of flamboyance and colour display rather than of harmonies. Because of my inexperience it was expensive and because of my lack of any reticence or discrimination it was futile. I am puzzled at this peacockism to this day since I had been naturalist, ruralist and topographer of my native land long enough to know better. I had surely studied the manuscript of nature, that "infinite book of secrecy," with attention enough to avoid laying out a garden in the spirit of a Bond Street florist. I went in not for great blooms, like those dreadful dahlias that look like bad engravings in 17th century devotional books, but great masses of bloom, such a riot of it that the subsequent clashes of colour were almost audible. I remember, for instance, that I had a cluster of *Wanda* primulas cheek to cheek with polyanthus of ochre and cherry-red.

As an example of the rawness and possessiveness of my then methods, I recall a certain day (some eight or nine years ago) when I had gone to the annual fair of the local market town. At that time I was clematis-obsessed—and indeed I have never lost my predilection for this noble and spacious family. I was weaving a way among the people who were perambulating the big field hugging great bunches of flowers, heaps and mounds of brightness, as though partakers in a May Day festival or a ceremony of the goddess, Kwang Yen. It was the time when Europe had begun to fall down the steep place and the sight was exhilarating against that vast cloudbank of minatory gloom. Ranged round the field were the tents of poultry, cattle-feeds, dogs, caged birds, vegetables, cutlery, Women's Institutes, handicrafts, flowers, mice, cats (next to the mice), and rabbits. It was a day when a Tyrian exuberance really was beauty and I had already bought some Paisley Gem dahlias and a trio of rock-plants. All at once I noticed a young woman walking about carrying a flowering *Clematis Henryi*, that Great White Queen of the tribe, in a pot. I was so entranced with it that I followed her, so that she began to look askance at me. She had no idea that I was following not her but the clematis. Her looks brought me to and I hurried off to the flower-tent where I secured the last of the Henryis.

When I got home, I resolved to plant it that very night against a little damson tree. I dug a hole, placed the torch in the grass to shine on it, broke the pot and placed the clematis in its bed. I took my hand away to knead the earth into mould when a gust of wind struck the slender stem, toppled it over and snapped it an inch above the roots. I was so vexed that I could eat no supper and felt physically sick for the rest of the evening. It was the fourth I had lost that year. Now for some reason or other I can grow them with ease and at this moment have some fifteen that flourish. But

I have never forgotten that instant when the queen fell off her throne, dead at my feet, and all because I had been in too much of a hurry to set her there.

I left this imitation, almost vulgar, Renaissance cottage garden, already decimated by the first of the great droughts that afflicted our temperate and once rain-blest climate, in the thirties. I had stocked this garden with considerable numbers and varieties of plants, mainly by attending nurseries, seeing something I liked and ordering it without any other thought in my head. But I had an uncomfortable suspicion that what I had really been sowing had been wild oats. It was possibly this vague consciousness of error that saved me from catastrophic follies and excesses when I came to take possession of my third garden. This, with the later addition of another half acre, I cultivate to this day. My previous gardens I had rented; this one I bought and so became a free-holder, a man who belonged to his native land.

It was a formidable undertaking since the ground now open to every rashness of experiment was open indeed, being, when I bought it, a treeless acre of cowsick pasture gently sloping to the floor of the valley. It was a blank sheet on which I might scribble another rake's progress or indite a set of copybook maxims or write something individual. Perhaps the magnitude of what lay before me had a chastening effect. I know that the act of becoming an owner-occupier of a piece of English land proved an educative force in responsibility and obligation which was one of the greatest "point-events" of my whole life. The influence of small ownership went far beyond the immediate requisite of making something good out of it. It extended over my whole mentality and stabilized it by giving me a now orientation. It seemed as though the springs of tradition welled up in me and that, in owning a plot of English soil, I not only became one with my forefathers but had contracted myself to the earth of England herself. It is difficult to explain an almost mystical experience like this, and indeed I failed to do so to my satisfaction in a book I wrote about it eight years ago. It may too sound a little presumptuous. All I can say here is that that experience did take place and that I have been in service to it ever since. As a result of land belonging to me I found that I belonged to the land. As the late Dr. Marett once wrote to me about the demesne of which he was siegneur in Jersey, you can see the sky in the raindrop.

I continued to make mistakes, some of them irreparable, the most injurious of these being the planting of the orchard at the foot of the slope. From the point of view of design, there was really nowhere else to put it; from the point of view of commodity and utility, I could not have chosen worse. Frost, like water, travels downhill and late frost in the much deforested southern Midlands, and in a garden where the protective trees, limes, poplars, wych elm, willow, chestnut, walnut, rowan, began as saplings, is, in the most ominous sense of the term, an Act of God. Though I did have the advantage of a bordering screen of well-established ashes, I have had but three plum-harvests in ten years.

In spite of this cardinal blunder and another as bad hereinafter to be mentioned, my horticultural promotion from tenancy to ownership and from a large pocket handkerchief enclosure to a tiny estate, proved rich in results. In the patterning of my new garden I am surprised to-day by their soundness of right relation both to house and environing fields. John Sedding in *Garden-Craft, Old and New*, quoted with approval by Gertrude Jekyll, declared for symmetrical architectural principles in planning that part of the garden which neighbours the house. You should proceed, he says, "from dressed to undressed and so to the open country." This was a compromise between the traditional formality of the old English garden with its walled rectangles and the naturalistic periods following the days of Capability Brown, itself put out of fashion by the Victorian coloured glass effects on the lawns. The William Robinson romantic school, in its reaction from the monstrous carpet-bedding of the Victorians, what a gardener I shall describe later (p. 126) called "jam-tart" gardening, went rather too far in its surrender to the seductions of wild nature.

How far it did go may be measured by looking up what Robinson had to say under the heading "Ivy." Robinson was a genius and went to war against the fancy pedantry and philistinism of Victorian gardening, with the gusto and gallantry of Taillefer at the Battle of Hastings. He restored an authentic taste to English gardens in his crusade against the pincushion bed, the carpet pattern, the coloured alphabetics of lobelia, alyssum, geranium and variegated grasses and all the shop-window stuff of the sham picturesque. But he gave those directions about the wreathing, training, piling, banding, edging and festooning of ivy, that python among plants, which overshadow the most genteel atrocities of the carpet-bedder.

His advocacy of ivy helps me to understand why the horticultural formalists spoke of the contrary school as "vulgar," and he does tend to condemn a geometrical layout, not because it is ugly but geometrical. Not only carpet-bedding but Milton's "nice art in beds and curious knots" must also fall under the sweep of his scythe.

Sedding's balance between the formal and the natural schools was thus a judicious one, sensitive to the virtues of both. I can therefore take a certain credit for having acted upon his precepts before I had so much as heard of him. My previous cottage garden was a parody upon that unerring rightness of instinctive taste which is the mark of the genuine cottage garden and was doubtless a legacy from the organic folk-art of the peasant. Thus, my conversion to a true canon was due simply to my having become a property-holder in land. As Arthur Young wrote when he had repented of his impetuous and short-sighted campaign on behalf of the Enclosures—"The magic of property turns sand into gold." So it was with me; only my magic was from an ostentatious imposition of my will upon the earth to a consideration of the not conflicting but dissimilar claims of a house in the country and the country round a house. The word "consider" in the sense immortalised by "Consider the lilies of the field" was the most valuable thing I learned from the acquisition of property. Not only had a rectangular house to be considered and the fields at all points of the compass about it but the slope between house and fields. This southern slope demanded a greater unity of treatment than a garden on the flat would have done. But it exacted the more not the less complexity because the transition between the architectural principle of layout at the top and the freer one at the bottom had, so far as possible, to conceal itself. This could only be done partly by slow gradation between the formal and the free and partly by modifying the one through introducing some element of the other.

The rigidity of the paved terrace separating house from garden proper and bordered by a low stone wall, I softened by growing clematis, fig, certain climbing roses, Ceanothus, jessamine, Cydonia and Viburnum up the south and west walls. These types of shrub or climber could be trusted to drape but not smother the linear outline of walls. In the middle of this southern front, I threw out a Muscadine vine on thin iron rods between the house-wall and the rockery walls, one on each side of a short paved walk at right angles to the terrace. These rock walls I made very low and broad.

At their ends they were continued into parallel herbaceous beds and the paved path between them ran into a grass walk. This interplay between stone and grass I followed up in other parts of the garden by making stone paths as connections between both beds and the grass walks which to me are one of the delights of any garden. From the east wall of the house to the whitethorn hedge I built later a high stone wall to shut out the north wind but, where the long beds ended some distance down the slope, I replaced stone with wattled hurdles. Of these long straight beds I had several, but I mitigated a too severe classicism of form by making their rectangles irregular. I think that on the whole this method of dividing a bare uniform piece of ground into three lawns of different sizes, divided by low walls and long beds and grass paths and in one instance by a continuous long line of climbing roses separating the largest lawn from the kitchen garden, the soft fruit cage and the espalier apples, must have been fairly successful. Ten years later, I have not wearied of it nor has an alternative design occurred to me.

What really were happy strokes were the terrace that a little raised and isolated the house and conformed to the principle of old gardens (usually a few feet lower than their houses), and the rockery walls. By forming part of the general pattern and becoming definite bridges between house and garden, they avoided the appalling irrelevance of the rock-dump or rock-cake set in a lawn or cleared space (often enough in a stoneless region). This pretentious fabrication is dignified by the courtesy title of "rockery." The anonymous letter-writer in the book, *No Music in Particular* (1943), describes the average rock-garden as

> "a brutal jumble of contradictory forms, a geographical nightmare about as inspiring to the true lover of Nature as a collection of postage stamps."

Yet an authentic rockery which fulfils a definite purpose in the garden and takes advantage of some natural feature in it, such as a retaining wall to a bank, can be one of its greatest beauties.[1] But to stone a garden in a stoneless region or where there are no stone walls is to cast a stone at beauty.

[1] A friend of mine in the same village has taken advantage of the long wall of a stone barn bordering his garden to lay out a rock garden of great elegance and propriety.

The orchard lay behind the wattled hurdles and the "shrubbery" in front of them. I tried to make the latter as gay and rich as possible with Siberian crabs and deep purple lilac and barberries and cistus and yucca and the charming kerria and forsythia and cotoneaster and Philadelphus and various species of free-growing old roses. The orchard grass was abundantly planted with daffodils, narcissus, iris and others, while its bordering beds were stocked with densely foliaged stuff like Bocconia, Michaelmas daisy, Siberian iris, elecampane, Daphne, pink Oriental poppy and the like, also with suckers taken from my species roses. My little Museum or "Hermitage," built on the model of Gilbert White's, I set up in the middle of the orchard. I even at one time carved out a rectangular pond in which a grass snake used to disport himself and surrounded it with cistus, flag, sweet briars, low flowering shrubs and divers creeping plants. This was balanced on the other side by a nuttery and a bog garden of *primula malacoides*, Kaemferi irises and other plants. Only the nuttery now flourishes, but the screen and drapery conceal the failure of the pond and the elm seat beside it is still seatable.

Another way I conceived of dealing with the slope was by colour. If there is a fixed association which a slope suggests it is travel, and so I attempted to group and arrange the flowers down the parallel herbaceous beds from the rock-walls according to an itinerary of light, volatile and what are called "petunia" colours. For both a slope and its crown have one a mobile and the other an aerial significance. What could be lighter than fleeting gossamer or whiter than mountain snow ? Of old stood freedom on the heights and the essence of freedom is release from fixity and bondage; when the butterfly emerges from the chrysalis it starts upwards. The summit of a slope also connotes purification, a shedding of secondary and complicating inessentials for the primary and elemental. So each of these long down-flowing beds should have a white rose for its headpiece, while the stream of flowers that glided airily down the slope should have a certain fragility, a cool and pristine quality. The blending of lilac, rose, primrose, mauve, light purple and various pinks and whites, was for the eye to be a butterfly among them and make no stay. On the other hand, when the ends were reached and the beds turned right and left, the eye should be caught and held by more potent and earthier colour-values—orange, scarlet, red and gold with admixtures of deep purples. Their intensity would call stop. The fierier lilies, blazing peonies and Oriental poppies, richly autumnal rudbeckias, helleniums and dahlias with a carpet of old red clove and an edging of ranunculus, zinnias, and anemone, those creeping earth-flames, with bold standard hybrid tea-roses at intervals along the borders, these would be like an inn at the end of the journey.

So I experimented in one way and another, making one bed of blues, whites and yellows after a recipe of Gertrude Jekyll, a visit to whose Munstead garden made me properly ashamed of my former barbaric phase. Another was of delphiniums among tufts of Madonna lilies and single sprays of various Michaelmas daisies with mounds of the Acris variety in front and cascades of the Climax behind. Up in the north of the garden I made a long rose bed in front of a double screen of sweet briar and a line of balsam poplars. Here I placed the strong colours in the centre and gave them light wings so that a crescendo should be reached from either side and the hues of a dwarf arras of anemones in front be "mingled and opposed." Among my beds of roses—and these gradually increased until they far outnumbered all other varieties of plants— I sowed in a quilt of violas and pansies, especially Engelmann's Giant, and this prismatic flooring I have never regretted. With the anemones I had for the first few years a spectacular success. Some of the corms produced as many as ten blooms to a plant and not a single day in the year was anemone-less, even garlanding old Hiems' bald and icy crown. I went very far in those early years; the stakes were painted jade green or light Brunswick and even the tying strings were rubbed with earth. I rejected all yellows from the Gertrude Jekyll bed which failed to come up to or tone down that excellent thing, a translation in terms of colour of Cordelia's voice. I attribute the fact that I gradually abandoned large-scale colour-schemes to their unsuitability for a small garden. In it drifts of colour make for paucity of it, and the sovereign purpose of all small gardeners should be variety, variety in *everything*.

Throughout this evolutionary stage of self-education, I was wholly preoccupied with making this new garden true to itself, to the house and to the landscape, to the very sheep and horses and cows on the other side of my western boundary that kept on browsing on my infant hedge and breaking down my wattled fences. But I was still sufficiently in thrall to my previous self-will to be oblivious to what was paramount over all. That was the nature of the soil. I seem to have regarded it as a kind of large-scale map into which I stuck little coloured banners. In other words, I was behaving just like the abstract urban planner who works out his preconceived schemes from the top downwards. Not for him to regard the vagaries of human nature, to study traditional social rhythms and patterns and consider the inward life of the individual. The soil of my new garden was simply a receptacle for plants and trees inserted within it according to certain groupings and arrangements. You placed your seed or plant or sapling into this conveniently yielding surface and waited for time and the inevitable cycle of growth to materialise the mental Utopia.

Now the earth is a patient creature, and she is ready to put up with a lot, especially from modern man. For his scientific ideas of conquest and mass-production are allied with inorganic methods and a predatory philosophy based, singularly enough, upon his more recent concept of nature as an intricate mechanism of pre-dictable actions and reactions. But there comes a time when that patience is exhausted. The earth goes sick on us or it dies on us; the winds sweep over the plains carrying the soil with them; the waters rush down the treeless mountain flanks carrying the soil with them; the plagues and parasites multiply; the blasted heath of Macbeth becomes the dust bowl of the American continent and the wilderness that once blossomed like the rose becomes as barren as the craters of the moon. "Misapplied science," wrote Jacks and Whyte in *The Rape of the Earth*,

"has brought to the world's richest virgin lands a desolation compared with which the ravages of all the wars in history are negligible."

Nature is having the last word.

This modern earth-history has been in a sense the history of my own pinshead of land. I do not mean that my ambitions for a pleasure-garden of rather subtle and intricate colour-schemes have ended in soil-erosion. On the contrary, the garden is twice if not thrice as fertile as it was when storing up fertility under pasture. What I mean is that every garden begins with its soil, just as every civilization begins with its peasantry. To neglect these foundations will in the end topple the superstructure. Though I did not actually

exploit my soil nor overdrive it nor omit to give it organic nourishment, yet in this demi-paradisal planning I was walking with my
head in the stars but without my feet on the earth. I failed to study,
to educate, to humour the nature and capacities of my soil and to
relate to its inherent faculties and variations the kinds of plants
I put into it. My garden, for instance, is hospitable to Great Scot
and Majestic potatoes and will just tolerate one of the Arans, but
uncompromisingly rejects every other kind. Just as plants have their
preferences for one kind of home rather than another, so soils
are like human beings in the sense that they have a welcome for
some and an antipathy for others. Is not this very natural when we
consider that soils are in part the ultimate composition of what
they support and that plants and animals and men (however they
may forget it) draw more than their sustenance from it ? Infinitely
complex is the interwoven fabric between what is upon and what is
below the earth, such as modern science with its separatism and
impoverishment of life into physico-chemical elements has failed
to grasp. It was not until I had properly elaborated my compost
system—and that took some years—that I could claim to have come
to terms of any real comprehension with my acre and a half of soil.

My retrospect of my former gardening career does in fact
largely resolve itself into a tally of losses. Perhaps one learns more
from misfortune even than from enthusiasm and assiduity; at
any rate I am sure that I am a better gardener in a chastened and
comparatively poorer present than when my garden was a blaze
of glory. Though I cannot but look back in somewhat of an elegiac
spirit, yet in understanding I am the richer for what I have lost.

The greatest of these losses have undoubtedly been my lilies,
in the cultivation of which I was extravagantly lavish. I might say,
indeed, that I once grew almost every lily that can be grown, though
even I had the sense to recognise that I could not in my sandy loams
and clayey loams with seams of unmitigated clay grow a lily like
the woodland Giganteum. It gives me a certain pleasure now to
enumerate the lilies that I did grow, the kind of pleasure that
Odysseus had when, at ease by his hearth, he related to Penelope
(or Othello to Desdemona) the surprising adventures and pomps
of the past. For the very names of these lilies are a pageantry and
bright procession in themselves—Thunbergianum, Testaceum,
Pardalinum, and again, Umbellatum, Chalcedonicum, Canadensis
and Auratum, and once more, Concolor, Croceum, Monodelphum,

Speciosum, Longiflorum and Superbum. Nor does this illuminated inventory comprise all the famous beauties and royalties that once graced my garden party, but names like Brownii and Hansoni hardly do justice to this Boccaccio company. And where are they now, the shining ones ?

I need not altogether round off the epitaph with—all, all are gone, the old familiar faces, princely but familiar. I still have one bed the length of the least lawn which is fairly well stocked with Regale lilies and among them a group of the white majestic Crow's Hybrid. Panther, Candidum, and Pyrenaean lilies, the survivors of a floral regiment that might have fitted Andrew Marvell's military parade, remain faithful. There was a time when, the day before the garden was open for the District Nurses Fund, I had six hundred white lilies in bloom. Had the Gardens of Aratäm— as described in that enchanting book, *The Gobi Desert*—better ones? Came a mighty rushing wind and the lawns were strewn with a snowstorm of their petals.

> "With the great gale we journey,
>   That breathes from gardens thinned,
>   Borne in the drift of blossoms
>   Whose petals throng the wind."

But what was that trifling annoyance to my present and permanent penury, when the earth has literally swallowed up my " garden of lilies" as the mountain did the gallants and fair women of Pompeii ? I no longer trouble to devise paper-nightcaps against the May frosts for the Candidum and Regale stragglers from these files of former Junes.

Irises have been other irretrievable casualties. I once possessed a number of highly aristocratic irises. Some of these came from the celebrated garden of Professor Seligmann, where they were perfectly grown in square enclosures among flagged courtyards; others like Purissima, the radiant Golden Hind and the strange and beautiful Susiana, the Mourning Iris, with its grey falls and head slashed and blotched with purple, were given me (and more than a few had R.H.S. and Iris Society labels) by the daughter of W. R. Dykes, the great iris scholar and breeder. Though I could not grow these and their peers among flags, I could and did under and among low grey walls and the Kaemferi round the borders of the rectangular pond. I still have square beds and crisp straight beds of English, Dutch, Spanish, Siberian and other irises among stone. and the little Netted Iris and the dwarf flag, *Pumila*, are still with me to colour and embolden the young spring. But nothing is left of these *grandes dames* among flowers except a few Kaemferi and whitest Purissima, that votaress of the moon. When she flowered with Golden Hind, could not one rather call them "blest pair of Syrens"? Truly my soil has been a hard stepmother to bulbs and corms and tubers.

The stern winters of late years accounted for all my dahlias, even the experimental single ones I bred myself. But it was a hostile soil that all but ended the polychromatic days of Cottage, Parrot and lily-flowering tulips, while of all that brave company of the lilies of the field, Caen, St. Brigid, St. Bavo, Fulgens and Feu Superbe, not one remains. What I regret most, perhaps, of these bygones are the Water Lily Tulip that came in the rear of winter rather than in the front of spring, the slender and elegant Clusiana or Lady Tulip and our own native Sylvestris, the best of all tulips because it is our own. Our native anemone, the Pasque Flower, the windflower of the open downs that I have found wild both in the Cotswolds and the Chilterns, I still grow, the only anemone, besides Blanda and Apennina, that will stay with me. But I can only maintain it by constantly replacing it—it survives on stepping-stones of its dead selves. Yet in the village a quarter of a mile away it ramps like a weed.

There were other examples of wasted obstinacy on my part, of a high-handed will-to-beauty, of trying as it were to grow wheat in Westmorland. Certain geniuses among families of plants I strove officiously to keep alive against the decree of my soil. *Gentiana Farreri* was one, with its grassy leaves and lustrous pale blue beakers, which drawing a limeless charmed circle about it could not save. Old Nick Culpeper said that you could cure the diseases of plants "by Sympathy," but preserving the shell of my morning egg for this jewel proved no armour against the estranging soil. *Salvia farinaceae* with its blue stalk to match its blue inflorescence was another of my hospital cases. The rather rare scarlet tufted Cardinal Flower from Texas faded out for lack of what it might have been presumed was the last thing it wanted—shade. The borageworts, Onosma and Lithospermum, would have none of my hospitality. My yellow tree-lupins and the tree mallows I grew in memory of their incontinent growth on the Bass Rock, they "liked it not and died." The Cape Hyacinth that used to shake its waxen bells among my white roses would have none of my ministrations. My white Everlasting Pea that used to twine among the delphiniums like epiphytes in the branches of jungle trees reverted to a dingy mauve. My two multicoloured flowers, Sparaxis, the foxglove of the Cape whose flowers emerge snowflake-fashion from reed-like foliage and little Portulaca that asked and received all the sun that even a buttercup can drink, here were two more brilliant travellers that joined the narrow cemetery of my acre.

I once had a little city of Eremurus spires, both *robustus* and *Bungei*, but they live in my memory less sharply than the loss of nearly all my Allwoodii Dianthus, many of them given me by Professor Tonks. In *Some Flowers*, Miss Sackville-West describes how on a visit to Robert Bridges at Boar's Hill she saw his two long bands of Cheddar Pink which he wrongly commemorated in

"Reading the Odyssey in my rock-garden
I espied the cluster'd tufts of cheddar pinks."

They were not in his rock-garden, but they were in mine and now they are there no more. And I have seen them growing where I am sure Bridges never did, in their home on Mendip. Let the Cannas go and even the Peruvian lily and even the Carpathian hairbell, but oh, my cheddar pinks! That Eastern star, the scarlet verbena called "Pleasure of the Kings" and first gathered from the walls of Persepolis, well, I am not a king and so its pleasure after a brief season was not for me. But why should I lose the Crown Imperial which, for all its name, is most at home, like a certain other King, in the plot of the cottager?

The record of such a holocaust, its victims gathered from all the flowery spaces of the world, would seem to point to me as a gardener indifferent enough. But I am inclined to think that it was the pitting of my will against the disposition of what it was exercised upon that was my undoing:—

"He that bends to himself a joy
Doth the wingèd life destroy."

My end was not wealth and the power to be derived from it, which is the only end to which modern civilization has hitherto put its enormous technical and mechanical resources. Yet in a sense I was using my ownership of my bit of earth as an instrument for the acquisition of a certain kind of wealth. I was tending to specialisation and forgetting the whole in the part; I was separating the cultural aspect of my activities from the organic. This has virtually been the purpose and the failure of our civilization. In my particular and private sphere it was mine. I failed and from that failure must be dated a radical change in my orientation.

II. A Gardener Looks Forward.

"Slowly, insidiously, while we have battled with deadly bugs, a new enemy has intrenched itself behind our lines; and in the struggle for health we have become like those wretches who bind themselves to a domestic tyranny in order that the same thing may not be imposed upon them by a foreigner. This new enemy is STERILITY: the sterility of our soil and therefore of our crops; of our crops and therefore of men and beasts. In vain we build Maginot lines of hygiene against the hordes of harmful bacteria: slowly but inevitably Life itself is on the ebb. Mankind is so surely dying that generations to come may like enough grow their first hair grey or white, and every child among them need spectacles from infancy."

REGINALD REYNOLDS: *Cleanliness and Godliness.*

THERE WERE of course other factors involved in this change of attitude. One was the war, which exposed the complete futility of all that modern society had devoted itself to achieving. Another was a very severe accident that removed from me all control over and indeed interest in my garden for a period of years and restored me to it minus a leg and with only one really workable arm. My faithful Dickory had been my under-gardener from the beginning in the work of construction and I his in all practical operations. But now he spent only half instead of all his working time with me. I was forced, therefore, to look upon my garden with new eyes, as the nation was forced to look upon the heritage of its native land. No longer could it be a gambling-board in site values nor a playground and escape-mechanism. It became a life-belt to save it from drowning in the sea of its own previous folly. The nation set to work farming its misused and neglected estate; I set to work farming my flowery one.

Yet this gives only a very partial and short-term estimate of a process of revaluation which the national and my personal tragedy only precipitated. The true causes lay behind both. During the years of my experimental work with my holding, it never occurred to me that my garden could be, much less ought to be, other than a pleasure-garden with a utilitarian annexe in the shape of fruit and vegetables. Why should it have done? Even that fairy god-mother among gardeners, Gertrude Jekyll, who made Munstead Wood into a work of art, hardly thought of it as more than a pleasance. What else is it but "a fine and private place" of delectation and refreshment? Even God so thought of it as He walked among the flowers "in the cool of the evening." We speak of "the flower of" something as the very crown of excellence, especially we English whose traditional poetry is garlanded with flowers.

Indeed the true tradition of Paradise (only the moderns have wrenched the Golden Age out of its matrix in the past and thrust it forward, a dreary Utopian substitute, into the friendless void of a distant future) is the perfect garden. But there's the rub: Adam did not stay in his ivory tower but had to leave it to cultivate the wilderness in the sweat of his brow. The hoary myth is a realistic avowal of what over-ripe civilizations are only too apt to forget, the dependence of short-lived man upon long-lived earth. No civilization has been so quick to forget it as our own. As a result, it has mechanically generated an unhappy, rootless, restless being who has done no good to himself and his fellows by ignoring the fundamental truths of man's conditional sojourn upon and tenure of the earth. For what actually happened when man became uprooted from earth at a definite point in time, namely that of the Industrial Revolution? He ceased any more to be either a spiritual or a natural being and his affairs have progressed from a chaos of appetites to a dead end. Out of this he is vainly trying to find a way by mere organisation, by mere machinery. Do they not deny even more flatly those spiritual and natural essentials of his being for the want of which he fell into his modern disorders?

This is a large issue. I cannot labour it here. But the making of a beautiful garden is a spiritual undertaking, occupied, like the work of any artist, with the creation of beauty. Let me put away any hedonist implications or escapist insinuations which the word "pleasure-garden" might suggest. But can the artist or rather does the artist ever create beauty in a kind of vacuum, without relating it to truth or goodness or the daily needs and works of man? I doubt it, and with all great works of art I am certain that he does not. But the mark of the Industrial Revolution was that it did so separate the arts from the crafts. Beauty was parted from utility, aesthetics from the common and ever more and more desperate needs of humanity.

So it was with my earlier years of manufacturing a flower-garden on my God-given acre. If the task began on the spiritual plane, it certainly degenerated into the ornamental. Considering my losses, I was struck with an uncomfortable idea. Had I been a rich man and built myself an acre-wide conservatory with elaborate devices of regulating temperatures, admitting and excluding light and of protecting my plants through all their stages of growth from analysed and sterilized potting soil to fertilizers and spraying machines with a host of horticultural gadgets, I might well have preserved all the flowers that are now mingled with the earth. And at what a price—the substitution of a glass-house exhibition for that beauty that comes only from man and nature working hand in hand. All the time I had been working against nature. Nature is never ornamental except upon a basis of use. That is why the true craftsman can never be mechanised, nor harnessed to the industrial machine. His inherent closeness to nature is an intimacy sprung not only from working in the materials of nature but achieving his beauty as nature does out of a foundation of utility.

I think that what gave me a truer idea of what a garden should be was a spring evening in my orchard. It happened to be a late season when an obdurate winter had been met and routed by an irresistible spring—exactly "bare winter suddenly was turned to spring." Consequently, the earthen daffodils had not given place to the skiey fruit-blossom and there were daffodils, narcissus, primroses, "frore-chaps" (as here we call the pied fritillary hanging out its Chinese lantern) all flowering with plum and pear and cherry and even the first of the apples in blossom. The sun-disc was balanced on the western hill and despatched long horizontal shafts to penetrate the yellow trumpets and render them transparent, while the blossom above was flooded by a great tide of gold. The grassy floor, the host of white and golden flowers, the branches that were both white and gold, the pink Siberian crabs overpeering the wattled hurdles, the very hurdles themselves, all were shot through and transfigured by a light that made unearthly their own. It was a veritable marriage of heaven and earth, a consecrated moment out of time in which experience was blended with promise, the seen with the unseen and the poetry with the service of the earth. Earth had seen a vision at the same time as heaven had visited the earth and so time itself was for that moment eternized.

I do not myself pretend that I saw a vision of what kind of a place my garden should be. These things come slowly and empirically, and I should have seen nothing had I not become predisposed to see it. By no longer believing in ornament except as a flowering out of utility, I was making an atonement or at-one-ment for urging my land to do what was not its nature to do. I saw it, that is to say, as an interdependent whole in which all the parts should interact with one another as a co-operative organism. Each section of the unity could not only contribute to another but receive from it something of the virtue and purpose of that other. Flowers, fruits, crops, all were indispensable members of a single commonwealth. To sacrifice any one portion of ground or type of plant for the sake of benefiting a different one would be to split the synthesis and unbalance the whole concept. What is more, this method of acting would defeat its own end, since beauty could not surrender to utility nor utility to beauty without mutual disadvantage.

I did not theorize about this. I proved it. Thus I had the sense based on experience not to fall victim to the imbecile campaign (instigated as usual by the urban busybody) for the ploughing up or cultivation of lawns. Personally I do not see how a kitchen garden, corresponding with the arable of a small holding, can possibly be kept going without a lawn, corresponding with the permanent grass of the holding, provided that the plot, whether called garden or holding, aims at some kind of self-maintenance. For one thing, a lawn is an invaluable source of protein; for another, grass cuttings make a very handy fertilizer, especially for raspberries; thirdly, they are a protection against drought and, next, superior to any chemical for speeding up the decomposition of the compost heap. Lastly, lawn cuttings and soil are all enriched by earthworms, which are killed by artificials. Worms not only till, drain and air the soil ; they are humus-makers of the first order, and, as Darwin showed, deposit 0.2 inches every year of earth loaded with humus and plant-food. Since compost is the garden-clearing-station, this store is invaluable.

I ploughed up none of my trio of lawns nor did I abandon a single bed of flowers. Of these, large and small, I have some forty, still, in spite of labour more than halved, almost weedless. But, like a man reshuffling a pack of cards and mixing kings and knaves and mere numbers, I abolished caste divisions between flowers, fruits and vegetables. On my second lawn the flower-beds ramping my sunk garden, on whose bottom roses grew like *Rosa canina* in the hedge, had always struggled against adversity. In the end I let them go to grape hyacinth which made strips of southern sky above the green hollow. But in the summer and autumn I settled them with the more decorative haricots. They had to be so because I look over them to the landscape. Its composure and magnanimity, the serenity of which makes the multicoloured crops in the foreground and the changing hues of the hills in the background the greater enchantment, are exacting.

There are too endless devices to be used in bringing fruit or vegetables to flowers and *vice versa*. A border of lupins to a kitchen garden, for instance, performs three offices in one; it saves space in the orthodox beds, enriches the soil with nitrogen and gladdens the place of bread alone. A similar service is granted by planting nasturtium round the apple trees. But as there is one glory of the sun and one glory of the moon and to mix up cabbages with kings may compromise the identity of both, discretion is necessary in these meetings between different classes of plants. A garden must not degenerate into cosmopolitanism. As a matter of fact, there is one place where every kind and class and order and hierarchy of plants do meet, commoners and aristocrats, whether for use or for beauty, flowers and fruits that you mean to grow and weeds that you don't—the site of the compost heap. For a garden which is an interlocking unity the compost heap is the key to the whole varied and composite structure. It maintains its continuity from year to year as the heart does the circulation of the blood-stream. It holds the entire complex together as the keystone does the arch, balancing the cycle of life and decay and decay and renewal like the hub to the wheel, all these and more, much more. As agriculture is to civilization, so is the compost heap to a garden. Consequently, in the revolution of values which I am trying to describe, it played a part of the utmost significance. In this chapter I only touch upon it by way of introduction.

I use the word revolution advisedly. The more my change of

attitude about the garden began to take shape and develop in my mind, the less I came to think of it in terms of a "pleasure-garden." There swam into my ken a host of issues and implications which the idea of a garden as a private delectation and a place of retirement hardly touched at all. The garden in fact became part of my mind, and indeed of the larger world without its boundaries. How could this be ? The compost heap, as I have said, became the key to the garden as a whole, the clearing house and station of communication between fruit, crops and flowers. I began, therefore, to think of it as a potential unit of self-sufficiency, a kind of microcosm of husbandry; without ceasing to be a gardener, I was in process of becoming a small owner. Thus, as soon as I began to conceive it as capable of being nursed and persuaded into an entity of self-support, it became linked with my whole life as a writer advocating certain principles and engaged upon working out a certain philosophy of life. In *Apple Acre*, my friend, Adrian Bell, has given a moving picture of Mr. Terrell and his wife who refused an old age pension and for forty years had without any capital maintained themselves and their family upon a holding of four acres. "I have met," he writes,

> "an English peasant-proprietor, that most honourable, rare and misunderstood of men. It is fineness, not boorishness, that is his hall-mark. A feast of English quality it is: this one man's success cancels a host of defeats in me: it is the very sweet and secret juice of England that has come to fruition against the bitterest weather, economic and political, of all time."

With my disabilities, together with the size of my holding and the obligations of journalism and authorship, I could not hope to emulate Mr. Terrell with his four acres nor even Tom Wibberly with his famous one acre. But I could do something more than write about such faith, such dogged independence as theirs: to some extent I could live it.

I wanted to live it. For I have a profound faith in the virtue and significance of responsible small ownership; to me in very truth it is the virtue of necessity. The social and economic inferences to be drawn from it are almost inexhaustible. But there are others that go beyond it and they are moral and religious. A virtue of necessity—is not this perhaps the key-phrase ?

Nor is the cultivation of the gardener as yet hampered and restricted at every turn by external interference. The small area is out of reach of officialdom: *De minimis non curat lex*, the writ of Leviathan does not run here; its little sky is unclouded by economic blizzards and hurricanes. It is significant that the Terrell family with its self-sufficient holding was the only one in the neighbourhood which mowed the graves in the churchyard and whose diminutive space had room for flowers. Thus, the garden can become "an island of example," a kind of symbol of the "ten just men" outside the unintelligible world of mechanical "efficiency." It thus contributes to the upbuilding of a new world in consonance both with nature and the Christian ethics of the value of the person. To think of it thus is to harmonise the practical and the realistic with the symbolic.

I must end with a brief outline, to be hereinafter developed, of what measures I took to make my own garden an embryo of self-sufficiency. As St. Thomas Aquinas said, "The more a thing is found to be self-sufficient, the better it is." There is, of course, far more elasticity in this respect than there could be on a farm whose output is controlled from without and is no longer independent of centralisation. Again, though all cannot become farmers, most people can be gardeners. Even suburbs and slums can to some extent educate themselves in the virtues of the organic life. Perhaps one reason why the garden continues to flourish and to make more and more converts in a denatured civilization is as an unconscious refuge of that traditional freedom which in England has always been based upon small property.[1]

I soon realised that a garden which could claim even a modicum of self-sufficiency could not afford to be without livestock. I did not aim at this primarily as a source of food-supply but as an inseparable part of its proper economy in the cycle of interdependence. How I came to grips with this issue I shall relate in a future chapter. To provide my own dairy-products was a goal beyond my horizon. But at least the house could drink its milk and eat its eggs *within* that horizon, even if the cows and the hens I could see over my fence were not my own. At any rate, the one did not

---

[1] "If it be true, as we are constantly being told, that man is fighting for freedom and his whole history has been a struggle for freedom, then a true rural life is the foundation of freedom, for you cannot bully and make wage slaves of those who can provide potatoes, vegetables, meat and milk for themselves."—*Alternative to Death* by the Earl of Portsmouth (1943).

come from a milk-factory nor the other from Canada. Propinquity here lent enchantment to the view. The variety of vegetables and legumes I grew and the cares of the orchard also belong to a later exposition. My cereals became maize and oats, and the latter crop does come within the range of this chapter.

I always bless the day when the rancid and acrid flavour of my morning porridge set me enquiring as to why I should not make my own. I came to the conclusion that there was only one way of defeating the conspiracy (it is nothing less) of big business to deprive one's food of its nutritional values, and that was to grow oats myself. I therefore squeezed an oat-crop within my scanty space, sowing both dressed Scotch seed-oats and English undressed, as what is called a "controlled experiment." A handmill had to be sought out or procured and I had to decide whether the linen cupboard or the rafters of my "outshut" would be an efficient substitute for a kiln. By what means, again, should I thresh and winnow my home-grown corn? Would one of the flails in my "museum" come in handy after all?

I debated whether I could brew my own beer by growing my own hops (to which my soil is favourable) or even making nettle beer out of the ditch. At least it would be pure beer, not coloured dish-water with isinglass in it to make it clear and quassia chips to make it bitter. The difficulty here was to procure a good traditional recipe and, besides, I prefer wine to beer. So I turned my attention to making wine out of my ample yearly harvest from my outdoor Muscadine vine. I found this easy because I happen to possess a noble pestle and mortar from Christchurch Kitchen, to crush the grapes in it, drain off the juice into a cask, leave it to ferment for a few days, remove the scum, and then bottle it.[1] I was to find later that a wooden wine-press is much better. No sugar is needed. Why is there so vast a difference in the price between Sauterne or Chablis and *vin ordinaire*? Because ordinary wine is made by crushing the whole bunches just as they are, but for good wine the grapes are picked over from the bunch, the bad and immature ones being rejected. To drink a light table wine daily is to banish rheumatism and be filled with a sense of well-being.

"If I had the power," recently remarked the Chairman of the

[1] This method uses no water. Another weighs the grapes, pours in so much water to the gallon, adds yeast on toast and bottles at all casks without corking or bunging until the wine has finished "working" and throws off its impurities. The loss from the "head" is replaced by water.

Council of British Shipping, "I would make a law which would prevent the consumption of any product in the country of its origin." The cultivation of the home-acre on as complete a subsistence basis as circumstance will allow is the true answer to such tyranny and perversion. Not only are health and sanity served by it. It is a means to recover that spirit of independence and self-reliance that once were our native pride and genius. A remark like that might arouse no comment among masses who are fed, clothed, amused, employed and discharged not as they but the money-market and what is called "the law of supply and demand" please. Not so with the small master who cultivates his own plot and pursues his vocational craft.

So much for the idea of a small garden as it gradually took shape in my mind. So much for its variation or mutation from the types of garden in my previous experience. I have now to relate something of the intercourse which took place between mind, body and estate and was concerned directly or indirectly with the cycle of a year in the garden as it now is and is in process of becoming.

In its cherishment of the soil and its craftsmanly development of the person, the husbandry of self-sufficiency is creative within the Creation. Gardening so comes within the fold of religion. It is in a garden that St. Paul's words—"Study to be quiet"—bear harvest, and man under the tutelage of God is first reported to have lived in a garden. In its combination of homeliness with variety, of self-support with delectation, the garden is one key to wholeness of living and wholeness comes from the same root-stock as holiness.

CHAPTER TWO

THE CROWN OF THE YEAR
(April—May—June)

I. A Forest Clearing

> "And here were forests ancient as the hills
> Enfolding sunny spots of greenery."

I LIKE to think that my plot is a kind of second-hand forest clearing.
The whole of my region was once forest and continued so long
after Anderida Silva, that became the Saxon Andredsweald and
our plain Weald, was separated from the jungles of the Kennet
Valley, and the forging of iron and the burning of charcoal were
letting whole lakes of sun into the Sussex Weald. So, if I am not
directly a forest-squatter, my garden not so very long ago was a
hole in the forest. And we set great value by trees in my neighbourhood because there are now so few of them. I can look nine miles
south from my terrace to the Chiltern scarp near its junction with
the Berkshire Downs and almost count the number of trees I see.
They form the structural pillars of the landscape, whereas an ocean
of leaves would offer nothing to delay the eye. Perhaps it was
this double consciousness of a multiplicity of trees in the past and
a paucity of them in the present that set me planting as many
trees of as many kinds in my plot as it would conveniently hold.
Especially as I am damnably exposed to one consequence of felling
that mighty forest. Mighty it was, this Forest of Bernewoode,
covering almost the whole ground between Buckingham and
Oxford roughly north and south and from Woodstock to the
Chilterns roughly east and west. In the amplitude of its sweep, it
traversed as varied a stratification as any ground of equal size in
Europe—Corallian, Portland Beds, Gault, Kimmeridge Clay,
Oxford Clay and Cornbrash.

In the immensity of its range this forest did not bear the same
name throughout but it was the same forest. Some score of miles
away from my clearing to the north and east it became the Forest
of Rookewoode, and it is possible to gather some sense of its wild-

ness and majesty from a tradition of it in this quarter. For Rooke-woode was the lair of a gigantic boar, the kind of boar you read about in the Mabinogion. According to Chambers's *Book of Days* (1850), this boar was the terror of the countryside. In 1283 the Lord of the Manor of Chetwode, whose family has held it since Saxon times, resolved to rid the neighbourhood of this scourge. He sallied forth, blew a blast on his horn or "welke shell" to the four cardinal points, encountered the monster and, after a four days' battle, slew him. A local ballad commemorates the fray and one stanza runs :—

"Then the wild boar, being so stout and strong,
  Wind well thy horn good hunter;
Thrashed down the trees as he ramped him along,
  To Sir Ryalas the jovial hunter."

Among the immunities and privileges granted by the King to Sir Ryalas in recompense of his deed was the right and power to levy the "Rhyne Toll" for a month in the autumn on all cattle "estrayes" found within the liberty of the manor. A horn or "welke shell" was blown after sunrise on October 13th, first at the manor and then at certain traditional points on the estate, as a signal that any "foreign" cattle found within the circuit would be impounded at a fine of twopence a month and a penny a foot on all beasts in the pound. Money was distributed to the poor at one of these points, for these were the days when charity was a local responsibility, not a State mechanism. In 1810 the bones of an enormous boar were disinterred from a mound close to the manor, and in 1942 I was handling in the manor the last of the horns known to have been blown "when that I was a little tiny boy"—a noble spiraliform instrument some two feet in length. This horn is the only tangible relic of a country legend all but proved (like most country legends) to be a fact. Not only have the mound and the Rhyne Toll disappeared but the forest as well.

Of the Forest of Bernewoode nothing is left but isolated blocks of woodland in which the butterfly orchis is sometimes to be found. One of these, Tithershall Wood of 109 acres (Tether-Hill, Tidershall or Titerselle) actually was part of my parish and the property of Walter Gifford, our lord of the manor in the early Middle Ages. It got its name from the Hundred, was part of the Forest and "wood

for one hundred hogs." Though the land has been so heavily deforested, to the attentive eye there are inferences and significations
of the greatness that once was. One such are the numerous hedgerow
oaks in a country where elm and ash are usually the hedge mono-
polists; the use of brick and timbering in the villages is another;
the dotting of little coppices a third. In Tudor and Elizabethan
times great estates were carved out of the Forest, three within three
miles of one another. These are of red brick with Tudor chimney-
clusters and extensive bartons and outbuildings in red brick and
tiling, showing the brick-making qualities of the clay on which
so much of the Forest stood. Even in the strictly stone areas, the
farmsteads and cottages reveal a rich medley of materials from the
abundance of what the Forest offered the masons. They will have
stone faces and brick sides; a window in a stone wall will be framed
in brick and have a brick cornice; a brick chimney with wide
shoulders will rise from the ground beside the stone wall of its
house; two right-angled stone walls will be joined by brick quoins.
Every farmhouse is like a patchwork quilt. Yet, when they stand
on hill or slope, they rise from the fields like flowers from their
soils, so softly attuned to their forest earth is the wherewithal of
their building.

Perhaps the most evocative of these memorials is the village
of Brill on its mount (Burghill, where Edward the Confessor had
a hunting lodge). It is nearly all russet tiling and brick with intricate
roof-angles and once had a fine tradition of wrought-iron work,
displayed not only on the church but inns and small houses. How
beautiful it must have been in the old days to emerge from the
leafy canopy, the dusky thickets, the massive pillars of the trees
into the clearing! From it the mount of Brill rose out of a green
sea with its multangular coloured roofs and the sails of the
postmill flailing the sweet vernal air. Now they are immobile
and now the Forest is no more. Yet the villagers still possess
certain shadowy liberties dating from pre-Enclosure days, certain
relics of former self-government and control over their own
lives. There is a strong liberal tradition among forest dwellers,
whether they call themselves Tory as in Whittlebury Forest or
Radical as at Brill. They have always been great lovers of
liberty: witness the revolt of the men of Otmoor against the
enclosure of a waste on the edge of the Forest that once supported 200 families. But at Brill there is no modern vent for

the effective and constructive service of this tradition. So it finds expression in a kind of art for art's sake. When trees were to be planted on the Common (long used as a rubbish-dump) to commemorate the Jubilee, the men of Brill planted themselves in the cavities as a protest against them, while the women of Brill fed and watered these tree-spirits until what time the proposal was abandoned.

Further south-west, the influence of the Forest is more realistic. Here still exists a small colony of woodsmen and small holders who cultivate their fields on the strip system. They produce well-tended crops whose average yield per acre is double that of the merchanized farms beyond the fringe of this traditional pocket of Bernewoode. The wooding has declined to faggotting, bean-poles and pea-sticks, but the "platts" in the surviving blocks of woodland are still divided in the ancient way. So my own clearing, cultivated so far as might be to become a unit of self-sufficiency, was true to the old forest custom of the squatter.

Yet, if the bosky environment of the giant wild boar has dwindled to a cluster of pigmy coppices, spinneys and woods, he, strange to say, has vastly increased his stature and multiplied his powers of doing mischief. Within the recesses of the larger woods lurk companies of bulky saurians asleep within the greening thickets, while the imprints of these beasts most dangerous may be discerned among the glades and in the clearings. Here broken branches and trampled underwood indicate that one of them has wallowed. And it would seem that it needs something more than the lance and the broadsword of the gallant Sir Ryalas to rid the places of Mother Earth of a brood of monsters more formidable by far not only than the wild boar he slew. More formidable they than even those huge reptiles of the prime and of the slime that roamed the Carboniferous swamps and tree-fern and club-moss and horse-tail forests many aeons before the appearance of the gentle paragon of animals. But oh, not the brood of Tellus nor spawn of the pregnant ooze; not—

"The stealthy terror of the sinuous pard,
 The lion maned with curlèd puissance,
 The serpent and all strong beasts of ravin,
 The scaly scourges of thy primal brine,
 And the tower-crested plesiosaur."

I was lifting the last of my winter leeks one April morning when there came over the brow of the hill a long procession of caterpillar tanks, the roar of them having been audible a quarter of an hour before they were seen. As the first *monstrum horrendum ingens* topped the rise, a bullock turned, saw it and died. Had but one of these Atlantosaurians spat at my trembling domicile from the crest or turned its snout towards my plot, the work of ten years would have been undone in a few seconds. A certain dignity and solemnity in their advance into our valley gave them a finality of terror. How could little man cope with engines such as these to which the mastodon was as a puppy dog? From dragon to man and from man back to dragon. The man's brain is the climax of the evolution and the man's brain operates the fiercer than brute powers of the dragon in a reversal to something darker than the darkest night of forebeing.

Yet we who live to-day can think of something worse even than the march of these devouring dragons over the earth. What but the alienation both from earth and from God of the civiliza- tions—Germany by far the worst example—which have repopulated the world with the dragons of destruction? Our dealings with the earth have become in a century's intensifying progress an expanding violence against the earth and bred a separation from it which ignores both religious and biological law. Science is as deeply implicated in this conquest as war and that economic friction which engenders war. This lawlessness of man in his violation both of natural and of eternal law is the real terror of our times. Man must work with nature if he is to return to God—there is a mystery of association between them which we are rediscovering from the catastrophe of our double heresy against them. Therefore I am glad to think of my plot as a clearing from the ancient forest. By looking upon it as a vocation of husbandry I am repaying a debt to nature and, I have come to believe, making an offering to God.

The extreme western verge of the Forest, at Horton-cum-Studley, a few miles from Oxford, best reveals its ancient characters. Here are marshy areas encompassed with oak and sallow and the sprays of ragged robin, the wiry speargrass and field-thistle taller than a man. These with burdock, darnel and the stately teazel in autumn, once among the most prized of arable crops, are altogether nature's. Here it seems possible to "fade into the forest dim" striding an age with every step and finding one's way back to hoary Saturn's

realm. What actually happens is a stepping from one age of the
earth to another, not of man's. It is the border of the cornbrash
country that itself merges into the oolite limestone whose scarp
is twenty miles away. Yet the technique of the drystone walling
is identical with that of the Cotswolds. Utterly different country,
oak for beech, valley for wold, clay for stone, and yet the stone
walls are after the high Cotsword fashion whose craftsmanship in
them has no rival. It seems as though the limestone had persuaded
men to build their walls in one way and one way only because
that way best suited the nature and characteristics of this particular
stone. In spite, too, of the dilapidation and the intrusive blotches
of modern building, the village from the forest is still of the forest.
The Almshouses are of brick (faithful to the clay plain), with half-
timbering in panels (faithful to the forest), while the framing and
the dripstones of the windows and the flat four-centred arch of the
porch are of stone (faithful to the borderline of the oolite limestone).
The village is still bosomed high in tufted trees, forest-trees that
tower over it and protect rather than dwarf it.

When man yields to this persuasion from nature, he is at peace
in his own being. He does not fall foul of his own nature nor suffer
that disintegration and purposelessness which have befallen him
to-day. I had failed to be persuaded by nature in my experimental
years of gardening; I had acted from self-will. But when I was at
Horton in June, I had learned from experience that it does not do
to set oneself up against nature. In the garden I was becoming a
pupil of the kind of craftsmanship which from the time of the
long barrows onward had built limestone walls in the sole way
they were meant to be built. This was another piece of forest lore
I picked up for my garden—accommodate yourself to the place
where you live and try to find out something of what it has to teach
you.

If Horton gave me a glimpse of the beauty of man, it added to
it a very special exhibition of the beauty of nature. I happened to
be in the Horton woods on Corpus Christi day, a day when all at
once full summer had entered the stage like an impatient actor
who anticipates his cue. I saw the first wild rose in the hedge, I
scented the first honeysuckle and the drowsy balm of the bean-
fields. These with the flowering grasses, the first ears of corn,
the dishevelled locks of the ragged robin, the trees in heavy blocks
of umbrage and the burning sunlight were all drawn together and

fused into one thing, the passion of the nightingale. Now I entirely agree with those few observers who maintain that there are half a dozen singers on the British list whose quality of performance is superior to that of the average nightingale. But in my limited experience there do occur in this region or that, this year or another, certain nightingales who are master-singers. They are unapproachable in power and range by any other singer who visits our western world. But this nightingale that I heard at Horton possessed a virtuosity and a brilliance of melody that excelled those of any other bird I had heard in all my life ; he was quite evidently a genius among singers. I heard him among the virile greens of an oak-wood, not one but two nightingales and, when they paused for breath, a blackcap broke the vibrant pauses between them. The pair were singing against one another; one of them was like any other nightingale, the other such a master and so absorbed in his outpourings that I was able to approach within five yards of the bough on which he sang. During the whole time his tail was depressed almost at right angles to the body, as though, if he let go, he would fall off the tree.

I stood spellbound. This bird possessed equal command of high and low pitch; his notes were uttered with a timbre and plangency as though a stringed instrument were struck with a brilliant dashing confidence. The high elfin peal succeeded by a tumble of colliding notes was so penetrating that the whole performance was what we call hereabouts a "masterbit." Crashaw's *Musicks Duell* describes in one passage the confused rush of notes (uncouthly called "jugging") which usually follows the rarer crescendo:

> "And makes a pretty earthquake in her Breast,
> Till the fledg'd Notes at length forsake their Nest;
> Wing'd with their own wild Echo's prattling fly.
> She opes the floodgate, and lets loose a Tide
> Of streaming sweetness, which in state doth ride
> On the wav'd back of every swelling strain,
> Rising and falling in a pompous train.
> Her little Soul is ravish'd: and so pour'd
> Into loose ecstacies, that she is plac'd
> Above her self, Musicks Enthusiast."

Crashaw's singer is feminine like most of the poets' birds. But the idea of this poem is founded upon a just observation in natural history, namely that a nightingale sings best when responding to or challenging other sounds, a thunderstorm, a rival male or, as in Crashaw's poem, "a sweet Lutesmaster." Doubtless my bird was stimulated into such nervous fire by the voice of the other oak-melodist in the same wood. That accounts somewhat for the intensity of his song, but not for its artistry. What Walton calls "the clear airs, the sweet descants, the natural rising and falling, the doubling and redoubling of *her* voice" reached in my bird a luxuriance, a lyric audacity, that transported me almost as much as himself.

How singular that these same poets should have followed the convention of a grief-laden, lamenting bird, uttering, as Vergil wrote, "*her* sorrowful strains"! This bird sang with an exultance that could have made nothing that Crashaw, Keats, Milton ("Silence was pleased"), Arnold and Walton have written about the nightingale an extravagance. The oak-wood throbbed with the jubilance of the song. It silenced the roar of all the guns in three continents, singing creation above ruin, an eternal joy above the temporality of chaos and anguish. In the burning heat, the tranced oaks seemed to stretch out their green boughs to catch the faintest syllables of these bursts of song and to watch the ringing and percussive notes leaping above their tops. As I listened, the irresistible impulse of the nascent summer seemed to burst its chrysalis and to ascend, by the instrumentality of this bird, into heaven. Its blue matched the singleness of purpose and sun the fire that informed the voice of one small bird singing in the ancient forest. The scent of the bean-flower, the fervent green of the oaks, the great plates of elder bloom and the flowering dogwood in the hedges, the valiant new greens of lime, hornbeam, maple and wych-elm, the fermenting odour of the earth's increase, the emerald of the wheat, the rush of wayside flowers, all were gathered into the voice of one small bird proclaiming the festival of the God of the Manger and the Cattle-Stall. A pagan glory? The pagan emphasis is of life's transitoriness; the Christian of life's eternity, the great Now of the fullness of life of which the nightingale had given a sudden glimpse in this quintessence of a summer's day. When Bridges wrote:

"Man's happiness, his flaunting honey'd flower of soul
    Is his loving response to the wealth of Nature,"

he was in the pagan tradition; when Smart wrote "Glorious the sun in mid-career . . ." he was in the Christian. They can well meet without strife on Corpus Christi Day.

If you buy a piece of ground in a particular neighbourhood and make a garden of it, you must do more than lay it out in harmony with the house and in league with the immediate landscape. You must cultivate the regional habit of mind. Alien and unfamiliar to the modern mentality, it becomes a labour of love. For it means gathering into the mind that directs and the hand that works the garden a wealth of association and experience. The mind continually draws upon and is refreshed by them, until, passing into the subconscious memory, they inform your doings and are the arbiters of your style. I do not mean anything so absurd as that the garden should be stocked only with local products. For all structural needs, indeed, thatch, stone, timber, hurdles, local loyalties should be an obligation. The garden, though it draws upon half the world for its stock, should yet be in every direction open to the gardener a cell of the regional life. I stocked my orchard with fritillaries because the "frorechaps" are a local pride and we even have a Frorechap Sunday, when pilgrimage used to be made to the wide meadow where they grow—or grew. Among the spring flowers round my terrace are snowflake and bluebells white and blue. This for a double reason, because they consort well with their neighbours but also because they are wild flowers within what I call my region.

What I call my region is not strictly the Forest; I include in it the beechwoods and the older mixed stands of the Oxfordshire Chilterns. Before the Forest was felled and grubbed up, there could only have been a thin line between it and the hangers of the Chiltern slopes which mark the line of the greensand, of the springs and of the Icknield Way. Though the Chilterns are not stratographically nor structurally nor pictorially part of my region, they are so organically because they are its natural watershed. Without the water from the chalk springs we should all die, plants and beasts and men, especially as our own resources in water are extremely sparse. This is a true regionalism, thus to regard the Chilterns as integral with my garden. But it is the very reverse of modern practice which carves out an administrative region pivoting on a great town arbitrarily centred on Whitehall through its satrapy at Reading.

Another reason for so regarding them is that I know them well and have recorded them intimately; I am better acquainted with their craftsmen even than with those of my own neighbourhood. And whenever I look south from my terrace, I see them moving like a great purple cloud on to their junction with the Berkshire Downs. I and my garden also belong to them as to the Forest. I retain, too, a particular memory of their bluebells in May. Upon six weeks of drought and east wind followed a day of warm still rain and I followed it up on the hills. The bluebells stood so thick in the beechwoods that, with the sun splintering down on them after the rain, they looked like lapis lazuli or glazed porcelain. The woods in their pendent vestments and verdure, sparkling with sweet rain, looked as radiant as a special creation, finished that very day out of the divine workshop. The juxtaposition of this green with this blue made the imaginations of saints and sacred poets about the glories of heaven seem like the windy verbiage of the hymn books.

How can one describe a bluebell wood under beech without picture postcard writing ? So obvious, so Tennysonian a beauty might be called a text of the Victorian picturesque. Yet must we be frightened off beauty by the hackneyed or conventional ideas associated with it? As I stood in the bluebell wood, it seemed to me that, if another convention could be overcome, the notion that the sky is above the earth and the earth below, it might be regarded as a symbol of the morning of the world. Take Tennyson's thought of the bluebell floor being a sky. Take it boldly; let it *be* the sky. And let the beech-leaves with the sunlight upon them be the earth, new-made, still shot through with the spirit of the heavens. Nothing like beech-leaves can convey this impression or illusion because the way of a beech is for twigs and secondary branches to spread out laterally from and at right angles to the mole-coloured trunk. The leaves themselves thus expand fanwise to catch every drop of light. When this occurs in a whole wood, thousands upon thousands of twigs and branches holding out millions upon millions of leaves to the sun, the effect is of a heavenly light itself being broken up and refracted into the shapes of shining leaves. This, one feels, was how Adam saw the world, or, at any rate, there it was for him to see. The sons of God might well have shouted with joy to see such a sight, peering out from that bluebell sky to see the newborn world in its first May sunshine. Ah, says he whom Wordsworth believed would botanise on his mother's grave, this is Genesis stuff, a good deal further back even than Tennyson. Are you not aware that tree-ferns and cycads and gigantic club-mosses and horsetails preceded the beech, one of the latest comers of the deciduous type and certainly unknown to Adam? And there were no flowering plants at all in the morning of the world. True, but when Antony said to Cleopatra—" O thou day o' the world!"—it is to be doubted whether he was sure of the date.

I passed on and came to an avenue celebrated in our parts. It was planted after the Armada with beech, sycamore, wych-elm and the two limes, the Common and the less familiar Small-Leaved. Their shapes lend colour to the suggestion that the Gothic church was a blend of Roman basilica and forest aisle. The taloned roots resemble the base-mouldings to Early English pier-clusters, the striated boles fluted columns and the pendulous boughs Norman arches. It is a Gothic avenue not only in the sense of architectural analogy but in the 18th century sense of the rude and the archaic. The effect here was of great fountains spurting out of the ground, huge gushes of green water shot out of the earth, soaring and returning to earth in parabolas and arcs of sunlit green. Here was another symbol of the Fountain of Life rising up out of plumbless depths of Antiquity, infinitely old, eternally young.

This was the way to Samuel Rockall's cottage on the heath, the 17th century cottage of Samuel the wood-bodger, where he has lived for 43 years and his uncle before him had lived for 50. In front, his miniature turf-lawn, upon which no bracken from the Common intrudes, was edged with the "fuzz" in flower, the worshipful gorse of Linnaeus. Fire now succeeded water—the entrance to his cottage on my journey had been by way of symbols of the four primary elements, earth, air, fire and water. But back of the cottage and past the stacks of seasoning wood a new aspect came into play. This was his garden of 40 perches in which he has elaborated a system of intercropping and rotations whose complexity only a French peasant could grasp in all its fine shades of conservation and productivity. I found him not turning the lathe for his dozen gross of chair-legs a month but mending shoes, soldering a kettle and sharpening a saw turn and turn about. Most of his neighbourhood was now coming to him to keep it going in the essentials.

In front of his workshop beside the cottage, a workshop where

wood passes through five metamorphoses, is a holly tree under
which stands his sawing block with piles of beech-logs in company
with it. At the tip of the holly bough that tents this natural shelter
a bullfinch yearly breeds, the nest of sticks, fibres, hair and wool
as conspicuous as an anthill in a field. The hen drowses on her
greeny-blue, russet-flecked eggs to the drone of the saw beneath
her. Yet Samuel is a great fruitarian. It was largely from the
example of his peasant frugality that I made a practice of collecting
all my apple windfalls and making a *purée* of them. But though
he grafts his own trees, bottles his own fruit, and makes his own
jam, he would not have a feather of his bullfinch ruffled. He is
indeed two beings in one, the changeless Woodsman, the universal
Craftsman both fused in the immemorial Peasant. He is older
than the Pyramids but always creating something new out of that
timeless tradition of Man the Maker of which the survivors are so
few. It was through the spring woodland and the ancient avenue
that I understood him; through him that I could dimly grasp the
meaning of them and in sympathy with him that I made my own
garden, the clearing in the forest, what it is now.

I have known Samuel for many years, and it is no longer strange
to me that he, the unprogressive, has always something new to
tell me. New even about wood, and we have talked about wood
for a decade. This time, as we took our dish of tea together, it was
all about leaning trees and the chain wound about the living wood
with an iron bar thrust through it just above the saw to prevent
the tree from splitting. Woodsman's talk, full of nice technicalities.
Wood too all about us—the semi-circle of the beech-woods round
the heath, the ceremonial avenue, sawdust round his paths and in
his compost heap, shavings wreathed and festooned round his lathe,
chopping blocks, sawing horses, draw-shave horses, wood in every
shape and process from tree to chair-leg, cabinet, stool, lamp-stand.
The subject of wood is inexhaustible, and Samuel's cottage is a
furnace of creation, a hub and pivot of interchange between nature
and man. After tea, he took me through the flaming gorse (all
of it on the heath has been smothered and killed by the bracken)
to where grew a sapling oak-tree. His apprentice son had planted
the acorn on Jubilee Day and he had gone out one morning to
find bramble trailing about it. So he cut away the bramble lest
it should impede the growth of his emblematic oak. But, said
Samuel, some idle boy will pass by, he will notice your oak-tree

and cut it down to make a walking-stick. So the pair went out and replanted the bramble round the tree.

Samuel has always something new to tell me, just as he always has something new to make, and for many years I have been his recorder. In him I found the archetypal peasant, the true pillar of society. But this, the story of the oak-tree, the most trivial of the many stories he has told me, seems to me the most significant and symbolic of them all. For it perfectly conveys the way he belongs to his native earth. It frames his sense of responsibility for that speck of it which he inhabits, forever turning nature into his modest art. It conveys more than that when it is seen as the foreground of that visible display of the Fountain of Life in the Avenue and of the new-born earth suffused with the light of first mornings in the wood. "Eternity," said Blake, "is in love with the productions of time." So Samuel, the patient woodsman, the diligent husband-man, the faithful craftsman, acquired the stature of universal man, of Man the Maker, through this trifling gesture of loyalty, of thanksgiving towards all that earth had given him. But the kind of thing that Samuel stands for means nothing to us any more: the whole drift of the age has for a century been away from him and the good works which are his form of worship. The age twists and turns in desperation to find a way out of the blind alley into which that repudiation has led it, but its best-laid schemes only lead it deeper and deeper into the labyrinth. It has turned its back upon the oak, the holding and the workshop.

Suddenly, an experience I had had the previous day became illuminating. I had gone round his estate with a man who owns not 40 perches but 4,000 acres. He is a man with great possessions— a fine house, noble wrought-iron gates, a formal garden, a park studded with groves of ancestral trees, lakes and woodlands, a herd of pedigree Ayrshires and a herd of pedigree Friesians, pigs, horses, calves. He even has a haunted garden, which strikes at anybody who tries to domesticate it. One of his trees is figured in Strutt's *Sylva Britannica*, while on his lakes breed wild duck and the Great Crested Grebe. How remote, then, this man from Samuel, going out to gather the wild raspberries, planting beans in his potato rows, keeping his wheelbarrow for thirty years without allowing a single shower of rain to fall on it, grafting his apples on crab-stock, making the furniture he sits in and the bellows that plays on the timber he had sawn from his trees, collecting pony droppings on the Common to spread on his compost heap with the shovel he had made himself in 1911!

But it was not the difference I was seeing between these two men, but the likeness. For the man with great possessions farmed his own land, bred his own stock and brooded over his own acres just as Samuel bent over his beans and Tom Thumb lettuces. All this he did in spite of Death Duties and the vindictive urban legislation and taxation against estate-owners, just as Samuel did his good works in spite of the economic leverage against him. They are as remote in station as they well could be, but both are equal in this, a common devotion to the principle of responsible ownership. Here is a real meaning of equality, that new slogan of the times. Therefore, they are natural allies, the peasant and the lord; through that common devotion they close in their respective spheres that great gap between the rich man and the poor man. A hundred years ago, the one drove the other off his land, and so established the reign of expediency and wealth for wealth's sake, not for the uses to which it is put. So was established the system of irresponsible property which made of the lord a traitor to his trusteeship and of the peasant a landless wage-earning proletariat. It is no accident that the Industrial Revolution followed upon the Enclosures.

It is upon the restoration of this principle of responsible property as a stewardship that the countryside can become once more united to rebuild its broken structure and refashion its dislocated pattern. It is the point of unity between all classes of countrymen, owner and tenant, rich and poor, the great and the small. It is the binding force between them and it is true to the tradition of them both. But it is true to something more than that—to the nature of man himself and to his purpose in this transitory world. For in making any good thing man becomes the owner of it by the act of creation, whether he keeps his control over it or not, and by owning something which he puts to good use, he becomes a maker. The two are inseparable and by separating them modern civilization is on the high road to the final disaster. And it is when they come together that that extra touch of timeless quality which is more than natural and indeed more than human displays itself—the light in the wood and the fountain of new life spurting up from the ancient trees.

When therefore I think of my garden as a clearing in the forest, I regard it in the light of these things I have seen among the trees and woodlands of my region. It has its own contribution to make to the life of that region, no less than the estate and Samuel's workshop and the bluebell wood and the famous Avenue have. It is the same with the Cotswold limestone I laid down between my lawns and grass-paths. They are not rightly local stone as is the stone wall I built to be a fortress against the north. But Horton in the Forest is on the edge of the noblest of all stone countries and Stanton St. John, a mile or so away, is as pure oolite as any Cotswold village. There is the link, just as there is another in the many Cotswold objects of craftsmanship and husbandry housed in the museum I built in the orchard.

But there is a deeper one. I had not been to the Cotswolds up to last year (1942) since 1937. On a May day streaming with rain I once more revisited them and in a region (the south) less familiar to me than the north. I could not have done so on a worse day, the rain blinding, the gale chill, the clouds sagging. Yet I realised at once that absence had counted for nothing. The high wild hills, the deep serpentining valleys, the paint-box quarries, the gold-leaf trackways (so few of them now), the suspended woodlands, the so solid and dream-like cottages and farms and manors, all had become as much part of my being as the shape of my nose. So, if the Forest is the authentic casket of my small plot, the Cotswolds and the Oxfordshire Chilterns are embossed in high relief upon it. My plot and its region are in their turn a representative piece of all England, the real England which is not the ephemeral England of to-day. This is my idea of the garden I have made.

What I have touched upon here is the organic relation of the garden to the region, a region in this instance that once was forest. But this primary fact has a much more practical bearing upon my garden than any I have indicated, even though that influence is negative. Like every gardener and every husbandman, I am much preoccuiped with the literally vital issues of climate and weather. Having studied the former pretty closely for a decade, I am convinced that it has quite definitely changed and for the worse. A decade is a mere toe-mark in the giant strides of time, but it is something to go on. The traditional idea of English climate has to be considerably modified by the contemporary phenomena in opposition to it. The traditional idea exactly corresponds with Enobarbus' celebrated words about the variability of the Egyptian Queen. Our climate has received many hard words on the score of its temperamental changefulness. It was a Zimri climate, a Cleopatra climate. Actually, this traditional idea has for many years become a purely conventional one for the simple reason that it is no longer true. The climatic change has been in the direction of a greater uniformity. Weather now occurs in slabs or blocks of similar conditions instead of being constant in inconstancy and rapidly alternating between hot and cold, rain and shine. This variable habit was, of course, the fundamental cause for the wonderful fertility of our islands. Though they are not yet predictable as in tropical countries, we now have our periodicities of rainy seasons and dry seasons. This was vividly illustrated in 1943. The east and the Midlands had one of the worst droughts in living memory; the south-west, west and north-west so heavy a rainfall that the Cornish harvest was ruined and in Westmorland there were 28 wet days in August. Thus slabs of uniform weather occurred not only in time but space.

What is still more to the point, drought in the east and Midlands is gaining at the expense of the rainfall. By means of my rain-gauge I have kept a record of the rainfall during the last ten years. It compares adversely in quantity with what it was half a century ago, though the data I gathered from the veterans of the village were necessarily inconclusive. But exact figures are available at Henley, some 25 miles from where I live. There the rainfall, on a five yearly average precipitation in a rainier district than my own, has between 1888 and 1942 declined from 26.72 inches to 26.37. The average rainfall in my own region is from 4 to 5 inches lower than this, so that we have very little marginal reserve to draw upon before inconvenience becomes anxiety. In 1943, the drought lasted from February 10 to May 23. Then came 2 inches of rain in 4 days, an amount almost exactly equivalent to the total rainfall for the previous four months. June, being for us a comparatively wet month, corroborated the traditional country maxim:

> "A dry May and a dripping June
> Brings everything into tune."

But the equilibrium was again upset by a further arid period, unbroken but for snivellings of rain, from the third quarter of June to the third quarter of August and resumed into the middle of October. Altogether the drought, though not pedantically continuous, lasted for eleven months and at the end the rainfall was six inches below the normal.

Weather, too, like man, can form habits hard to break. After a period of drought, rain-clouds for a long time fail to discharge rain. This is especially true of my region and place within the region where some peculiarity of land-surface causes cumulus from the south and west to swerve from its course. I remember numerous occasions when rain has occurred two miles away and even much close without moistening my own area.

Coincident with this decline in the rainfall is a corresponding increase in the violence and frequency of our gales. In 1943, these winds blew violently through most of the whole year. I have studied gales for so long in my exposed garden that I know something about them. The two phenomena synchronise and I believe their relation to one another to be one of cause and effect. The gales are usually westerly or south-westerly, the rain-winds, but the rain as often as not is retained until the gale has shot its strength. Then the depression of which the gale or gales were a symptom has been succeeded by an anticyclone. These great rainless winds, not infrequently gaining a velocity of from 60 to 90 miles an hour, are caused, I believe, by deforestation; the wind bloweth where it listeth, but it can be and often is partly man-made. Havoc from a gale may be an act of man rather than of God. The woods both pull down the rain and check the gale; when they are felled, the rain lacks their gravitational influence and the gale has a free run. This is not mere speculation; such phenomena have already happened on a far vaster and more intensive scale in Libya, the east coast of the Adriatic, Central and Western Africa and Northern America. There, the felling of the forests has been followed by great winds that sweep away the soil and the sand that has succeeded the soil through over-cropping, monoculture and the exhaustion of the humus content.

It is a commonplace how greatly two world-wars, the cupidity of land-speculators and the impoverishment of the landlords who have sold their timber to them have peeled our woodlands off our soils like the skin off an orange. By thus stripping the land naked do we expect no consequence to follow? Are we to dislocate nature's equipoise and adjustments without paying the cost? And these gales, of course, intensify the actual effects of the drought by drying up the soil. A three-days' gale will result in a greater degree of aridity than a six-days' sun. During a hurricane I have watered polyanthus twice in twelve hours to save them from dying of desiccation. Buds and shoots are dried up and leaves withered by the loss of warmth and moisture, the increase of radiation and the hardening of the plant-cells.

We are now exhausting our soils by overcropping, the unbridled use of artificials, monoculture and big business farming, as fast as we can. Let us not then flatter ourselves that we shall escape the erosion that has desolated so many other countries of the world. For these predatory and makeshift methods loosen the crumb-structure of the soil from which the humidity of our traditional climate has by its binding qualities hitherto preserved us. Not altogether, since in Lincolnshire and Bedfordshire, two of the least forested counties in England, erosion has already occurred. A friend of a friend of mine, travelling down the east coast from Hull into Suffolk during the great gales of spring (1943), passed the whole way through sun-hiding dust-storms or rather soil-storms. This was erosion due to the excess use of artificials.[1] I recently received a letter from Vermont, New England, in which occurred the following passage :—

"We were much interested in what you described in your book as a result of soil-erosion. We have seen with our own eyes the dreadful desolation in this country over immense territory caused by this, as a result of bad farming methods and destruction of pasture lands. Soil has darkened our skies a thousand miles from the farm lands where it was blown in the great dust storms."

In the face of such evidence can we continue to think that our highwayman attitude to nature, abetted by orthodox science, will let us off scot-free from the laws of nature? In this way and that way and another way, we are destroying England.

Has not my garden, then, a profound if secretive relation to the forest whence it came?

[1] The appearance of eel-worm in the potato crops is another symptom of soil-exhaustion.

II. *The Visitation of Birds*

"Four globes shone in the dark,
  Like lamps of dew,
In folded secrecy
  Of my dwarf yew.

Caved in her womb of night
  My linnet sleeps,
At the flame of her breast
  Her charge she keeps.

Her lover to the day
  Aloft in bliss
Sang this tremendous act
  Of genesis.

His day has met with her
  Procreant night,
And these their hidden gems
  Shall soon take flight.

In this benediction
  Darkly I see
Eternal paradox
  And mystery."

DUBIOUS as I am of the justification of these verses, they serve to introduce a further paradox, that of the playfulness of work and the workfulness of play. Of all the paradoxes at the heart of life this is one of the most essential for the contentment of man and the fulfilment of his proper nature. It is beautifully illustrated in the true function and purpose of a garden. Year in and year out it is nothing but work from morning to night. But it is work which continually sees the end in the means to achieve it. It satisfies the two primary needs of man, to nourish his body and delight his spirit. It is a perennial exercise of craftsmanship and freedom of choice and is at the very base of reality. The beauty and use of a garden come to fruition from the work-in-play and the play-in-work of the gardener.

No work indeed is worth doing unless it be a kind of play, and no play yields such intensity of satisfaction as when you have

worked for it. It is a principle that runs right through nature.
The flower is the pleasure no less than the purpose and function
of the plant, and what a furnace of workmanship has been stoked
and fed by plant-energy to produce it ! I take a casual glance over
my hedge and there are the April lambs playing like mad in order
to become work-a-day sheep. How perfectly then the bird fit into
the economy of the garden! The lives of birds are so interwoven
with the strands of work and play that it can only be an artificial
separation which says—this is work and this play. The bird sings
out of the joyousness of his strung being but also to attract his mate
and define his territory. The emotionalist sees only the one, the
card-index type of ornithologist only the other. But reality sees
both at once. "The wagtail," Sir William Beach Thomas has
written, "finds amusement in its own skill." The linnet broods
her eggs and feeds her young with such a devotion of labour that
will stick at nothing to achieve her ends. But only because her
duty is her pleasure and her work her play. The cock like an
actor in a masque displays before his mate; his performance
is the peak and epitome of ceremonial pleasure, but the more so
is it profoundly functional, and purposive. And in like manner
the birds both grace the garden and execute one of its most indispensable services. They are the pleasure of flying flowers and the
use of the insecticide. In getting their livelihood they make the
garden workable and in singing on the spray they add a lustre to
its blossom that neither earth nor sun nor rain can quite accomplish.
The poet described something of the effect in his idea of heaven:—

> "Where the daisy is rose-scented
> And the rose has got
> Perfume that on earth is not."

I will go a little more closely into this economy of birds in a
garden and relate it to my experience both of my own birds and my
own garden. On April 4th, I was coming into what I am pleased
to call my stackyard (the stacks consisting of timber, peat and coke)
when I saw two boys enter the gate from the lane and approach
a bulky and conspicuous thrush's nest in the fork of a damask rose
against my outhouse. They did not see me till I had one of them
by the collar. What I said I will not repeat; the point of the story
is what they said. They were about to rob my thrush because they

had authority behind them. Here were "sparrows" the B.B.C. and the Ministry of Agriculture had instructed them to destroy. I forebore to wring these young hooligans' necks; their mentality was indeed that of the Cockney who described a skylark as a "sparrer 'ollering." But what of the authority that provokes it? This was only one more example of what the countryside suffers and has suffered for a century at the hands of its urban masters.

The incident brought home to me a recent conversation with a friend of mine who, before taking charge of three flax-mills, was a farmer in a big way. By this I mean not that his farm was a "large-scale economic unit" after the model of the Roman *latifundia* but, what every farm ought to be—a large garden. A Pests Officer suddenly appeared on this farm one day and ordered him to annihilate the rookery on his land and his father's and grandfather's before him. There is no doubt at all, of course, that finches, blackbirds and whitethroats take fruit. I have myself counted 13 mistle-thrushes, 4 linnets, 4 magpies, 3 jays, a yaffle, a yellowhammer, a pair of sparrows and a tree pipit, not to mention countless throstles and blackbirds, all at one time in a large whiteheart cherry. The tree was in an uproar and the leaves shook as though in a high wind. The great drought of 1943 was an Egyptian tribulation both to birds and gardens, and I myself lost my loganberry crop, part of my oats and even some of my apples to busy beaks. There are also, I think, "rogue" birds who make it their business to turn robber and are aware of what they are doing. This is particularly true of certain blackbirds with fruit. Nor is there any doubt that rooks take arable seeds and seedlings—another farmer friend of mine lost his whole crop of winter beans from them. But rooks do not follow the plough for nothing (or did, for I never see them behind a tractor-drawn plough), nor did our forefathers hire boys with the clappers (I have one in my Hermitage) just to keep them out of mischief. Civilization has made the part (the town) into the whole; science abstracts the part from the whole and specialises in it without considering the whole. Both are blind to the balance and interdependence of that "web of life" which is nature's whole. The result is that the delicate complex of these adjustments has been so dislocated that repressive measures leading to yet worse disequilibrium to some extent have had to be adopted.

I said to the farmer whose rookery was thus threatened: "Do the rooks destroy any of your grain or young peas and beans?"

"Yes," he said, "but I consider they have earned it." This, of course, was but carrying into practice the old saying:

> "One for the pigeon,
> Two for the crow,
> Three to rot
> And four to grow,"

and some of the old diligent dibblers I used to know always planted for the birds no less than for themselves. This was not, of course, sentiment but an empirical knowledge of and a sound instinct for the economy of nature. In that economy, they knew the value of birds as insecticides and modern figures have corroborated the validity of their actions. A modern poet has too:

> "Nothing to eat
> In Stupidity Street."

I too can corroborate it. One side of my rose-walk is bordered with espalier apples, three of which are within the fruit-cage which I shut up when the fruit is ripening. In May, 1943, I found these three apples, a Beauty of Bath and two Coxes, in ribbons with some twigs quite naked and hardly any fruit on them from the attentions of six hairy caterpillars, the food which appears to make the cuckoo such an ill-conditioned bird. The six espalier trees outside the cage, four Coxes, an Allington Pippin and a Worcester Pearmain, were undisfigured and crowded with fruit.

This husbandman I have referred to is indeed one of the wisest of men and possesses one of the subtlest of minds. I delight to listen to him talking because of his extraordinary earth-knowledge. In many ways, he has been one of the greatest of pioneers in the return to husbandry. He was the first to restore flax-growing, the first to fold large pig-herds over his land and the first (see p. 73) to grow wild white clover. We once visited Avebury together and were walking along that mighty rampart which enfolds the village. I gazed at the line of the Avenue and the monoliths, many as big as a cottage wall, round the lip of the internal fosse, with the interest not only of an amateur archaeologist but of one who had been present years ago when Alexander Keiller was excavating them. He in a seemingly distrait mood bent his head to the ancient turf as often as he lifted it to the greatest prehistoric monument in Europe. When we left, he remarked in a musing tone—"Poa, cocksfoot, fescue, rest harrow, rye grass, bent—we should always try for the natural association." No man living knows more about the inter-relationship between soil, plants, livestock, insect-and-bird-life. As he talks, I catch a glimpse of the endless convolutions and intricacies of natural law, as a single richly embroidered fabric. Yet, if you analyse what he says, it is always a conscious elaboration of old country knowledge and never departs from the organic as modern chemistry not only radically but aggressively departs from it.

Because he is a wise man, he is also a poet. Not the magazine poet who rhymes birds with lowing herds, nor the modern Bloomsbury poet who rhymes them with surds, if it ever occurred to him to mention anything so Victorian as birds. If he wrote poems instead of, as he does, making his poetry part of his husbandry, he would be more likely to rhyme them with turds—thinking of the wheel of life. He is a poet in the sense that this interwoven pattern of life is to him the music of life. When he sees a bird, he considers what that bird may be thinking of him rather than *vice versa;* when he hears a bird sing, he thinks of it in terms of Genesis—the sons of God shouted for joy. He would admit that the competitive-territorial-biological stimulus was not to be despised, but he thinks also of the marginalia, the overtones, the "more than bread alone." In other words, his faith in the creation is such that he believes any brusque disturbance of natural balances to be an error against good husbandry, and that the incidence of insect-pests, blight, virus diseases are the consequences of imperfectly understanding them. The sole dominance of self-interest or other ulterior motive is but taking the liberties of short cuts or quick returns or the abstractions of the laboratory with these laws. Imagine, then, the effect of some agronomic pedant or brisk young Commissar just incubated from an agricultural college bursting on this man's wide-acred farm, pointing to his ancestral acres and commanding "away with those rooks!" An old Cheshire countryman had his cottage condemned by an Inspector and, in describing the visit, remarked, "An' I condemned '*im.*" I fancy such were the feelings of my friend. In fact, he often reminds me of a sentence in G. K. Chesterton's *Life of Cobbett.* Cobbett, said G.K.C., had the sharpest eyes in England. He carried observation to a fine art—"from the shade of ripeness in a cornfield to the shade of rottenness in a Cabinet Minister."

Years ago, I had to cope both with plant-disease and infestation, together with the depredations of birds in my garden. I have almost eliminated both, though I still have slight trouble with Sweet William rust, black spot, peach leaf-curl, apple sawfly and codling moth. But I have reduced them beyond all computation and to the barest minimum by a painfully acquired adherence to the principle of the wheel of life. I never use poison-sprays, but I take (when I have time) the precaution of lime-washing the orchard, espalier and cordon trees. I never discourage birds and my garden offers plenty of nesting sites for a variety of species. But I tie up the pears in muslin bags. I take the precaution of wire-guarding the young peas and black-cottoning some crops and the smaller fruit such as cordon pears, outside the fruit-cage. This cage cost me a lot when it was made and now saves me a small fortune in fruit-returns. I came to recognise that everything hangs together in our dealings with the earth. The scientific habit of always beginning at the wrong end and elaborating more and more curatives to undo the effects of its own inorganic methods and *a priori* reasoning has been a failure.

One of the things my friend the husbandman told me was that in the United States they were doing exactly the opposite of what we do.[1] While we think of nothing but expansion and prairie farming, they think of hedgerows, small fields and conservation. More than 80% of all farm-land has been brought under more or less intensive soil-conservation practices, while the Tennessee Valley Authority has perceived the intimate connection between free and responsible small properties and the reclamation of land from erosion. Bulletins, reports and scientific papers I have seen published in official journals all speak of the chain of continuity between soil-fertility, the return of wastes and human nutrition. While we talk of grandiose drainage schemes on a scale which would infallibly lower the water-level and put large tracts of arable uplands out of cultivation, Americans plant natural water-weed in the watercourses. Why do they do such things? Not because they are naturally wise but because they have learned the beginnings of wisdom from that large-scale policy of soil-robbery, the exploitation of natural resources and the persecution of wild life that have

[1]See p 113.

been so disastrous to them.[1] They are beginning to learn the rudiments of the deep-versed knowledge and philosophy of life which my farmer friend expounds. Therefore, my birds are welcome. Not only am I honoured by their nesting on my land and enchanted at their singing among my trees and flowers, but also because I have come to regard a garden as what I have called a microcosm of husbandry. Husbandry, contrary to modern orthodoxy, is not a conquest but a decipherment of the natural order.

We could do with three times the number of birds in my neighbourhood, whose lack of undergrowth, paucity of woodlands and brooks and open shelterless country are decidedly unfavourable to them. The scarcity-value of birds has also increased of late years when the more interesting small bird life, like everything interesting in country life, has steeply declined. Thus a bird is more than a ball of feathers to us. The day of the first chiff-chaff round about April 10th is a day of consequence and inward celebration. How did the little leaflike creature escape being blown into kingdom come these latter springs of wild west winds? Where did the frailty get to while the world was being blown about like a leaf? Had he the powers of Ariel for whom the blast was a charger?

Bring unmolested, the birds throng to my garden in considerable numbers, and latter June in it is full of the metallic din of venturing nestlings being fed by their parents. This frequentation is a definite index of soil-fertility, since a rich soil with plenty of animal life in it carries a larger number of birds than a poor soil. I can always count upon a pair of linnets to nest with me year after year, and they always line the nest with the hair of my sheepdog, Friday. As it is extremely doubtful whether the life-cycle of a linnet can be longer than, say, five years, it looks as though the children and possibly the grandchildren of my original pair inherited this use of raw material from their parents. With me they behave just like regular migrants, arriving in April and leaving with the family in the autumn. In 1942 I had two pairs, one nesting in the hedge, the other in the dwarf Irish yew I brought from my home in Gloucestershire. The cock used to sing to his mate in her dark grave-like bed from the nearest ash or perched at the apex

[1]My friend once arrived at Illinois when the floods that eroded its soils were out. He found that they had become dust, to such an extent had artificial manuring disintegrated their crumb-structure. The dust blew into the river which in consequence overflowed its banks.

of the stiff pyramidal little yew. The making of the nest nearly always synchronised with the flowering of my Star of Bethlehem. It is possible, I think, that the failure of these annual birds to make any attempts to conceal their nests (though in darkness the yew nest was near the surface of the tree) was due to the recognition of home over a number of years of security. Owls and hawks are rare. It was seldom that these successive pairs crossed the frontier of the garden; if so, they never flew out of sight. "Sweet Stay-at-Home, Sweet Love-on-Place" was the right name for these small-holders whose landlord I had been for many years. Yet their territorialism was not exclusive since the two pairs nested only twenty yards apart.

The same is true of my blue tits, dunnocks, blackbirds, chaffinches, greenfinches, wrens and thrushes, whose songs soar to the peak of summer and fall with its decline. I had a very true-toned blackbird who every evening from the same place sang a stave of his own invention or perhaps an imitation from a whistling boy—a third, then a fifth and back to the third, all the notes being quite perfect. In the mothy dusk or when the enormous moon climbed through the misty-leaved branches of the trees in early April, this tuneable bird sang his own particular catch until the night dropped him to sleep. In my experience, these nesters were all most conservative home-birds, their area of flight being remarkably circumscribed. Thus, the garden is full of wings in spring, and in the spring of one year I had more than a score of nests. In 1943, I had two very curious nesting sites—a bulky wren's nest (not a cock's) in the hedge and a willow-warbler's, a mere twist of hassock grass, at the end of a row of Laxtonian peas in the arable garden. The wren's nest was not five yards from another in a cranny of the stone-wall. When the young willow-warblers left home, they found the peas in full pod and promptly stripped those nearest the ground. These and other depredations (such as those of the whitethroats slipping through the meshes of the fruit-cage and finches dehusking my oat-bells until I black-cottoned them) I regard as an Excess Profits Tax upon the plenty these birds help to produce for me. At their worst, the whole tribe has less nuisance value than one rabbit or grey squirrel.

This avian regionalism is graciously illustrated at dawn. In the fields of the ridge above my house, it is the lark who rings in the day:

"When the first lark on high hath warned
   The vigilant robin of the sun's approach."

But in my garden it is not the robin

"Whose slender pipe calleth the nesting tribes
   To awake and fill and trill their myriad warbling throats,"

but the blackbird. So in the fields about my plot, it is the lapwing
who serenades the stars, but in my garden the humble dunnock.
The wren that nested in the compost heap at the bottom of the
garden never, so far as I know, crossed the boundary of the wren
that nested in the stone-wall at the top.

A garden warbler I could hear singing every morning from my
bed last year, though mateless, never appeared to leave a strip of
lane just opposite my front gate, bordered by tall elms and ashes.
If I drove him to the limits of his range, he would always return
by the other side of the hedge to his former platform. Though he
often sang in the air, he preferred definitely customary stances,
pouring out his melody in fits and starts, like a stream winding
among boulders. The whole body partook in the song, throat,
wings, frame, until every feather seemed a song. It was invariably
in snatches, whether from a spray of wild parsley or a topmost
elm-bough. But, though he skulked like a whitethroat back to
where he was singing from when I met him, he never reached the
territory of the whitethroat, ranting and gesticulating away like
a mob-orator, fifty yards away among the nettles at the bottom
of the lane. Some years ago, a pair of willow-warblers nested in
my orchard grass and I never saw them at the top of the garden.

Even the goldfinches who never nested with me before 1943,
though twice they nested in the sycamore just outside my hedge,
remain, volatile as they are, in and about the garden until they
depart to revisit me in April. A food they delight in with me is
the seed of the weeping wych-elm, encased in its flat bract-like
"samaras" from which these brightnesses extract it, spitting out
the membranous sheath on the grass. But in the year I write, at
last they did nest, and how could the nest of such a pair be other
than a work of art? They choose their site in the pillared rose-walk
with the flowering arms of the espalier apples on the other side
of the grass path and just at the point where the Lemon Pillar rose
meets the copper *Rosa Moyesii*. Here at Goldfinch Corner I have

some of the best roses in the garden. But even the cups of the Chinese roses could hardly compare with the cup of moss, lichens, wool (also from my sheep-dog) and thistledown in which lay those eggs of cream with what Dickory calls "Chinese writin'" of red and purple inscribed on their top ends.

Perhaps of all these stay-at-home birds the most so were the flycatchers. I have watched a flycatcher in the orchard for an hour on end until I was tired of looking at the spiritless little creature. During the whole time, he never fed but deviously passed from plum to pear, pear to apple, apple to apple. The flycatcher habit was so strong that he would double or treble the distance from tree to tree by the loops, swirls and right-angled turns accomplished between perch and perch. But then why should the flycatcher be a time-saver? It was through this bird's tenacity of place that I was able to cast some doubt on the text-book statement that the flycatcher is a silent bird. Except in flight and for day after day this bird never ceased uttering his harsh, guttural, long-drawn churr, taken high or low, like the noise of the swinging pendulum in a grandfather clock. Once, after rain, when everything burst out singing, so did he, if so faint a sibilance could be called a song, and it is sufficiently rare to hear. In 1943 the mate of this flycatcher or another nested in my thrush's nest built in the crotch of a damask rose against the wall, only a few days after the young thrushes had left it. By May 27th there were five minute eggs laid in the enormous cup which, a fortnight before, had been congested with the craning and insatiable brood of the original builder. The thrush nested again at the same time in one of my clematises over one of the south windows, thus moving house from the back to the front of my own. She and her mate used to threaten my sheep-dog, Friday, with arched backs and bristling plumes when she ambled between them and the nest.

The most curious example I can give of this passionate sense of place in birds is an incident that happened on June 7th of 1942. Some seven families of starlings, adults and young, were congregated on a small ash in my hedgerow, making a shrilling almost as tedious as the hiss of a leaky pipe. Suddenly a sparrow-hawk sheered the top of the hedge, charged into the midst of the tree, seized a starling and flew off with it. Instantly, the entire tribe dispersed with yelps of terror (a very different note) and for ten minutes there was a blessed silence. At the end of it the stampeded

birds reassembled and I was able to compare the shrilling this time
with the needle of a gramophone record. The episode reveals not
only how short-lived is fear in nature and strictly utilitarian, but
how compelling are the ties of place. I often used to sigh for that
sparrow-hawk to reduce the starling proletariat. In my orchard,
quiet on the earth though never in the skies, they are as obstrapulous
(to quote my Dickory) as a crowd at a football match.

But for the bird who concentrates the home-sense into a burning
point, commend me to my 1943 song-thrush. She beat even the
chaffinch who nested at eye-level on one of my balsam poplars,
the hen-bird never stirring even when I touched the nest in passing.
As for the thrush, she never moved when, to keep the polyanthus
going in the drought, I filled my can from a water-butt and in
so doing could not avoid my head touching the rim of the nest.
No wonder that even the dog (see above) could not keep her from
her second nest. Her mate was very definitely a ventriloquist and,
when I searched for him singing high in the high elms on the other
side of the lane, he was actually at my elbow in the hedge. His
voice but not he had left the garden.

The autumnal gatherings of the swallows and house-martins
on my roof, whose blessed twitterings I never heard until the combined business-cum-pleasure, beauty-and-use, work-and-play of the
pre-migration flights begin, is as striking though paradoxical an
example of the sense of home. For the urge is countered by the
reluctance to leave home, and these birds are caught in two minds.
Then my garden offers as diverse, thronged and active a scene as
a mediæval church. The church was the refuge, playground,
law-court, theatre, assembly room, concert hall, college, picture-
gallery, recreational and educational centre of the village. So the
doings in my garden were a medley of pleasuring, feasting, labouring, instructing the young, remembering back and desiring forward,
resting, travelling, celebrating and singing all in one.

My garden is a home for many birds. The more they make
it a home for me.

III. Proserpine

"When wheat is green, when hawthorn buds appear."

"It's a warm wind, the west wind, full of birds' cries;
I never hear the west wind but tears are in my eyes.
For it comes from the west lands, the old brown hills,
And April's in the west wind, and daffodils."

FINE, but it is seldom that it works out quite like that.

So confusing and multitudinous are the impressions of late spring in the garden and so ephemeral is their incidence that I have to concentrate on a very few images of uncommon beauty. My site particularly exposes me to great winds, late frosts and a chain of droughts. But there are moments when I have to struggle against gardener's vainglory in thinking what I see beyond compare. It is not, of course, but the illusion is strong. One of these will occur on any calm and glowing evening when I walk down the eastern grass-path into the orchard. The "when" I cannot place. In mid-April of 1942, the daffodils in the orchard were not more than half ablow and the cordon pears on my left as I walked down the slope were but in bud. In 1943 at the same time, not only had the daffodils come and passed before the swallow dared but the narcissus and fritillaries were fading, while the pear-blossom had lost its virginity. But late one year, early the next, there does occur a brief, a very brief conjunction of clemency in weather conditions with simultaneity in time of blossoming which makes that walk an appointment with Proserpine. But as for a decade

"When that Aprill with his schowres swoote
The drought of Marche hath percèd to the roote"

has been no more than a poetic convention, this felicity is only too closely linked with Robin Herrick's hail and farewell to the beautiful things of the young earth.

Yet the moment does come. It is when most of the cordon pears look like Aaron's rod, whiter than whiteness against the fresh green of the tall quick-hedge. Their formal line is interrupted at intervals by Japanese double cherry, one of which I look upon

with redoubled pleasure from having cured it, two years ago, of
a vile leprosy by no other means than the application of compost.
No patent medicines, nothing but the means of curing itself. The
children of darkness recommend lead arsenate that poisons the
boughs, poisons the grass under the boughs, poisons the earth
under the grass and poisons the bees that set the fruit. I will use
no poisons. Nasturtium Essence for American blight, on the
other hand, is a legitimate spray, if you do not grow nasturtium
at the roots of the fruit-trees.

Where the pears end, there stands as a gateway to the orchard
a single thorn which in its profuse blossom of a very pale pink
looks dressed in muslin. The path then turns right, the pears being
exchanged for shrubs. At the corner, I can look back from their
whiteness to the shell-pink of the thorn and the cerise of a pair
of Siberian crabs with gold barberry and kerria (forsythia earlier
in the year) under them. The rose-red clouds of these crabs might
well have drifted down out of the sunset. It is a sign of the irregu-
larity of flowering periodicities that these barberries, out before
mid-April in 1943, did not blossom until May 20th the year before.
On the right hand of this pear-walk, across the rose-bed where
the Engelmann Giant pansies are velvet maroon or indigo black
with yellow centres, are two long beds of nothing but grape
hyacinth succeeded by tulips and later by the more brilliantly
coloured flageolet beans. My soil compelled me to leave these beds
to the grape hyacinths and they grow with me like they do in the
Alpes Maritimes, shedding a faint aroma when the bells are rustled.
From the pear-walk they are a solid block of sea-blue and the
bordering grass is a coast.

But under the cordon pears there is something more "eyeable"
(Howard Spring rescued this expressive country word from oblivion),
and that is the groups under each separate standard rose of that
form of the Poetaz Narcissus called Cheerfulness. The perianth is
creamy-white with a frilled double centre of white and eyebright
yellow, while the flowers stand on very tall and erect stems. If such
preferences are not wholly arbitrary, it seems to me, the Lady
Tulip (Clusiana) and perhaps the jonquils and Star of Bethlehem
excepted, that these are the most spring-like of spring flowers. If
the lustihood of spring is made visible in the opening leaf-buds
of horse-chestnuts, its blissfulness is in these flowers.

I have these, the Barrii, Leedsii, poeticus, polyanthus and sweet-scented jonquil types, everywhere in the garden. In the orchard, along the grass-paths, round the house, in the kitchen garden, under the espalier apples, in the shrubbery, behind the long line of catmint, they gladden and lighten our heavy senses with their bright gradations of colour, their subtle modifications of form, their airiness and grace of poise. I delight in nothing so much as to wander among them, gazing at them and thinking of nothing, but absorbing their light-heartedness and dancing motions with the nostalgia of us who live in this most flowerless of ages. But Cheerfulness is best in regular groups under the loaded trusses of the cordon pears. These are themselves so formal that the whole scene of this eastern walk is like a tapestry of flowered arras, punctuated at set intervals with the equally formal Irish yews, the strips of azure grape hyacinth, the crabs, thorn and cherries.

In the orchard itself the value of Cheerfulness becomes more relative. Here it is joined by a host of forms in daffodil and narcissus undersown, as it were, with primrose, fritillary, periwinkle and forget-me-not succeeding the rings of crocuses round the fruit trees and overcanopied with plum and pear blossom. I judge that I am not over-weening about these orchard daffodils and narcissus because of the number of people who, before the hedge conceals, stop in the lane outside and say, "I say!" In return I glow. The reasons are twofold: my livestock which in a manner most marked has increased their size and height and one of my very rare acts of wisdom in the past. Before I stocked the orchard with them, I ordered them, regardless of expense, from Jager of Heiloo, a firm whose very catalogues used to be *de luxe*. What is more, I ordered them in great variety, long and short, white, yellow and bicoloured trumpets, single and double, thick and thin-stemmed, slender and robust. I am bound to say that this original outlay has justified itself at compound interest. The diversity between the types and between trumpet and perianth gives them in the mass (but there should be an archipelago, not a sea, of them) a striking distinction. Lastly, their multiplicity makes for continuity of flowering over a much longer period. When the apples blossom, there is still an abundance of flower in the grass beneath them, the procession being closed by the pheasant eye and that ghostly thing, the white daffodil. And the last of the pheasant eyes synchronise with the first of the moonflowers.

Yet what is most to be remarked in the orchard is not these.

not even the chequered frore-shaps; it is the twigs of pruned plum and apple I pushed into the grass to mark the first daffodil shoots in February. In April, half a dozen were in blossom, one, six inches high, having 17 flowers. I was reminded of the ox-goad that St. Theodulph plunged into the soil so that it blossomed into a holy tree. Such is this east walk. I confess there are moments when, perambulating it, I have a fleeting understanding of the immortal words, "And God saw that it was very good." For the beauty is, now and again, ravishing, and in part I had created it, or persuaded nature to do so. As Aquinas said, citing Dionysius, "It is of all things most godlike to be God's co-operator."

If you own fruit-trees, the pleasure of their blossoming is incomparably greater than if your emotion were purely aesthetic. I have a small Codlin whose every rift year after year is loaded with ore, every bough, spur and twig clustered with crimson flowers on their green platters. But not in confusion nor improperly spaced. Fruitfulness, order and décor, three graces in one. The May month pageant of my 35 apple trees ends with the Bramley Seedlings of the shapeliest forms and largest blooms. Only Crawley Beauty is later.

But the pleasure is attended with carking care. Abundance of blossom is by no means a forecast of abundance of fruit: more often, it is the reverse. The heavy falls of my apples in June and July of 1943 were no doubt partly due to more of the damnable gales and partly to the frost of May 8, because the plums and pears, earlier set, hung gamely on. Modern droughts, again, are nearly always attended by night frosts and cold winds at the most sensitive period of the tree's annual cycle. The alarming precocity of renewal in 1943 after a dove-like winter was greeted in cloudless April by days with temperatures of 70 degrees and nights of 28. Yet the fruit of that year escaped bad mauling by a hair's breath, though nothing could be more upsetting to the metabolism of plant-life, nor weakening to its constitution, than extremes of temperature. The non-producers who take weather at its face-value did not notice the drop in the milk-yield from lack of the "early bite"; they were not aware that the frosts that followed these days of blowing cold and withering heat would, but for the dew that damped their powers, have blasted every blossom in the land. Since not one in ten of modern Englanders knows the difference between wheat, oats and barley, I doubt whether they would have known that there was any connection between blossoming in spring and fruiting in autumn. Into such measureless unreality has our economic system drugged their understanding in a scientific age of what has been called "ignorant knowledge." But the gardener and the husbandman do not see weather in the absolute sense at all—fair or foul. They consider it in relation to the prosperity and happiness or the reverse of what they grow. They detest to see the dislocation of the due order of seasonal rhythms; they feel and fear a disturbance at the heart of things when January apes April and April usurps the robes of June.

True, they see marvels, as in 1943—elder and wild rose both flowering in May, blackthorn, crab and apple all blossoming simultaneously, a portent unknown to the hoariest of villagers. These sages say that there can be no rain till the blackthorn fades. Quinces, strawberries, my *Clematis montana rubra*, flowered from four to six weeks prematurely and the May hedges a month before their due coming of age. They were met by Buchan's Three Ice Men, the Eismanner, riding at the head of a long procession of Viking gales. We growers are not compensated by a sunset of banks and streamers of light feathery gold with pearl-grey gulfs between them for a boreal wind under the burning-glass of the sun scattering the petals of the plums like its own snow. There is always a flaw in the beauty and a beauty in the flaw—that is life.

The July days of late April-May in 1943 made speed-addicts of the flowers and the planting-out problem a knotty one indeed. But, as the adjacent surroundings of my garden are meadows with uncut hedges, it was ramparted with snowy ranges of May blossom. The orchard advantages of a gentle winter are visible in the cleanness of the blossom. A hard winter keeps the insect tribe snug in its hibernacula, while a mild prematurely entices them out of doors with consequences fatal to their survival. A dry March makes a good seed-bed—the peck of March dust worth a king's ransom. But hot dry Aprils with cold venomous winds make the orchardist scan daily the green hearts of plum and pear blossom for the tell-tale black spot that aborts his harvest. And the gardener goes not so much by the look of the weather as by his charges' reception of it. When flowers look pinched and as though they had gooseflesh, when they very literally take to their beds, he knows that foul is fair and fair is foul; when a ten-days' gale drives the bees away, he is rightly concerned for his cross-pollination. The moles too tunnel his beds and let in yet more drought.

In 1943, spring precipitated itself into the arms of summer without waiting to be wooed. In my garden, heuchera, columbine and sunroses were all blooming by mid-April. In mid-May, I was dead-heading the Isabel Rose and the first campanulas and white pinks were in flower. In the third week of May, we were bottling the first gooseberries, just as in the third week of July the harvest had begun and was more than half over by the end of the month. Before the middle of August I had gathered the first apples— Worcester Pearmain, which is eatable if plucked green before the crimson flush of an inward worthlessness. But the real reason was the birds. Driven by famine from the interminable drought they were attacking apples and pears as hard as stone.

During these recent Mays, the gardener goes about with his heart in his mouth, and his brow furrowed with black care. His morning round is tremulous. When he has inspected the fruit, he walks delicately to the early potatoes. The first marrows are examined for frost and the seedling sprouts, cauliflowers and others for the deadly flea-beetle. One compensation there may be. Fruit blossom in these drought years comes and goes as though seen in a film. In 1942, the blossoming season lasted a fortnight and escaped; in '41, ten days and was frosted ; in 1943, just over a week and the blossom was about halved. The quickest over, the more chance for the expanding leaves to afford protection for the embyro fruit, if it has not been too dry for it to set. But the real compensation is a spiritual one. Clash between inorganic adversity and the upthrust of organic life in its will to live and fulfil its functions is as much a law of life as adaptation. But the gardener is enabled to observe that vegetation does in spite of loss master and utilise for its own purposes the forces of the elements. This is the supreme argument of Dr. Barlow's able confutation of neo-Darwinism in *The Discipline of Peace.*

The April and May hurricanes that raged with idiot fury during the "blackthorn winter" of 1943, reaching on one day the velocity of 80 miles an hour in my region, made the spring flowers look like a group of aristocrats mauled by a revolutionary mob. They gave a toy exhibition of the senseless furies of our destructive age. Their havoc upon flower and blossom was like the savagery of modern war against the graces and liberties of human life. They lifted

my thrush clean off her eggs and she could only remain on the nest
by pressing her tail and underparts against the wall and her breast
against the rim of the cup. Many of the wattling rods of my hurdles
were wrenched out of their frames and strewn about the grass,
leaving the hurdles a "looped and windowed raggedness." Yet,
though some of the polyanthus were killed not by buffeting but
desiccation, the daffodils and narcissus remained upright by the
strength of non-resistance and a week later but little wreckage
could be detected.

The only other scene of massed spring flowers I can claim,
apart from that of the rockery walls and certain borders, is my
west wall. The middle of it is spread with an exceptionally shapely
Cydonia (I refuse to call it "Japonica," which is as though you
looked through a wine-list at a restaurant and ordered a bottle of
French.) There are two Cydonias, one blood-red in flower, the
other coral. But I reap the advantage of both in possessing the last.
At dusk the innumerable flowers darken and deepen into a redness
that glows as though from hidden fires. In the day, its coral-red
is all softness and lightness, and so close are the clusters along the
short spurs that it becomes a kind of coral tree. It is flanked by the
"glad light grene" of the spring foliage of *Viburnum fragrans* on
one side and winter jessamine on the other. At its foot is a bed the
length of the wall whose dominants are multi-coloured polyanthus
and the slender snowflake, the green-edged bells hanging two or
three from the tips of the long grass-like stems. Star of Bethlehem,
gem-like vernal squill, intermediate stock (which usually survives
the winter with me), various primroses and butter-coloured jonquils
accompany them. A narrow paved walk separates this bed from a
parallel and narrower one that reaches the edge of a low dry-stone
wall. This bed has a double line of soldierly grape hyacinth and
another of polyanthus, interspersed with fritillary and white and
pink bluebell. The overhang of the wall is tufted and matted with
rock-rose, thrift, houseleek (once a country cure for pneumonia),
aubrietia, saxifrage and a handsome yellow-flowered rock-plant
with fleshy glaucous leaves. This was given me by a great gardener,
Ernest Blackburn, who told me it was rarely to be seen in gardens.
Between the foot of the wall and the lawn is a yet narrower bed from
which rise the tall blades of *Iris ochroleuca*, six feet high in June and
flowering a bold yellow and white at the end of the month or in
July. The aubrietia climbs right down to and winds among the

tubers of these flags. When the drought-winds are not plaguing this western idyll, it reminds me of a 14th century illuminated manuscript I once saw at Malmesbury, one of the few relics of the celebrated Abbey library ravaged by the villainous Stump. Or it is like one of Morley's or Henry Lawes's song-books what time the music of England matched the loveliness of her native land.

These fritillaries (*fritillus*, dice-box, from the square markings and *meleagris*, guinea-fowl) Miss Sackville-West felicitously calls "our own private English lily of the fields." They are never seen wild except in hosts when they look like brown furrows in green pasture. Since that effect is impossible in a small garden, I experimented by growing them singly among other spring flowers or in small groupings on or near walls, round trees and, of course, on the grass. Under my medlar I had one such grouping both white and purple brown that grew 12½ inches in height, each plant hung with three lanterns. Miss Sackville-West surprisingly calls it "a sinister little flower in the mournful colour of decay"; to me it has the elegance and romantic formalism of English (and it *is* English) 17th century Baroque.

I persistently grow polyanthus, not only along this west wall but all round the least lawn, because they agree very well with my soil, making abundance of flower at the ends of those long stems (the lover of these flowers achieves these by yearly planting seed) which are an essential part of their quality. Another "secret of their charm," as we say of film-stars, is the fidelity to the yellow or orange centre in spite of all the freedom of colouring. They grow so well with me that I have had several a foot in height. But our modern desiccated wind-blown springs make it a toil and a trouble to keep them alive by almost daily watering. Evening after evening they take to their beds with a silent cry of "water, water." Unless the drought is very severe, they are the only plants with the exception of transplanted seedlings I ever do water, compost being the great drought-resister and the hoe the most effective of watering pots. I observe that the most progressive scientific theory now abroad disclaims the hoe. Science which claims a more than papal infallibility is positively womanish in its fads and whimsies, and I continue to hoe.

It would be tedious here to enumerate those group-associations of colour and form which every fastidious gardener loves to attempt but more often achieves by accident than design. I will mention two of the very simplest. One a group of pumila iris, deep purple and creamy-buff in a small square paved bed under fig; the other the globe flower with fold within fold of beaten gold-leaf among wallflowers of rusts and browns and browny-yellows and velvety warm reds like the old England of russet tiling and rosy-red brick and brown smocks. A right similitude, for the wallflower was of old the "yellow gilliver." Wallflowers of "murrey," that is neither maroon nor puce nor plum.[1] They are just the setting for the soft balls of sun-colour. One wallflower whose stem could not be seen for flowers and leaves measured 23 inches wide by 21 high. I need hardly say that it was self-seeded. It was the wallflowers which presented me with the most startling indication of the pre-cocity of the season in 1943. On April 23rd, a date so early that I shall hardly be credited, I saw a humming bird hawk-moth probing their nectarous centres with its long-drawn-out proboscis and hovering before the flowers in a velvety mist of vibrating pearl-grey wings. This year, too, the blue tit nesting in my gutter was feeding her young at the end of the third week of April.

Nature often confounds our artifice. And sometimes relents when we give up going against the grain of things. I have related my misadventures with plants I tried to grow against nature or my particular speck of nature. One of these was a wonderful arum-like lily, like a Brobdingnagian *Hyacinthus candicans*, that I bought on speculation in 1933. Another was the Lady Tulip which had disappeared from my garden for five years. In 1943, they rose again like Lazarus from the dead.

[1] See *Norfolk Life* by Lilias Rider-Haggard (1943).

IV. Roses

"Among all flowers of the world the flower of the rose is chief and beareth the prize."

J. RAMSBOTTOM: *A Book of Roses.*

"Oh, no man knows
Through what wild centuries
Roves back the rose."

WALTER DE LA MARE.

ALL beauty in nature comes from movement—a blackbird alighting with upward tail-heave, a fleet of clouds in sail, grasses swaying, wind-blown trees, a running fox, a creeping snail, a gliding shark. a breaking wave, wind in corn, growth, seasonal change, the kneading of the earth's crust, the underlying rhythm of things like the circulating blood and the beating heart. This perpetual motion is immanence, but the transcendant is eternal fixity, the source of motion, the absolute. So, though summer's lease hath all too short a date, we seek in a word, Midsummer, the crown of the year, the sense of a changeless finality, a something which expresses the eternal truth and idea of what summer is behind the appearances of flux and transience. And since we can do no other, we seek it in some symbol which for us sums up summer, though the symbol itself, being concrete, passes onward and is gone. Thus it is we who, by our power of conceiving the absolute, in a sense deliver nature from the flux of time.

I look round the garden for this epitome of summer. The moon-daisies open among the flowering grasses of the orchard. They break like foam[1] from the high tide of summer; they are the white crest that records the full surge and swell of the year before it ebbs, or they are the white fire of midsummer at its full burning.

Maybe it is the flowering grasses that are the heart of summer, as haymaking is its immemorial rite. They are of supreme interest and value for the countryman. So, though the book-names, cocks-

[1] In my garden, there is a summer foam rather more literal but just as representative of middle summer. This is Tennyson's "froth-fly" with which I am abundantly plagued. I sometimes spend an hour ridding my lavender walk of this pest, dissolving the green ogre's palace of glass between finger and thumb.

foot, timothy, foxtail, fescues, Yorkshire fog, rye-grass and oat-grass, are countrified enough, yet for mine, for ours, we have vernacular names as well. Rye-grass (*Lolium perenne*) is "Jacob's ladder" and also Shakespeare's "darnel" (*Lolium temulentum*); the villainous couch is "squitch"; bent-grass with its pyramidal feathered head is "bennets"; the purple Molinia is blue grass, and "hassocks" is our regional and expressive term for those coarse tufts that even the geese leave to the last to eat down. Foxgloves, too, are for me "flowers of middle summer," and I take pleasure from them the more because I never planted a single one. They drop in on me like my goldfinches and linnets. Better still, they place themselves at the points of vantage where one tall flower will be the pivot of a whole design, while a self-sown plant, set in the ground by nature's green fingers, beats a very Gabriel Oak's.

Noble effects are produced by accidental siting of self-determined seeds. Sweet williams and snapdragon, expelled in former years because of the rust, find unerring homes at odd corners and among the flag-paths; pale blue cup-and-saucer campanulas place themselves in front of sweet briar, salmon pink Oriental poppy, yellow cistus and yellow iris round my neglected pond and a blush-coloured musk rose chose to flower under the white lemon-scented Phila-delphus. Nature is the first of farmers; she can also be a gardener to instruct even Gertrude Jekyll. And these self-seeded plants are indeed the very flower of summer, so rich is their growth, one reason no doubt being that those dropped by birds are coated with fertilizer.

Summer's opulence is in the Oriental poppies, her peak of living in the beflagged standards of the delphinium bed (and I still have survivors here of lavish days at Chelsea). Her depth of colour is in the Kaemferi irises, the flaming gaillardias and red hot pokers (*Tuckii*) and the gromwells deep in colour as in antiquity (gromylle, gromel, gromil, grosmyl (1318), gromylle (1425), grummel (1589)— all from *granum milii*, *grain de mil* from the shape of the seeds.) But the white splendour of midsummer nights is in *Clematis Henryi* and that matchless iris I have already mentioned, Purissima, her joyousness in the densely flowered clumps of the little Stresa daisy (*Erigeron mueronatus*). It is quite different from Chaucer's daisy:

> "That of alle floures in the mede
> Than love I most these floures whyte and rede,
> Swiche as men callen daysies in our toun."

It is much more delicate and symmetrical than our native daisy, has slender lanceolate leaves, neatly cut petals, and a tuft-like habit of growth in the interstices of my terrace paving. The more sun it gets, the more it branches and proliferates into gay and airy patterns, studded with careless and impulsive flowers of a deeper crimson than the common daisy. The great white blooms of Henryi look superb when the plant clambers about freely in a red climbing rose or riots interlocked with a purple Jackmanni clematis on the wall of the house.

At the foot of the rose-climbing Henryi I have a group of Cotswold Queen Verbascum whose stems of pale primrose flowers (I cannot understand why Miss Sackville-West speaks of them as "musty, fusty, dusty") accord extremely well with it. A cloud of bee-loud catmint and the languorous sun-roses all-Danaë to bright Phoebus in his strength but as short-lived as the May-fly, these are the softness of high summer. I have such a liking for sun-roses that I continued them as an edging with perennial candytuft right down my parallel middle beds from the paving under the rockery walls where I originally planted them. Against the grey stone they have a kind of incandescence, but behind the columbines of various types and shades they look like basking butterflies.

Among all these emblems and qualities of midsummer I am not sure that I am not best pleased with the white clover in the orchard. It recalls me to my husbandry, since clover means herbage and humus, clover means nitrogen, clover means fertility, clover means sweetness of soil:

> "The even mead, that erst brought sweetly forth
> The freckled cowslip, burnet and sweet clover."

I have, too, a special feeling for wild white clover because that friend of mine, the great husbandman who plays an important part in this book, was the first to cultivate it. He made the brilliant suggestion that the prussic acid which appears in some plants early in the spring and then disappears, is nature's tonic to the cattle after the long wet or cold winter. This is the kind of man he is. I never can make out whether it is wild or a survival from former leys, but probably the former. It is as much a signal of the goodness of the earth's increase as the richest and most gallant of flowers. It differs from the late-flowering red clover with its long tap-root that penetrates the soil-pan by the greater number of four-leaved plants. To find these in your grass used to be considered lucky but nobody looks for them now. There is no time and nobody believes that any talisman or amulet or prosperous find could bring anybody luck any more. I look for them still; if this minor sign that my soil is in good heart is given me, then so am I.

But of course the true, the inevitable no less than the conventional symbol of summer is the rose, as the crown is the symbol of monarchy, the mitre of episcopacy, the sword of the soldier, the eagle of power, the lion of strength, the dove of peace. And the rose is the choice of my soil as indeed it is the pride of the garden. At the Flower Show I always took first prize for roses; other gardens easily surpassed mine for gentians, for lilies, for the lime-haters, for the Pasque Flower I have tried in vain to grow, for many excellences. But I have never seen a garden that can grow roses like mine. Thus my boast since it is not my virtue. I have merely to push a bush or standard into the ground for it to luxuriate in a very heaven of a home. I have detached suckers from my old-style roses in January, replanted them and had them in flower in May. In consequence, it is the only plant in my garden which has steadily increased its range and where I once had scores I now have hundreds.

I started off, as all but the very discriminating do, with the hybrid teas and hybrid perpetuals and I did achieve a sumptuous kind of beauty with them. Indeed, the opulence and enormity of their blooms made them almost vulgar. I have a north bed of them, for instance, backed by a tall screen of sweet briar (not the Penzance which is scentless) and a line of balsam poplars behind this. Seen from the bottom of the lawn with the white pinks in front and a lake of blue violas at the roots of the bushes, the bed has a Renaissance pomp, both in massed profusion and the remarkable size of the individual blooms. Not that I have ever made the smallest attempt to grow exhibition specimens. Far from it; I do nothing for or to them but prune lightly by the "long pruning" principle on Lady Day and give them a banquet of compost once a year. Only two roses have died on me in ten years and only one—Rosa Mundi—has never properly fulfilled itself, never reminded me of what Miss Sackville-West calls "red cherry juice generously stirred into a bowl of cream." Many of the roses I now have are nameless because they are sports or variants of parent free-flowering traditional

roses. The roses grown up the walls of the house, Ophelia and
Isabel, for instance, have to be few in number or they would have
given no chance to vine, fig, jessamine, clematis, Viburnum and
others.

My change of attitude towards my roses illustrates a similar
change not only towards the garden as a whole but towards life,
towards economics and in philosophy. During the pleasure-garden
stage, I was content enough with the modern roses, especially as
they were content enough with me. Then of some I began to tire;
they had a kind of confectionery look about them and an unclean
blending of colours, while too many were scentless. Not that others
are without a beauty of their own. General MacArthur with its
fine red and McGredy's Yellow are among the best of bedders,
while the single *débutante* rose, Dainty Bess, with its girlish com-
plexion and almost black centre, looks legitimately like an old
rose brought up to date. The white Marcia Stanhope has a stately
and sophisticated excellence, and I am fond of the flat, shell-pink,
multipetalous Lady Waterlow which flowers twice a year. If well
placed, Paul's Scarlet can be very effective. More by chancing my
luck than planning a design, I placed two weeping Paul's Scarlet
standards on the edge of my sunk garden opposite the pair of Irish
yews. More than once I have been told that these rose-trees, when in
full bloom, reminded their beholder of a child's picture-book of
fairy stories. Also the long walk of climbing roses of many varieties,
trained up posts and along wires, excels in richness of colour and
freedom of growth through many weeks of the summer. I trained
many clematises of different kinds to wander among the rose-
branches and a long bed of delphiniums and Candidum lilies and
another above it of mixed herbaceous plants show their flowers
beneath this long arcade.

But more and more I found myself inclining towards the more
"old-fashioned" types like William Allen Richardson, La France,
Frau Karl Druschki, Gloire de Dijon, Hugh Dickson, Zephyrine
Drouhin, a long-flowering hybrid of the exuberant, sweet-scented
and aristocratic Bourbon group, the Noisettes and Caroline Testout
whose huge pale pink flowers against the wall of my Hermitage
look very fine entwined with the even larger flowers of *Clematis
Henryi*. I began to prefer those of recent culture like Etoile de
Hollande which were not a revolutionary break with the tradition.
So in time my new roses became nothing but old roses. This step

I have never regretted, fully aware as I am of the brevity of not a few in flower and of a luxuriance of growth in others which made me sigh for threefold my space. The ramblers I abolished one and all and made the long walk of poled roses whose lateral branches meet and mingle on wires nothing but climbers. And, so far as I had the time, I began to take an interest in the excessively complicated and recondite and obscure and bewildering and ramifying history of roses and to regard with awe the erudite rosarian. My garden was new-stocked with Gallican, Chinese, Persian, Damask, moss, musk, Provins, Provence and Cabbage roses, roses cultivated by savants and with a tradition behind them. They had a habitation among gardeners to whom beauty was a normal characteristic of life and a prerequisite of education, not, as it is now, an eclectic or exclusive pursuit remote alike from livelihood or recreation. I am sure that is one reason why the modern rose is as often uncomely as not. It is separated from nature and in an age of specialisation and fragmentation beauty has been separated out both from use and from ordinary living.

Consequently, I came to value the associations and historical lineage of my old roses. My little double yellow rose, *R. Persica*, for instance, that produced the *Pernetiana* group, is a hybrid of *R. lutea* (the very handsome Austrian briar) and related both to *Xanthina*, my earliest rose to flower (in 1943, it did so in mid-April), and the exquisite single yellow, Hugonis. All are hybrids of *Spinosissima*, the original burnet rose with its bright black hips and bronze foliage in the autumn, also responsible for the fine Stanwell Perpetuals and Harrisonii and, with me, flowering twice in a season. This Persian rose is a shy bearer, as Xanthina is not, every twig and spray being garlanded with the white gold-centred flowers, hundreds to a bush. But there is no other rose except Hugonis to touch Persica for its pure and rich butteriness. My other Persian rose is a Damask, a family of late Tudor introduction and said by Kinglake in *Eothen* to "load the slow air with their damask breath," and by Parkinson to be "of the most excellent sweet pleasant sent . . . being neither heady nor too strong, not stuffing or unpleasant sweet." The York and Lancaster rose is a variegated type of Damask which I expelled for its inferiority and my Persian Damask is no great shakes. Though Jason Hill in *The Curious Gardener* calls it "brilliant and floriferous" and I give it every chance in a square raised bed of English and Dutch irises, I can find it nothing more than a pretty thing, cherishable for its associations rather than its own charms. This is possibly because the corner I have chosen for it happens to be in June one that takes some living up to. Then, this FitzGerald rose is fronted by a cluster of tall aristocratic *Pallida* irises. Behind them rise the yet taller bosses of the straw-coloured Cephalaria; behind them, again, the early summer Torch Lilies (*Tuckii*); behind them the purple Jackmanni clematis and arching over the whole scene a wax-white, full-bodied Noisette rose. Still, it is the authentic Edward FitzGerald rose, planted on his tomb in Suffolk whence I received my own cutting, while itself was a cutting from the rose planted on Omar's grave at Nashipur.

Three of the most floriferous of my old roses are *Sancta* or the Abyssinian rose, Danaê and Penelope, both Pemberton hybrids of the Musk Rose. The first is presumed to have come from the tombs of the Ptolomies and to be the rose in the mediæval *Coronae sacerdotales*, single white with yellow centre and only a little smaller in diameter than the now celebrated Mermaid. Mermaid is a cross between Gloire de Dijon and *R. bracteata*, a white rose with gold centre introduced in 1792. As I have all three, my family holding has become a hostel for the most intricate and circuitous family relationships. Both Danaê (in which my linnets once nested) and Penelope flower for at least four months of the year in great creamy trusses of bloom. Penelope blooms so prodigally that from above (it is in the sunk garden) the leaves at the zenith of its flowering can hardly be seen. The flowers press against each other so closely that each spray looks like a single mammoth bloom, two and even three feet in circumference. Perhaps my oldest rose is the Cabbage (*Centifolia*), mentioned by Herodotus, the "rose noble" of Rhodian coins and apparently cultivated both by Midas and the Minoan dynasty at Knossos. My Chinese Monthly Rose that flowers at the ends of the branches also is in bloom at intervals from the opening to the falling leaf.

The puce-coloured *R. moschata*, Keats's "mid-May's eldest child," Gerard's, Parkinson's, Bacon's, Hakluyt's and Titania's Musk Rose, has downy blue-green leaves, long buds and fine spread of limb. Bacon said that it "yields the sweetest smell in the air" next to the Violet. It is not, of course, to be confused with the Moss Rose (*Muscosa*). This is a Provençal rose with many varieties, of which the white (La Neige) is in my garden. Nor is this Provençal rose to be confused with the Provence, which is not flat but globular.

This is Shakespeare's "Provincial Rose" (see Jason Hill) and was brought from Palestine by Thibaut, Comte de Champagne, when it became a Mediterranean industry for syrup of roses.

The Tuscany Rose, pleasantly described by Miss Sackville-West· and by Miss Sinclair Rohde as "a small semi-double rose of deepest velvet and very fragrant," is with *R. Mundi* (named from Henry II's Rosamund) and *R. Harrisonii* called by Jason Hill a rose "rescued from the rosewood coffins of the past." It has thick flat otiose petals almost exactly the Tudor Rose in design. It is a Gallica, like the carmine Provence, a group of which Gertrude Jekyll said, "no one group of plants has ministered so closely to human sensibility or has so greatly promoted human happiness." The golden boss and very dark crimson petals of this "velvet rose" of the 16th century are of a peculiar beauty against the light yellow-green leaves. Though it is short-lived like most or all of the Damasks, it flowers most profusely with me. Its flat clustered petals resemble those of *R. Lucida* except that the latter is a Tyrian pink with gold centre. This ruby-fruited rose I also have and the great rosarian, Andrews, calls it the Virginian Rose. It has been agreeably described by Miss Rohde, whose knowledge of "old-fashioned" flowers is matched by a sensitive discrimination.

This is a handful of what we call hereabouts my "garland" of roses that possess what Miss Sackville-West truly calls a "mediæval quality." Most of them are heavy "doers" and no trouble at all to grow; all are crowned with a double beauty, their own both in flower and habit of free growth, and the love that has been lavished upon them by the worthies of past ages. Budded on briars, they make, too, splendid standards—*Alpina*, the spineless rose, for instance, described by Gerard as with its "shining deepe greene leaves" "of a colour between the Red and Damaske Roses." Also, their foliage is usually fresher and greener and more delicately cut than that of modern roses. Lastly, we make a delicious hip-honey from them. Perhaps my best corner of them is at the northern end of the long rose-walk where the copper-red fringed Rugosa hybrid, the rosy-spined rose, *Sericea Pteracantha*, the wine-coloured *Rosa Moyesii*, the Austrian Copper, Musk, "Velvet Rose" and *Rosa Hugonis* grow together. All, with their far-flung sprays and the arched Chinese beauty of Hugonis and Moyesii, require plenty of room to display their full graces. Years ago I said in a book that the primrose yellow Hugonis with its luminously green foliage and carven cups poised on the sprays was the delicatest rose I had ever seen. I see no reason now to modify that opinion. It goes well with the delicatest of nests, the goldfinch's, a few feet above it.

Another advantage of these old roses and Chinese roses, especially the single ones, is that they keep one *en rapport* with the wild rose of the hedgerow. Well was England called Albion from her white roses —*Rosa alba* of her first Romano-Celtic gardens and the dateless rose of her wild places. If there are three symbols of the true England that can be picked out from a host of them, I think they might be the parish church, the brown clod and the wild rose. The inconsequent wayside revelations of Rosa *canina* or *arvensis* are not like anything else in the world; its beauty in itself is supreme and the Queen of Sheba in all her glory was not clothed like one of these. Even roses like Hugonis cannot better it; they are a variation upon it (my pale pink *R. macrantha* actually is a Canina), since the rose form of the wild rose is rose-grace in itself, one of the few perfections of an imperfect world.

V. Garden Economy

"We should ask of an enterprise, not ' will it pay ' but ' is it good,' of a man, not ' what does he make ' but ' what is his work worth,' of goods, not ' can we induce people to buy them,' but 'are they useful things well made,' of employment, not ' how much a week ' but ' will it exercise my faculties to the utmost.' And shareholders in—let us say—brewing companies, would astonish the directorate by arising at shareholders' meetings and demanding to know, not merely where the profits go or what dividends are to be paid, not even merely whether the workers' wages are sufficient and the conditions of labour satisfactory, but loudly and with a proper sense of personal responsibility: ' What goes into the beer?'"

DOROTHY SAYERS.

THERE are really only two questions relevant to the economy of a garden—what can you grow on it and what labour can you put into it ? Both these questions are more or less covered by the quotation I have given from Miss Dorothy Sayers's *Why Work?* But for convenience I shall take them one by one, inseparable as they are in reality. The first may be introduced (though the second is concerned in it too) by another quotation from the same author, hardly so wise:

"There is no longer any real reason why anybody should go
short; we know how to make the barren places fruitful . . .
how to combat diseases which used in former days to destroy
whole civilizations. . . . So far as sources of supply go, there is
no longer any economic problem."

Begin Here.

The fallacy underlying this extract is the Fallacy of the Age of
Plenty which is almost undisputed. We only half know how to
"make the barren places fruitful." We know how to reclaim them
with our machines but we do *not* know, except very partially, how
to cultivate them. But we know very well how to make the fruitful
places barren. Though we know how to combat diseases, we do
not know how to build up a health to prevent them from occurring.
The Dust Bowl on the one hand and the mounting scale of the
malnutritional diseases of soils, plants, animals and men on the
other are a sufficient reply to Miss Sayers's none too prudent statement.

Miss Sayers makes it because she believes that machines on the
land can do the work of men. So they can but only up to a point,
and one reason why we are in the pickle we undoubtedly are as to
the potential exhaustion of the resources of earth is because we have
passed that point. Every gardener, for instance, will regard what
Miss Sayers says as a downright absurdity. *He* knows that in his
garden machines *can not* do the work of men and that nothing can
be a substitute for the work of hand and eye. As a craftsman and a
cultivator, that is to say, the gardener looks upon the Work State,
by which I mean not only the employment of machines to do the
work but of men *as* machines, with utterly different eyes from those
of our industrialism and, I regret to say in this instance, from those
of Miss Sayers, whose genius of insight should have known better.

The salient fact about a garden is that its work is never done.
Since that work must be Adam's after his expulsion from Paradise,
the gardener never ceases sighing for more human labour. While
there is nothing our civilization despises so much as a pair of hands
being used, the gardener looks upon them as a benediction. They
are a very present help in time of trouble, a means to that control
over the husbandry of his garden for which he longs. And this
is not only true of the gardener but of every holder of a small
property and indeed of every true farm, large or small, in the land.

It will be remembered that in the first chapter I spoke of a garden as a unit of husbandry.

The economy of the gardener is based on a thrifty use of his resources and, I repeat, as much labour as he can get. But this economy of the small man is a very different thing from the economics of those who would gladly be rid of him. Even to-day, at a time when thrift means self-preservation, the dice are heavily loaded against the thriftiest members of the community. Take the backyarder and his or her hens. If he were encouraged, everybody knows that he could double or even treble the desirable output of eggs. A man and wife very well known to me get a "balanced ration" (much of which looks like sawdust) which suffices for two hens; it just suffices to keep them alive and is to real poultry feed exactly what watering a plant is to rain on it. Yet they keep 14, 8 bantams and 6 pullets. How then do they feed them? Partly by miracles of economy with kitchen waste and partly because they have the foresight and laborious willingness to collect 5 sacks of "leasings" (gleanings) in the autumn harvest. They are extremely productive, that is to say, through their own local initiative, care and prudence against the official attempt to prevent them from being so. They have told me how it went to their hearts to see an invaluable source of supply in the tail-corn of chaff and cavings from threshed corn burned for four days and nights almost literally under their eyes. No objections were raised to this abominable waste, every obstacle is opposed to their thrift. Had they kept thirty (or is it twenty-five?) chickens they would have registered with a poultry dealer who in his turn sells the eggs to the Ministry of Food which may send them hundreds of miles away. More waste of transport, of labour, of time and of food-values. Food is, in fact, allowed for poultry on condition that its produce should *not* be locally distributed. It is hardly surprising in such circumstances that poultry which A. G. Street in *Hitler's Whistle* (1943) has declared indispensable for folding over the land to fertilize it, has declined by a quarter of the pre-war stock and the pig by half.

In this same village where these backyarders live, some cattle got into a ten-acre field of standing corn. It was so trampled down that the farmer procured some Irish labourers to reap it with scythes and fagging stick. It was then horse-raked. But before a single grain could be used by man or beast, three tractors arrived from the W.A.C. and ploughed it all in. A native of the village told me that

it would have fed the poultry of the entire village for a twelvemonth.
Before a spectacle of such wantonness of official waste as this one
can but stand aghast. What nemesis is not in store for us who
repay the earth's bounty with such profligacy in high places?
What judgment can be too harsh? Contrast it with another example
I know of where a man keeps 3 cows, 3 pigs, poultry and bees and
feeds two families of 9 persons almost entirely from a diminutive
holding of 10 acres. Are not these men "efficient?" Of course not
in the accepted modern meaning of the term. But the right name
for them is the salt of the earth. Let the gardener regard them
with humility and admiration; they are his exemplars.

It is said with truth that the owner of a small holding, be it
garden or farm, works much too hard. Why so, when much of the
work *is* drudgery? The profits are infinitesimal or nil, the returns
are often incommensurate with the energy and skill expended
and the temper of the age is all against the small unit. Because
by it he preserves his independence; through it he satisfies his
natural skill-hunger, his "artistic sense" and at the same time
feeds his family. He keeps his self-respect and his liberty of choice
and can (more or less) snap his fingers at the obsession of the
"Economic Man." Because he is the master of the work and, under
his diligent hands and painful aforethought, his holding blossoms
like a flower. He is a creator, and so true to the Creation. So the
meanest drudgery is dignified, and even sanctified.

Do I enjoy cutting grass edges with but one natural leg and one
useful arm? No, but I love to see the straight line when it is done
and that straight line is the measure of a well-tended garden which I
neglect at the cost of my responsibility for it. We are the trustees
of our native land and the stewards of the earth, and we are Englishmen with an historical sense of individual liberty. Thus, there is
only one problem for the gardener, the peasant, the yeoman, how
to get enough labour to do his duty by his land, not to *save* labour
but increase it. And since the last thing the economists, the states-
men and the planners ever think of is to repeople our native land,
I can see but one "solution" to this one "problem." It is that
gardeners and small holders should form local associations of mutual
assistance and co-operative buying and selling as a modern adaptation of the traditional village community of the open fields. I
have no space here to develop this idea, but the independent, self-
acting co-operative Growmore Clubs started by Hampshire farmers

that have no connection with the official W.A.C.s are the best example of how to execute it. We have to remember that distributed small ownership is *naturally and traditionally* co-operative. Sir Henry Slesser tells me, for instance, that the small farmers of Dartmoor, descendants of immemorial copyholders, "all help one another when wanted at harvest, lend each other tools and labour, cut each other's hair, etc." It was the *laissez faire* individualism of the 19th century which broke up this universally co-operative habit. It needs not to be created but restored.

The second question of the garden economist is—what can he grow on his plot? As in other issues, the answer will be the reverse of modern orthodoxy, because he will aim at two things only— the widest diversity of crops combined with a purely qualitative standard. He will be like the artist who accepts the limitations of his medium but elicits the utmost of its possibilities. Every year he will experiment with novelties, as many as possible of which will be traditional cottage garden crops that the average seedsman knows nothing of. You have to know the cottagers and those who know them for that. The Hamburg Parsnip, for instance, whose top is parsley-like and root of a much nuttier flavour than that of any of the catalogue parsnips, originally came, like the Jersey Bean, from the cottage garden. After long trial and error and with many a lamentable failure, I have endeavoured to put these dual principles into practice. First, the broad divisions, flowers, fruit, crops and herbs but not kept in separate compartments—when Capability Brown and the landscape gardeners thrust the kitchen-garden out of sight, they degraded its status and broke up the comity of civilized plant-nations. My kitchen-garden is edged with flowers such as lupins, irises and the variegated Cheiranthus, espalier fruit-trees and the Mermaid Rose. It is a herbarium as well, so that as many dishes as may be shall be a *bouquet garni*.

The arable ground also serves as a nursery for soft fruit and annuals and is topped by a miniature orchard with Viburnum and other shrubs as a kind of by-product of the main orchard. I grow as great a variety of fruit as possible—apples, pears, plums, peaches, greengages, figs, grapes, medlars, red, white and black currants (the fine *Boskoop Giant*), Alpine and other strawberries (including the heavy cropper, *Ober Schlessen*), raspberries (the white, usually called the yellow Antwerp, the best eater I know, and Norfolk Giant, the best cropper, not only far superior to Lloyd George but later in fruiting so that it does not clash with the strawberries), filberts, walnuts and Kentish cobs, loganberries, gooseberries, cultivated blackberries and quinces (in a dry garden one of my failures). But I also cultivate as many species within each family as are consistent with so small an area. I even tried eccentric fruits like the strawberry-raspberry which tastes like cotton-wool and served me right. But the Boyson Berry and the Hailsham autumn-fruiting raspberry which I now grow are, like the Atlè wheat, new crops to the credit of our own age.

Thus, in an assembly of 17 pear trees, there are Conference, Doyenné du Comice, the golden brown Beurré Hardie, Jargonelle (this kind with its troubadour-like name is one of Cobbett's recommendations), Winter Nelis, the yellow, green and russet Joséphine de Malines, the October Louise Bonne and Williams' Bon Chrétien. Such are pears for one month and pears for another, the prodigal in any single year compensating for the niggardly as is the way of hard fruits. Catillac pears, the best of all cookers, I always get from my Dickory. The apples are as varied, though in this class Cox's Orange Pippin predominates. Fortunately, monoculture is impossible with hard fruit, and correct interplanting is essential for ample cropping. Even though I have only one kind of apple (Bramley's Seedling) which is a "triploid" (viz., a bad pollinator with 51 chromosomes) needing the "diploids" (with 34 chromosomes) to pollinate it, I freely mix even the diploids.

As for arable crops in the kitchen garden, the annexe to the orchard and in the orchard itself, I raise hardly fewer than fifty in a year, roots, cereals and vegetables. I confine myself to two cereals, oats and a new variety of maize given me by Lord Portsmouth and bred by himself. It has the advantage over other maizes, including Golden Bantam, of early ripening.[1] Perhaps, like many modern discoveries, it is a recovery of what has been lost, for Cobbett declared *his* maize ripened in the coldest of summers. Whether for himself or his livestock he did not say, for cattle like a dry and yellow grain, while we men can eat corn off the cob as soon as the tassel, to use Lord Portsmouth's words, is "like a sick negro's hair." Coke of Norfolk actually grew good maize earlier than Cobbett in 1828 and obtained it at the beginning of the 19th century from Massachusetts.

My lettuces I carry right through the year by growing corn

[1] In 1943, the crop was ready for the table soon after mid-August.

salad, land and other cresses, Arctic lettuce, smooth-leaved (the best) and curly endives and chicory, all of which make winter and early spring salads. Purslane is an addition to Cos and cabbage lettuce in the summer and autumn. The endive I bleach by the simple process of inverting over it the largest of my flower-pots. The onion gap (I also grow garlic) I close by planting in late summer and autumn as well as in the spring. I thus can afford to take a good spring culling from the earlier crop before they have achieved what Sir Thomas Browne called their "circinations and spherical rounds." Since I have no glass but for cold frames, I plant for "cowcumbers" the Stockwood Ridge, said to be the hardiest and most prolific of them all, and three other ridge cucumbers, one of them for pickling. The best of these is the small oval Russian cucumber of a delicate flavour and devoid of the tartness incident to ridge cucumbers. I have, too, Mammoth Pumpkins that flourish on the compost stack, the Hubbard Squash, a new edible gourd and, as well as the Common Marrow, the Russian and South African varieties, the last cut green and no larger than a cricket ball. Together with the customary vegetables, I grow Salsify (which Cobbett grew), Skirret (which Cobbett also grew), Calabresse and Celeriac. The Chinese artichoke serves me for two seasons without replanting and (to me) tastes better than the oysters to which it has been compared, and for a dual purpose that wonderful vegetable, Seakale Beet. This, besides coming in for the pot when the Savoys and Heading Broccoli are veteran, is a kind of asparagus when the glistening white midrib is cooked like celery and a spinach when the elephant ears of a rich glossy green are shredded from it. I have even grown a fine sugar-beet crop, but desisted owing to the lack of means to convert it into sugar. I wish I had had the prevision, years ago, to grow sugar-maples, whose beauty is as rich as their usefulness. The younger most of these vegetables are eaten, the better.

Purslane Cobbett in *The English Gardener* called in one of his racy prejudices "a mischievous weed, eaten by Frenchmen and pigs when they can get nothing else." It is to the best of my knowledge another dual purpose plant, a salad with stem and leaves, three cuttings in a season, and cooked *à l' épinard*.[1] Besides the ordinary broad, French and runner beans, I grow others to be shelled out as flageolets in the winter or eaten in the young green pods. I love to experiment with these, Comtesse de Chambord,

[1] It is, however, subject to black fly.

Little Green Gem, the Brown Dutch, the Stringless Green, the noble Jersey Bean, the brilliant Robin Bean, the refined Princeps, a Scarlet Runner, the Golden Butter Bean,[1] a bright-podded dwarf eaten after topping and tailing, the Blue Coco Bean, whose long pods are of the royal purple and as excellent for beauty as the table. No living plants could better illustrate the junction of the two sovereign principles of beauty and utility nor more fruitfully minister to the fundamental purpose of a smallish garden.

For peas I also so far as possible go outside the stock-in-trade of the nurseryman, so often exhausted by mass and over-production, and, as in the notorious example of the Lloyd George raspberry, liable to virus and other diseases. So I grow peas that provide me with dishes from latter June till October and are less easy to procure than others. Such are Alderman and Onward, but there are others rarely if ever printed in catalogues. These are Petits Pois, the epicurean pea which is not a good cropper with me, the Asparagus Pea with its prostrate ramifying growth and a bright vetch-like red flower, whose rectangular pods, each with its quota of ten peas, are cooked whole. We gardeners of small-holding principles, who are rightly suspicious of buying seeds produced by mass-production and nine times out of ten on chemical manures, owe a debt to Eleanor Sinclair Rohde, who not only grows a number of the seeds I have named but on composted humus, and to George Bunyard.

Some of my French seeds—self-hearting Winter Endive from Touraine, an Early Stump Carrot, one of my Seakale Beets (*Race de Paris*) and the Summer Cabbage Lettuce called *Grosseblonde Paresseuse*—I owe to a learned friend who is a doctor at Cambridge and the inventor of Derris Powder. Lastly, I may mention the halfbreeds such as the climbing Pea Bean, a superior kind of Mange-tout which is neither pea nor bean and is a wonderful cropper, tenderer than the best French bean and perhaps the best for salting down. I also grow the Sugar Pea whose virtue, in these days of preserved and transported foods, is that it will not travel, and the Sucrene Lettuce, one of the crosses between lettuce and cabbage. I grow yet another cabbage lettuce—*Cos Craquante d'Avignon*, the most cracksome and toothsome of all summer Cos. In a mild winter, these Coses, planted in September, are ready in April and

---

[1]The climbing *Mont d'Or* Butter Bean is the best of all runner or French beans, the pods of the dwarf inclining to rot in touching the ground. This climber can no longer be bought, but I am obtaining seeds from a friend.

almost drip their sweet juices. So far as is possible, too, I make a
point of planting my own seed.[1] I have a suspicion that much of
the American seed imported nowadays is responsible for plant
disease and nurseryman's seed is as often old as new, thus making
for very irregular germination. Cobbett in *The English Gardener*
devoted three pages to the primary essential of soundness of seed.

When the individual soil-preferences and characteristics of
growth of so great a diversity of food-plants are considered, he who
has to fit them to their exigencies, to educe their capacities and
study their rotations may almost consider himself a husbandman.
Not only so, but he must also contrive various intercroppings and
inter-row planting. Such are spinach and runner beans. Other
plants are suitable for nurse-crops, if he is to pursue multiplicity
upon the realistic basis of economy in space. Some of my oats, for
instance, are a nurse-crop to beans, potatoes to leeks.

The moderns, whose doctrine of automatic progress has turned
ignorance of and contempt for the past into a prime virtue, imagine
in the vanity of their hearts that by undersowing a clover ley to a
cereal nurse-crop they are inventing a novelty. The *Nouvelle Maison
Rustique* of 1804 describes how the Flemish sowed together vetches,
peas, lentils, beans, barley and oats to make a "dragle" "than which
no forage is better or comparable." Cobbett, again, was well
acquainted with the principle of the long-term ley. On a downland field at Uphusband (Hurstbourne Tarrant) he would, he says,

"sow thick with sainfoin and meadow-grass seeds of all sorts
early in September: let the crop stand till the next July, feed it
then with sheep, and dig up all thistles and rank weeds that
might appear, keep feeding it but not too close during the
summer and the fall, and keep on feeding it for ever after."

It is obvious what Cobbett's opinion of our modern practice of ley-
farming without animal husbandry would have been. Rye-grass
and clover alone have indeed become a kind of fetish in these days
of expediency farming. But true countrymen notice that cows so
fed snatch at docks and nettles on their way to the milking shed.
In Switzerland, they allow a great variety of "weeds" to grow on
the pastures and at about 9 inches cut four times a year for hay.
The Swiss cowman, the best in the world, goes out on Sundays to

[1] This does not apply to potatoes.

collect these "weeds" which he hangs up in the cowhouse. If a cow
goes sick, he mixes them with the feed. But nature's principle of
variety is forgotten by modern industrial States. Is this one reason
why 80% of our cattle are diseased and the average life of a dairy
cow is $2\frac{1}{2}$ lactations? Such nutritious grasses as the fescues, cocksfoot, foxtail and others are usually omitted from modern seeds
mixtures. Not to mention legumes and deep-rooted "weeds" like
burnet, kidney vetch, melilot, and others. One of the sovereign
principles of our older husbandry was a variety akin to nature's.

In Mysore, the peasants plant millet as the main crop but every
sixth or seventh row is maize or sorghum with mustard and beans
sprinkled among it. Five miles from where I live, a small-holding
community, cultivating its acreage on the strip-system, sows its
beans among the wheat. Since dredge corn and other mixed crops
on the same ground are peasant practice, which the progressives
regard as obsolete, its motive was soil-fertility combined with
productivity. Robert Elliot in his Clifton Park system (see p. 264)
of sowing down a ley with a great number of different grasses and
legumes, was merely developing that practice. Ours is rather to
use the conventional ley as a means to continuing the use of artificials and the disuse of livestock.

Here and there we learn from our own errors which we might
have avoided from the example of our forefathers. Thus, in Hampshire, a large area of barley, potash-poor, was in 1942 completely
burned up by sulphate of ammonia, and a farmer set to work
inventing a machine for turning compost—to the making of which
Speed in *Adam out of Eden* and Evelyn in fifty folio pages of *Terra*
had given full directions three centuries ago. So did Cobbett in
1828 (*The English Gardener*), also recommending the use of salt
upon the heap or on the ground which certainly conserves moisture
and perhaps releases potash. Well do I remember a farmer of my
neighbourhood standing on my terrace a year ago. He stretched
out his arm and said, "Look at the colour of that field and that
one and that one. Starved. They are alcoholics, those fields, but
they get no food.[1]   Bags of sulphate of ammonia and superphos-
phate as substitutes for the dung-cart (one was put up for auction

[1]Lady Eve Balfour in *The Living Soil* (Faber; 1943) records that a salesman said to
her: "Use any soluble phosphate fertilizer and keep the rabbits away." Another said:
"Use enough nitro-chalk and you will get big greens that rabbits will scarcely touch;
if they do, they die." Yet men and livestock now "live" almost entirely on food grown
from soils so treated.

in my market-town and failed to fetch a bid) make profits for the
big firms but to beggar the fields. This agricultural jerry-building
that science, government and big business enforce will appear a
kind of profanity to the husbandman of few acres who makes the
very intensity and multifariousness of his cropping a means to
observing the golden rule of fertility.

A little I have come to understand this peasant mentality by
making my own field three times as fertile as it was when it was
cowsick virgin pasture. And how? Because I have made this variety
of crops and flowers and fruit support itself. In myself I have been
nothing but the medium for this circulation between life and
decay and renewal, nothing but an agent to secure its smooth
functioning. It is true that I have gone to the ditches outside my
boundary for the nettles and to the fields I can see out of my window
for the dung of the cattle and horses that feed on them. But for
this, my garden makes its own fertility by the law of nature which I
merely supervise.

I have no theories about the use of compost, old Tusser's "com-
pas," with which I shall deal more fully in the next chapter. I do
not theorise because I know by two infallible tests that this is the
true and only way of reaping the fruits of the earth in perpetuity.
First by experience; since I properly organised and regularised the
return of all wastes and plant residues to the soil, the health and
prosperity and fecundity of the garden have changed out of all
recognition. Secondly, by the *taste* of what I eat from it. I know
the difference *in taste* between food grown by natural and organic
manuring and that grown on artificials, between nature's way
and the way of modern civilization. This for me is proof positive
that the latter way is a pernicious delusion and heresy from the
way of truth. It is the way of the father of lies by the pressure of
vested interests, and the way to the death of the soil. I speak strongly
because composting is so very obviously a universal law. The
whole of life pivots upon the necessity of death for ministering to
the health and continuity of life, of the katabolic as the spring-
board of the anabolic and of decay and decomposition as the parent
of fruitfulness.[1]   Year by year we are disintegrating our soils by

[1] At long last a learned and historical work upon the third of these antitheses has
appeared in the bookshops (1943). This is Reginald Reynolds's *Cleanliness and Godliness.*
It is a book of merriment and gravity, wisdom, wit and freakishness, with a very un-
modern Rabelaisian flavour, pungent as an autumn bonfire. It is a vindication of nature
and an indictment of chemical manuring to gratify biologists, gardeners, historians and
men of letters alike.

the abandonment of good husbandry for banditry, as our whole civilization is disintegrating unless we can learn before it is too late to reinterpret our traditions and so to arrest the dissolution of our ancient culture.

A year ago I had tea in an old manor house of my neighbourhood. It was the kind of benedictive tea that should not have been eaten without at least a silent grace, without the sense of sacrament. Set before me was a great wooden platter of home-ground, home-baked bread from the stone-grinding mill on the estate, a glass dish of innumerable pats of butter from the cows feeding by the stream and a huge jar of honey from the apiary to the left of the cows. All but the mill I could see from the window as I ate and I knew exactly where the mill was and what it looked like. I was absorbing the very scenery, the rich meadows, the towering trees, the mill-race, the comfortable cows, the flowers, the bees taking in their cargo of nectar and setting sail for the hives. The purity of the guelder roses which we call "Whitsun bosses" hereabouts, the prodigality of this June painting in the window-frame, Blake's exuberance and Spencer's white chastity, as I ate I was drawing it all into my very being. How incredible it is that men now spend more than their food-bill on their doctors ! They pay through the nose for a patent medicine, a patent breakfast food (made of the wheat germ extracted by fraud from their daily bread), for the extravagance of what they call cheap food, vamped up, sterilised, produced from exhausted soils, transported over thousands of miles, when they could give themselves the health and vitality they need by shouldering the responsibility of growing it for themselves or at least within the orbit of their own neighbourhoods. Is that the rub? That in our hearts we have come to dread and fob off responsibility? Perish the thought or perish ourselves!

I cannot practice a self-sufficient economy so complete as this. But I also have my view from the window which I have known for ten years. Its composition is so true that I have never tired of it. The copse on the left thrusts out like the prow of a ship, the hedgerows swing out into the plain, the thickening of vegetation is the course of the little river, there is a low swell up to the clean bold line of the downland whose colour pales or deepens with the moods of the skies. That view saves me from the isolationism which (now that the old co-operative habit has been broken) is the only vulnerable point of the holding that attempts to support itself. If I cannot wholly feed myself from it, I can partly supplement what I grow myself with what I can see from the terrace, the Rhode Island Reds whose eggs I eat, the herd of Herefords whose milk I drink, reclining there in the distance with their white faces like bridal bushes. The chalk range bounds all and thence I have brought chairs and stools and many a furnishing for my house. But there is more in this view than that. If it is part of the economy of regionalism, it also links my garden with the virtue and significance of husbandry. I think of the fields in terms of my garden, of the garden in terms of the fields. They have taught me much, they and the men who till them, of that virtue whether in its observance or its violation. For I can also see from my window part of a farm of 200 acres without livestock on it all the year round, which I find indispensable for my one acre.

If I do not clothe myself in the wool of the sheep I see, I store my mind with them. Over my northern hedge is a June flock of Border Leicesters and Ryelands. The former do not go further back than Bakewell who first bred them. But Ryelands (so called from the sandy tracks of Herefordshire where rye was once grown) go back to the 12th century, Leominster having been their chief centre. Hence Drayton's "Lemster ore," which he called Colchos:

"Lemster for her wool whose staple does excel
And seems to overmatch the golden Phrygian fell."

Drayton took part of his description from Camden's *Britannia*, and John Philips his from Drayton in *Cyder*—"Can the fleece Bocalic or Torentine compare with Lemster's silken wool?" Were they called "golden fleeced" because they were once ochred as I have seen the Cotswold Lion breed, which date back to the 13th century? Yet Australia clothes us!

Over my eastern hedge is a flock of Southdowns—I have a crook from Pyecombe in my little museum and Sussex sheep-bells. These sheep keep alive in me the true England of my mind which the years of an evil age have trodden underfoot. And over my western hedge is a cross-bred flock of Kerries and Hampshire Downs, being "dagged" in April just before lambing. They are feeding down the wheat. This is the true traditional economy with which our economic system has nothing to do. For these sheep should fulfil a sextuple purpose. Their fleeces, their lambs, their mutton are the primary and obvious services. But they also consolidate the dry arable, prune the blades of corn so that they will tiller out and restore food and potash to a land starved of it. But the town dictates that it is not economical to keep sheep, and during the war, the time of greatest need, it became the deliberate policy of the urban powers to drive the sheep altogether from the lowlands and confine them to the mountains. Our farmers only keep sheep because from time to time they *have* to in order to save their land. Our economic system takes care there shall be no money in them. It does not agree with Tennyson's *Northern Farmer*:

> "Dubbut looak at the waaste: theer warn't no feead for a cow:
> Nowt at all but bracken an' fuzz, an' looak at it now—
> Warnt worth nowt a haacre, an' now theer's lots o' feead,
> Fourscoor yows upon it an' some on it doon in seead."

The traditional sheep-shearing time was Oak Apple Day. That is all forgotten now and all the shepherds of my region have gone. But I keep in touch with my countryside in another way. In the memory of the countryman, the cultivation of the earth has always been associated with its festivals, his work inseparable from his play. So we always plant our runner beans on May 8th, the date of the Club Feast, now obsolete, in all the villages about. And in my planting programme I always go either by my weather and vegetation or by local custom, never by the book. For there is an intuitive wisdom behind these punctuations. The books says that a camel's hair brush or rabbit's tail should be the medium between the pollen and the "fruit"-bud of the marrow. We never dream of so doing here; the little flies do it for us. So with tomatoes (which I plant with the peat of my winter fires), we water the plants from a rose to secure pollination. How so? Consider night-scented stock and tobacco-plant. They only smell at night, when there is more moisture and less evaporation than during the day, and after a shower, and what we do smell are not the petals but the pollen-grains. Hence watering the tomato-flowers is a means of their fertilisation. In spite, then, of the policy that fomented the war, we are as self-contained in our economy here as the urban powers permit us to be. There would seem to be good sense in it. In April, heading broccoli was fetching 7d. a lb. in the open market. I had one that weighed 5½ lbs., while I had an espalier of 200 large Coxes selling in London at 4/- apiece.

Garden economy is thus to be a cell in the regional body, a cell which at the same time is an entity and an identity in itself on the principle of self-sufficiency. This is one of the home-truths that England has forgotten for a century. Even my wheelbarrow (which is twenty years old and as good as new) was made in the village a quarter of a mile away. But this self-sufficiency is subject to one irrefragable condition. Our holdings must be held in trust—to our native land, on behalf of the responsibility of property, and to God. And to God, for if God is left out, words like responsibility, independence and indeed any valuation whatever are totally devoid of meaning. By the paradox of life, self-sufficiency has nearly always been achieved by the dependence of the community that practises it upon God, while the parasitism of the modern industrial state is accompanied by man's self-glorification. Godlessness is another word for irresponsible power in the exercise of which no values, Christian or otherwise, can survive. Our own State has not yet gone to the extremities of other States in the use and so the abuse of irresponsible power. It is still restrained from so doing by the traditions of Christendom and our own historical liberties. But these checks weaken year by year and almost day by day. They can only be strengthened by the restoration under God of the principle of responsible property of which my garden, any garden, is a warden.

The following is an extract from a Tudor Garden Prayer:

"In Thy Name O Lorde, we set plante and graffe, divining that by Thy Mighty Power they may encrease and multiplye uppon the earth, in bearing plenty of fruits, to the profits and comfort of all thy faithfull people thorow Christe our Lorde,

AMEN."

It is not obsolete.

CHAPTER THREE

THE AFTERNOON OF THE YEAR

(July—August—September)

I. Food and Fertility

"Every event in nature has its inception in the alteration of substance or change of action that preceded it. Spring is born of autumn; to-day's roses are nourished by the fragments of last year's leaves; the liquid burble of a wren outside your door is only the energy of yesterday's insects whose crushed and digested bodies are transmuted into song and joy, into flight and avian activity."

GILBERT KLINGEL: Inagua.

"You do not breed good men and women on tinned meat, canned tomatoes, foreign eggs with a rubber stamp on them, imported bananas with a band round them, or 'breakfast foods,' milled, grilled, baked-up, dried-up, puffed-up, roughed-up, packed in cardboard, kept for months, and sold at the pistol point of publicity campaigns. . . . Food from our own soil, fresh, unspoilt, full of irons and the salts of the earth—English beef, Southdown mutton, new milk, wheat with the grain in it, green vegetables and fresh fruits—these are the guarantee of health, the aids of the good doctor, the enemies of the quack."

J. WENTWORTH DAY: Farming Adventure.

IN *The Way of the Land*, Sir George Stapledon describes the progressive and industrial town of Slough which has spread like dermatitis over some of the richest market-gardening land in Western Europe. The building of Slough no doubt made large profits for estate companies, absentee landlords, building contractors and factory shareholders. But the promoters and builders of Slough never thought to attach gardens to the new houses sprawling out with all the latest amenities. Where, then, do the inhabitants of this milestone along the road to Utopia get their greens and potatoes? What were left of the market-gardens on the fringe of Slough sent their products to Covent Garden from which in the fullness of time they returned to Slough.[1] For some native of the Slough of Despond to take a few steps into his back garden and dig

---

[1] Lord Portsmouth records an example of a Hampshire market-gardener forced to grow carrots which were transported to Ipswich, there tinned and thence returned to the village to be sold.

up his own potatoes would have been putting the clock back. To do this over the length and breadth of our native land would be more destructive of modern economics than a dozen revolutions.

I take it, then, that in relating the details of a few of my summer suppers, I am helping to found a new order more advanced because so utterly backward than anything of which our planners ever dreamed. To go out and pick one's own peas swelling after a day's rain, a kind of bloom of rain, lingering, spectral, noiseless, windless, is almost as good as eating them. Nothing indeed could be more revolutionary than this interaction between producing and consuming within the compass of a single holding. It is the luxury of simplicity. It is a step towards wholeness of living, the key to something more than health of body, to a frugality inwardly rich in association and satisfaction. A meal that is good in itself and for yourself, that is the reward of work, and what Eric Gill, speaking of his French family farm, called "agricultural righteousness." It is a meal that should be a true sacrament, the crown of a covenant and partnership with the earth. Everything you eat has overtones and memories; you know all about it from A to Z. So the good woodsman remembers the tree, the wood, the landscape, his own skill and care, in the finished article.

Take, for instance, purslane, that I mix with my salad early in July. The seeds were sent me by a learned Cambridge friend and they made compact bushes with sedum-like leaves, blunt and rounded at the tips and of a pleasing light green. Greenfinches recognise the pods—how do they know that such an unlikely receptacle contains edible seeds? As you eat, with something of the deliberation of old Iden in Jefferies's *Amaryllis at the Fair*, you compare it with the various cresses you grow; it is more palatable than land-cress but lacks the agreeable tartness of chicory and endive that, failing autumn-sown cos in a hard winter, were your winter salads. To grow it revives a traditional dish, and so, as you eat, you partake in the life of the old comely England which the economics of cheap imported food has temporarily submerged. My first purslane of the year I had with salad, new potatoes, broad beans (cut young), mint, garlic (rubbed round the salad bowl), lemon thyme, strawberries, white and red currants and raspberries— all out of the garden. Did Heliogabalus fare better? Did Lucullus know as much about food-values? Still more to the point—do we or rather the powers that rule us know anything whatever about them? In 1943, a Somerset Women's Institute made 112 lbs. of "excellent seedless blackberry and apple jam, pure fruit and set like music." It was condemned by a government inspector as "sub-standard," so that it could not be sold to the public. Yet jam so sold with the government stamp of approval contains only 3 per cent. of fruit.

The Alpine strawberries I have had in the garden since 1935, sowing fifty plants in April and having a thousand in October. I still keep one or two beds of them, but the best and largest are self-propagated and sown in any odd places where they can hide from the sun's eye—in the stone-walks, on the terrace, even in the cold frames. The other strawberries, Walton's God's berry, are Royal Sovereign and Ober Schlessen,[1] a marvellously prolific strawberry (no doubt because it has not yet been mass and over-produced from runners alone) but barren unless grown in proximity with others, Royal Sovereign, Fillbasket, etc. Raspberries I eat with scalded cream from the top-milk or Les Battus or the curds taken at the consistency of whipped cream or Coeur de Jeanette, heart-shaped from a wicker basket and more solidified. Les Battus we make from my farmer-friend's cows over the hedge, suspended for 24 hours to exude the whey and mixed with the top milk. I owe some of my soft cheeses to the recipes of Mrs. Constance Spry, a self-sufficient craftswoman in garden and kitchen invention and quality. It is a pity, therefore, that she adopts a chromium-plated style which succeeds only in being pretentious. Why should a country writer dress up her wares in a Bond Street smartness? These raspberries are Norfolk Giant,[2] another soft fruit but not yet exploited to exhaustion and disease like the Lloyd George raspberry and in moist years lasting me till October when I get several dishes off the next year's canes. And if the "cream" for this abundant fruit is not out of the garden (though I still think of getting one day a tethered pigmy Dexter cow), at least I can see the cow out of the window. There is much to be said for a mathematics of food; it is good in inverse ratio to the distance you get it from. With the invention of dehydration, which enables foods not only to be dried but much reduced in bulk so that they can be transported in aeroplanes instead of ships, food-mobility will be carried to greater extravagance, fresh foods will be yet fewer and even the "protective" foods of our farmers be subject to as fierce a competition from abroad as the

[1] See page 83.　　　[2] See page 83.

staple ones. So the contemporary world discovers ever more ingenious devices in the circumvention of nature and to its own destruction.

I had my first dish of calabresse early in August with cold meat and cooked in vegetable juices. Salted (with rock-salt), peppered and nutmegged with the top milk on it, it is superior even to purple sprouting broccoli and much better than the coarse curly kale which it superficially resembles. All my cucumbers and tomatoes are grown in the open, and from two very short rows of the latter I can get at least a bushel every year, a household sufficiency. Both to my palate are superior in taste, as they certainly are in food-value, to the green-house ones. My cucumbers, including the striated, blunt, oval Russian cucumber that looks rather like a sea-urchin, are richer in juices than frame-cucumbers which sell for half a crown each in the market. To a woman complaining of the price the boothman said: "I'll cut it in half and sell you each one for 1/3 each."

I thus acquire a multifarious palate by quantity in the number of kinds of vegetables I grow. But I also acquire a selective one by concentrating on quality through using nothing but compost, saving my own seed and fetching the food whenever possible straight from the soil to the pot. My friend, the husbandman who has already figured in these pages, used to set on his table tomatoes grown from compost—and by modern methods. His guests invariably chose the former and believed they were a superior variety from the latter. Indeed, the humblest of self-grown, whole-eaten foods are both more palatable and more life-giving than the richest and most exotic, meretriciously dressed up and deceitfully doctored. It is tragic to think that nine-tenths (probably a much higher percentage) of the entire population of Britain never knows the natural, essential taste of any vegetable[1] and never consumes its full nutrients and vitamins. And Sir George Stapledon declares it to be the most vitalising of all foods. With craftsmanship in the cooking (and I am fortunate enough in that essential to have a housewife in the old lost 17th century sense of the word), you are eating not only natural but highly civilised food and with none of

[1] Mr. L. F. Easterbrook, the agricultural writer and a good composter for years, writes:—"We have not enjoyed vegetables of such flavour and succulence since the fabulous days of childhood. One member of the family, for instance, who formerly hated parsnips, has become a complete convert since growing them with compost produced a soft succulent vegetable that almost melts in the mouth."

its nutritional powers wasted in the process. A shoppy old marrow, for instance, tastes like wood-fibre. But cut young, cooked whole, stuffed with unpolished rice, wrapped in grease-paper, garnished with chopped up egg, suet, chopped bacon and wholewheat bread-crumbs and dusted with thyme, sage, chives, tarragon, mint and parsley fresh from the garden and grown on compost, it is a dish not merely for a king but for a gardener.

I could fill this book with an inventory of my summer meals, like a 17th century account book. There shall be but one more, eaten on September 12th. Cold rabbit pie with cucumber, tomatoes, Great Scot potatoes in their jackets, lettuce, the last of the peas and the Robin and Jersey beans. I usually contrive to make the last of the peas coincide with the first of the Brussels sprouts just about the end of the third quarter of the year. The main dish was a rabbit shot over the hedge of my garden, not imported from Belgium, sold as a hare and regarded as cheap food. It is beyond me to describe the taste of a good bean. I have to call in the aid of another organ of sense, the sight. One of this pair (the Robin) hangs in August a pod splashed and mottled coral-red on green, like a swimming goldfish, and under a canopy of overlapping lanceolate leaves coloured a pale lemon-amber, as though dipped in the afterglow. The large beans, each in its downy white pocket, are white with splashes and filaments of crimson, not unlike the hieroglyphic eggs of the yellow-hammer. Their "exterior semblance" does not belie their eating qualities, and as they com-bine beauty with utility in the garden, so palatability with honest nourishment in the mouth.

For a change, I move on to the pea-bean, like a superior French bean but with a softer skin and a delicate left-motif of pea flavour. It is, of course, cooked whole: nothing so betrays crudity of taste in the moderns as their habit of slicing up French or runner beans. Had I the pen of a Charles Lamb, I could write a beautiful essay about the different flavours of a dozen different beans I grow in my garden of an acre and a bit. When the tulips are over, I plant some of the highly coloured Robin Bean in the beds round my sunk garden, where they could easily be mistaken for exotics. I propose to combine these next year in the same beds with the blue cabbage to which Chesterton devoted a prose-poem. As this kingly cabbage also tastes like chestnuts, once more use marries beauty. Feed it with diluted urine once every three weeks and it is a giant.

Yet modern civilization with all the world as its handmaid is as barbarous in the food it eats as it is barbarous in its treatment of the earth that grows it. A civilization devoid of the sense of wholeness of living, such as the smallest garden properly cultivated displays, is beneath all its chromium plating uncivilized.

Of that wholeness the compost heap is, as I have said, the linchpin. Without this generating station of humus, the whole edifice of self-sufficiency collapses,[1] and with its collapse go all the food-realities. Fetch your food from the garden as fresh as you please; if it is not grown from humus, that is to say, out of the flesh and blood of the garden itself (with a bit of aid from over the hedge), it might almost as well have come out of Covent Garden. The vital link is missing. I once heard a B.B.C. talk by one of the Rothamstedians to children. It advocated certain kinds of fertilizers they should use in their gardens for different types of plant. There may or may not be something to be said for the use of artificials on the large-scale mechanised farms (our modern *latifundia*)—and from the point of view of organic agriculture nothing at all can be said for it. But there is not the faintest shadow of an excuse for them in any self-respecting garden or small holding over and beyond that of swelling the profits of the enormous interests whose business it is to see that organic husbandry shall become obsolete. It is not only completely unnecessary for children to buy artificials for their gardens but positively corrupting to their general mentality to be instructed in their use.[2] Why? Because it gives them a false conception of the kinds of laws, intricate and exquisitely disciplined, which nature employs in maintaining and repairing the architecture of plant-life. The inorganic plays the lowest part of all in this great drama of interdependent and interacting life-in-death and death-in-life. But the children would go away from that lecture with the idea in their budding minds that chemistry—a clever trickster—was the real hero of the play.

I do not say that the man giving the talk intended to convey that impression, but that must have been the effect produced. It

[1] In the Highlands, for instance, the decline of the crofter's self-supporting husbandry corresponded with soil-exhaustion.

[2] Not to mention their lethal effect on the soil. "The fertility that produces the most luxuriant plant association is all contained in the vegetation itself; the soil is . . . a passage-way through which nutrients are rapidly transferred from the dead to the living plants." Jacks and Whyte: *The Rape of the Earth.*

could not fail to distort and falsify the child-sense of the wonder and mystery of organic life. Every child should have a religious view of life, and this is a religious view.[1] It is an abomination that a child should believe chemistry to be the dominant power in life. Leave it to the adults to assume that nature is an atomic force that sets us "problems" in the manipulation of matter and energy. The only possible inference to be drawn is that the actual life of nature, if it can be said to exist, is an irrelevant epiphenomenon, a kind of froth exuded out of the complicated energies of heat, motion, light, radiation, electrons. It is singular indeed that, while material-ism as a philosophy of human life is now utterly discredited, it should be assumed to be valid for plant-life. If human beings cannot be kept alive on chemicals, how should plants? There can be no real doubt that plants can suffer from deficiency diseases, the effects of malnutrition like our own. Observers *in the field* have noted that insects, virus and other infections rarely attack other than weak and leave virile ones alone. They are in fact nature's sharp warning that her plant is being improperly fed. Not only does this vicious doctrine teach the children to see nature "as in a glass darkly," but to be lazy and parasitic. They learn how to take the short cut. Chemical pellets save them from observing the dietetic preferences of animals, how, as experimenters have now proved, mice, rats, rabbits, poultry, sheep and cattle will always choose foods organi-cally to inorganically manured. Yet what child has so much as heard of the great name of Sir Robert McCarrison? They grow up in the magical superstition (like the sacred congealed blood of St. Januarius) that what makes the garden grow is something out of a bottle, a sack, or a tin. Science originally made war on super-stition and has now enthroned its own. No wonder that the majority of the nation's children believes that milk comes out of a pasteurised milk-bottle. Educate them from magic to truth. It comes out of a cow.

Fortunately, the orthodox science that everywhere supports big business (they have made the Dust Bowl between them) is not the only one in the field. Let the compost heap be approached through Sir Frederick Keeble's *Science Takes a Hand in the Garden*.

"Is it not time to take stock of the situation and to ask not only

[1] "Divinity," runs the Oriental saw, "sleeps in the stones; stirs in the plants ; wakes in the animals; is conscious alone in man." Quoted by Miss Maye Bruce in *From Vegetable Waste to Fertile Soil* (1943).

what are the benefits but also what are the inevitable evils that follow in the train of scientific progress? There is a curiously unconscious presumptuousness about science. It is always assuming that the things it describes explain the things that happen. . . . It is the humus of the soil that pins the earth down. Destroy that and the soil is destroyed and with it the human society that subsists on it. . . . 'Who feeds well manures well' is the peasant's most advanced scientific opinion. . . . It is the interest of every consumer to see what he eats."

A significant comment upon this extract is that one of the largest seeds merchants in Great Britain makes contracts for seed only where it is grown with no artificials.

The principle of the compost heap is both the principle of nature and the principle of wholeness. Thus, orthodox science, in opposing it as it has repeatedly done, has progressed from the interpretation of nature to setting up systems as hostile to nature as are its specialisations to wholeness of living and thinking. The true but heretical science of earth-culture is that of Sir Albert Howard's now celebrated Indore Process. This is simply an analytical examination of nature's own methods of regenerating her forests by means of the mixed humus of the woodland floor, and the constructive adaptation of natural humus manufacture through bacterial energy to man's own need for regenerating the soils which he plants and cultivates for his own purposes.

Like most of the more genuine discoveries of modern days, its roots are in the past, as far back indeed as Tusser's *Five Hundred Points of Good Husbandry*. An Arabian wrote a treatise on the properties of compost in the 10th century. According to contemporary testimony, the Islanders of Barra made compost in 1794, and the Aran Islanders made their barren rock fruitful by the use of it. John Evelyn made a prolonged study of it in *Terra*, and Speed in *Adam out of Eden*. In *Leaves of Grass*, Whitman has a poem called *This Compost* whose last stanza runs:

"Now I am terrified at the Earth, it is that calm and patient,
  It grows such sweet things out of such corruptions,
  It turns harmless and stainless on its axis, with such endless
    successions of diseas'd corpses,
  It distills such exquisite winds out of such infused fetor,

> It renews with such unwitting looks its prodigal, annual,
>   sumptuous crops,
> It gives such divine materials to men, and accepts such leavings
>   from them at last."

Cobbett recommended compost with his usual lucidity of detail
(" A great deal more is done by the fermentation of manures than
people generally imagine"), and Dr. G. V. Poore, a consulting
physician to many London hospitals, born a century ago, advocated
the saving of city wastes and the use of night soil for conversion
into humus in his *Essays on Rural Hygiene* and other works. The
traditional practice of the French is to make " terreau," very well
rotted dung mixed with soil and frequently turned. This produces
4 market garden crops between January and July on the same
soil every year. The Chinese[1] have, of course, been compost-makers
for centuries and for 4000 years have held the belief that every
person with access to land can support himself from *his own* waste
products. This is one good reason why they have preserved their
civilized structure from the collapse that has befallen other cultures
less tough than theirs.[2]   These systems knew from traditional
practice the processes and results of composting. But, if Dr. Poore's
pioneer work be excepted, they were unaware of what actually
took place in the translation of organic and vegetable residues
into plant-food. To establish this on a scientific basis has been the
work of Sir Albert Howard in his *Agricultural Testament*, and, to a
lesser extent and with some occult suggestion, of Rudolf Steiner
and Dr. Pfeiffer. To these honourable names should be added those
of the botanist, Prof. Bottomley, who invented the formidable
titles of "auxinomes" for vitamins of plant life which are found
only in organic substances, and of Prof. Gilbert Fowler, an erudite
and zealous exponent of the "rule of return."

Hamlet remarked to his mother:—"Spread the compost on the
weeds to make them ranker." But what makes plant-growth rank
is not compost but the use of chemicals as a plant-food rather
than a plant-stimulant,[3] just as the face of a man who drinks

---

[1] See Prof. King's *Farmers of Forty Centuries*.

[2] Our progressive intellectuals, of course, think differently. As one of them (Peter
Cromwell in *Horizon*, August, 1943) puts it, China "so long asleep" is soon to be awakened
by the trumpet of the angel of industrialism.

[3] The effect is well seen in the rank growth of the straw in cereal crops dosed with
sulphate of ammonia. This is the main reason for the "lodging" of so many cornfields
in these days. That and disease, and yet no farmer now dares plant his seed without a
mercurial dressing.

too much whisky becomes puffed and mottled. A closer analogy is perhaps the use of drugs for insomnia. In a neuropathic condition, a sleeping draught may restore the normal rhythms of the patient's metabolism; if persisted in, it destroys the very sleep it was its purpose to induce. Humus is the daily bread of the living soil. If for one reason or another its condition is impaired, a phosphatic or nitrogenous fillip may well repair it; to continue such treatment is, when it asks for bread, to give it a stone. In a garden where I was staying, the cabbages, artificially manured, were twice the size of my own. But they were all without hearts, whereas mine, compost-fed, had all dense and tight hearts.

The Rudolf Steiner school uses certain coloured essences kept in darkness and coloured bottles until used on the heap. They are then said to exert a "dynamic" (a favourite word) influence. The blossoms of camomile, dandelion, valerian, yarrow, nettle, have to be gathered before midday, moistened with rain-water, pounded in a mortar, wrapped in butter muslin, pressed out in a potato or fruit squeezer, strained and bottled. Essences are also extracted from pure run honey and powdered oakbark, the last of which is steeped in 2 ozs. of rain-water, stirred, left for 24 hours, strained and bottled. When the compost stack is completed, a dram of one or other of these solutions with a pint of rain-water is poured over it, whether with appropriate incantations and invocations is not recorded.

The "etheric anthroposophists," whose prophet was Rudolf Steiner, also build elaborate compost stacks within sleepers fastened by hoop-iron or planks of seasoned timber or brick or stone walls and on layers first of stone rubble or gravel and second of charcoal. They reject pig manure and they insist on unslaked lime, pulverised on the spot. They are very particular about the density of the layers of soil, grass cuttings and vegetable residues superimposed sandwich-fashion, about watering in dry weather and protecting from heavy rains. Occult "Forces" radiate through the air, interpenetrate the soil, quicken the seed, harness the roots to the earth and enable the plant to "defy the Laws of Gravitation." Thus the acolytes who minister to these influences regard the compost heap as a kind of Ark of the Covenant to which ritual and herbal sacrifice are meet to be paid.

It would be easy to deride this religiosity and its articles of observance, and to regard them as an elaborate and pantheistic cultism. It suggests an up-to-date white witchcraft like that of culling simples under the waxing or waning moon. It tends to frighten people away from its eccentricity, nor in eschewing animal manures is it true to nature. I cannot pretend that my own compost heap is a pagoda of such shelved, buttressed and composite architecture as this.[1] There is not the time nor labour for it for one thing, and, like all true field-labour, composting takes plenty of both. I do floor the heap or rather stack with rough stuff, hedge-cuttings and the woody stalks of Brussels sprouts and I do build it exactly like a rick, some five to six feet long and four to five broad. Like the rick-builder, I make up its sides before filling in the middle, I keep it properly cornered and the sides clean-cut and slightly battered. I dress away any ragged edges and cover it with sacks and an old carpet against heavy rains and drought, but also to intensify the heat. It is a structure, not a heap, and so far as possible I keep the soil, the animal manure and the vegetable refuse in blocks or stories. It is often inconvenient to do so, since the residues pile up every day, the soil and manure are added but seldom.

For it is difficult to spare quantities of soil out of a garden whose every square foot is in use for one purpose or another. Fortunately, I have a good dyke outside my eastern hedgerow whose oozy bottom makes one pinguid layer and nettles another. I cannot praise the nettle too highly. There is a yeoman I know whose one reason for buying his farm was the nettles on it; if nettles grow on it, he said, anything will. Good for making paper and linen, good for brewing nettle-beer, good, as Shakespeare knew, for growing strawberries under them, good too for guarding plums from wasps and good again for ripening the plums on beds of them, good for raising the temperature of the stack, good for salads when young,[2] good for the whitethroat or nettle-creeper, a fort of a million spears for her fragile cradle and very good for the compost stack from their potential wealth of calcium and potash.

All the household wastes I also use with the exception of those that go to the livestock or have printer's ink upon them. And nothing that grows in the garden but finds here its last home and

[1] A very much simpler version of Steinerism is given in Miss Maye E. Bruce's *From Vegetable Waste to Fertile Soil* (Faber; 1943). A much more comprehensive work on soil-vitality, the functions of humus, nutrition and the Indore Process of Sir Albert Howard is E. B. Balfour's *The Living Soil* (Faber; 1943).

[2] Here is a recipe from Dr. Fraser Darling's *Island Farm*: the four top leaves of each stalk of young nettles put into a saucepan. Press. Add a little water. Cool for 7 minutes, moving nettles and gently pounding. No straining. Add fat, pepper and salt.

bed, to feed the living by the due end and course of nature and by the mysterious cycle of life, decay and renewal. Even the prunings and hedge-clippings I strip of their leaves in death's service for life. Stout woody stems like those of Brussels sprouts and other Brassicas I either crush with a maul or use for foundation or aeration. Urine swells the offerings, though I have not yet had the courage or the means to experiment with night-soil,[1] which Cobbett advocated for its uses in fermentation. Luckily, I am surrounded by small farmers and so can make use of horse and cow manure, apart from the ample contributions of my own livestock. For mixed organic manures are the best.[2]

Four stakes are thrust into the heart of the fermenting and decomposing mass for the air to sweeten and aerate it. I turn and rebuild it, keeping the green stuff on the inside, when time permits. When the complex processes of metabolism are completed, the result is a rich currant cake, highly compressed but breaking down into a friable mould that will go through a sieve, odourless and of the consistency of potting soil. The only "chemicals" I use are lime and potash from the ashes of my peat and wood fire or from burnings of hedge-cuttings and prunings. But it behoves the composter to be careful with lime. It tends to dry the stack.

Many gardeners who adhere to the principle of the compost heap use sulphate of ammonia or calcium cyanomide for hastening the processes of fermentation and decomposition. Even the excellent No. 7 Ministry of Agriculture Dig for Victory leaflet approves of the use of chemical fertilizer on the compost midden. This is characteristic of the modern superstitious magic of the Djinn in the bottle called by some heavy-armoured name in bastard Greco-Latin. But all it really means is the modern passion for short cuts and dodging nature. These chemicals certainly dislocate the balance of the stack, as does excessive dung, by encouraging the anaerobic at the expense of the humus-forming bacteria and fungi and so releasing the nitrogen into the air as ammonia. For, though humus contains all the chemical ingredients in proper balance that are now applied piecemeal to the soil from factory by-products, its organic action is not chemical

---

[1] Dr. Pfeiffer, the Dutch farmer and bio-dynamic composter, used to say that by compost you gave your plants not this or that food but a restaurant.

[2] It has been suggested that small communities should pay rates not for a garbage man but a gardener whose charge should be the conversion of night soil into compost, together with pig manure from the community's own pig-clubs.

at all. The real function of humus is "to stimulate the activity of soil fungi" on which the plant-rootlets depend for their vitality and immunity to disease. These fungi "feed on the humus in the soil and it is the product of their metabolism which is of such vital importance to the complete and balanced nourishment of the plant."[1] Humus is a substance that comes from the once living.

This discovery goes to the heart of the illusion that chemicals feed plants and explains why disease always accompanies the use of chemicals without humus. The activities of these soil fungi *on which all life ultimately depends* are inhibited. Chemical fertilizers also affect the closeness of texture in the ultimate mould and so its moisture-retaining qualities. Their brusque interference with the natural workshop (like an inspector bursting in on a factory and hustling the work-people) hardly ever accomplishes its purpose. Fortnightly applications of lawn-mowings most effectively expedite the formation of humus. The chemical changes are brought into action by intensification of heat and it is impossible to put one's hand into the stack after the lawn-mowings are on. Come a shower and it smokes and will sink two or three feet in as many days. When a stack is thus treated according to the prescription of nature, it is quite free of flies and odour and is ready for use in three or four months, rather longer in winter and if the weather is very wet or dry. If it is made in a workmanlike fashion, all weed-seeds are killed, all spores of virus and all "pestilence-stricken" leaves. When weed-seeds germinate (as they sometimes do), the fault is in the composter, not the compost.

I have already described the almost miraculous effect of a well-made compost upon the fertility of the soil and the vigour of plant-life. These in their turn ensure freedom from disease and the good health of men and animals that feed on it, while the vitality of the plant is expressed in the palatability of the meals made from it. I have certainly all-but cured my sweet-williams of rust by ceasing to grow them for two years and resowing in my composted nursery. The oats I grow in compost rise to just under six feet, are quite free of rust and have heads twice as heavy and carrying twice as many kernels as I have seen in cornfields.·

But there are other advantages, and one emphatically is the release it affords from much of the boredom and drudgery that accompany all hard work. The modern revolt against work comes

---

[1] *The Living Soil* by E. B. Balfour, p. 101. (Faber; 1943).

primarily from its excessive dullness. What could be duller than minding a machine in automatic repetitions which call for practice rather than skill? In their products the worker has neither share nor interest and over their processes no control. But there is necessary drudgery even in the craftsmanship of gardening. This is lightened by composting in three ways. First, by the extraordinary interest of directing and manipulating a garden to support itself. Secondly, by the elimination of all the niggling, highly specialised and fragmented labour of biochemical analysis in studying the inorganic requirements of your plants. For the enormous benefit of humus manufactured by composting is that it is its own laboratory. It supplies all the oxidation, all the chemical salts necessary, the nitrates, the phosphates and potash compounds, which are absorbed by the roots and carried up in the sap to the green leaves. Thirdly, and this follows naturally upon No. 2, the toils of weeding are carried upon a new plane.

Weeding considered *per se* as a pursuit has little to recommend it. Yet weed you must. Charlock is the host of the flea-beetle and cruciferous weeds are of the slime fungus that brings club-root to cabbages. Weeds compete with food-plants and flowers for the supply of nutrients, especially nitrogen, and no gardener worthy the name can bear to look upon

> "an unweeded garden
> That grows to seed; things rank and gross in nature
> Possess it merely."

To an authentic owner nothing is more unpleasing than a dirty bed. But if the weeds go to the compost heap, the process of getting them there acquires a new significance, both practical and psychological. The weeder is acting one of the rhythms of nature but at the same time controlling it. And as he weeds he educates himself. For weeds are indications of soil deficiencies, and by a curious paradox—and life is a perpetual paradox—weeds in a garden are rich in the particular minerals that the soil lacks. The more vigorous certain types grow in a particular area of soil, the more lacking that soil is in those needs. Bad drainage, for instance, is betrayed by marestail, ranunculus, mosses, meadow sweet and other plants. Acidity is advertised by dandelion, plantain, daisy, dock, self-heal, bents, sorrel and others. Nitrogen deficiency is registered by the presence of the nitrogen-fixers—clovers and vetches. It is an interesting fact that nitrogen-fixing legumes like clover, if artificially overfed with nitrogen fertilisers, become consumers instead of producers of nitrogen. If the weeder glances at the nodules on their root-hairs, he can tell by their presence or absence whether his soil is rich or poor in nitrogen.

Thus, the weed extracts from the soil exactly what the soil needs, and the prevalence of one type of weed over another is a pointer to reading the soil like a manuscript. The absence of boron, cobalt, manganese, potassium, sulphur, phosphoric acid, sodium, zinc, iodine, silicon, copper, iron, or some other essential or trace-element in minute quantities becomes a language to be deciphered. The profound error of modern science has been in separating minerals and vitamins *from the plant*, whether in health as food for beasts and men or in decay as food for the soil. This is the root of the matter.

But let not the student be dismayed. The compost heap shoulders all the burden and he can lean back on nature's erudition. She is the librarian. Trundling his barrow filled with weeds, the weeder flings the whole bundle on to the stack. In time the fungi and bacteria, on whose activities the whole sensible world depends, reduce them to mould which in the spring or autumn is forked into the soil or laid on as a top dressing. Thus are restored those very elements whose shortage of supply was announced by the living weeds.[1] The compost heap is the most precise of chemists and its prescriptions are impeccable. How then can the weeder regard his task any more with distaste and weariness? Bent to his toil, he is also the student bent to his book. He bows his head to the widsom and economy of nature, and, acquiring this knowledge, perhaps offers a silent prayer to the Creator both of nature and himself. For the compost heap corrects the fallibility of his judgment and redeems a prosaic task of its pedantry and tedium. It gives him learning without tears.

There is yet another thing he learns—and that is the real obstacle to making this garden Horn Book a lesson of universal application. For, quite apart from the mutually contributory[2] relation between

[1] Most literature, including government pamphlets, advocate the digging in of refuse, not in the least realizing that, during the decomposing process, plant-growth is, as Billington pointed out in *Compost*, retarded. The plant feeds on humus when prepared, not in process of being prepared.

[2] Scientific jargon calls it "symbiotic."

plant and fungi of humus which penetrate the root-cells of the plants by threads rich in protein ("the mycorrhizal association"), the humus is itself mineralised by the soil bacteria. Thus NPK *and* protein are prepared by nature, the minerals seeing to the size and growing power of the crops (the yield) and the protein the quality. If, that is to say, the preparation of humus was extended from gardens to the whole earth, the vested interests in artificials, poisons and soil-dopes of all kinds would cease to be. With them would pass the equally powerful and enormous ones in patent medicines, "the pedlars of Rheumo, Slobbo, Scabo, Gobbo, Blotto, Pimpo, and the rest of the tribe," as our Rabelaisian author, Reginald Reynolds, aptly dubs them in *Cleanliness and Godliness*. That on the contrary they are extremely active and prosperous is a measure of how commercial and scientific forces combine to obscure truth and to block a right standard of nutrition. They are enemies not only of the soil but the whole human race. "Do you imagine," writes Reginald Reynolds in this brilliant work, "that powerful chemical industries will allow themselves to be replaced without a struggle? Here are the druggists of the soil, offering quick results, dearly bought in the final reckoning; potash, nitro chalk and sulphated ammonia used (as all drugs are used) in ever-increasing quantities, until the soil bacteria (by which good *humus* is formed) are destroyed, and with them the earthworms, the *Ploughs of God*." Not persuasion but catastrophe will break this coalition.[1] "There is only one real law," wrote Dorothy Sayers, "the law of the universe; it may be fulfilled either by way of judgment or by the way of grace, but it *must* be fulfilled one way or the other." But the dust-bowl and the diseases of malnutrition are our creation, not the Creator's, and the judgment is but the logic of causation. So is fulfilled God's beautiful and intricate but also inexorable purpose. As the author of *Cleanliness and Godliness* expresses it: "The fertility of this planet is running out through open sluices as surely as a clock-spring unwinds itself till the clock stops." The judgment

[1] Sir John Russell says of the notorious Broadbalk field at Rothamsted: "The Broadbalk results show that, apart from disease, the yield of wheat can be kept up indefinitely by proper artificials." He then proceeds to say in the same article (*The Countryman*: Autumn, 1943) that "diminishing returns" from doses of nitrogen have began to operate (in Plot 8), that the straw is weakening and the plant "easily tumbles down." Also a fungus recently discovered "accumulates in the soil, and is probably one of our coming tribulations, for it is spreading widely in the country." Yet he does not admit that this disease is the consequence of the nitrogen! Broadbalk has not, again, been continually cropped for a century, as is claimed. It has been frequently fallowed and fresh seed is imported every year.

has already occurred on a vast scale in the Sahara, the Middle West, north-west China, the Tigris Valley, the Mississipi Valley, South Africa and many other parts of the world. The great level plain of the Middle West where the bison once roamed and fed the soil is now over thousands of miles a barren desert of naked rock, torn into gullies and fissures by the unimpeded wind and water, a very landscape of Dante's Inferno or El Greco's paintings without even moss or lichens to show where miles of cornland once revealed the fatness of the earth.

Another benefaction of compost is its conservation of moisture in the soil, and what this has meant during the present cycle of drought-years cannot be conveyed on paper. When a period of drought has set in, a depression means nothing, the appearance of the sky means nothing, the direction of the wind means nothing. Rain-clouds look as promising as a telegram of confidence, sombre, dragonish and big-bellied. But they are no more than fancy-dress clouds, impotent and inglorious with no fatness in them to drop, no balm to distil upon the thirsting fields. How often in my region have I not seen the roots of the peas turn white, the potatoes flop, the turnip-leaves go bleached and yellow, the hard fruit lose its hold for lack of sap, the soft fruits look as woody as they prove to the taste, lawns turn sere and the soil yawn into cracks that will take your foot! The drought-winds of 1943 shrivelled the very leaves off the plants three months before the fall and shrank the kernels of the dry-loving wheat to half their normal size. Often I have had to rely upon mist and dew for rain in essential planting out. How petty and abortive have been storms that were preluded by a cloud-pall black as an Aethiop's skin ! We have welcomed rain that did at last break the spell as though what Gilbert White might have called in his Journal a cold, wet, dark, dank, dour, sour day were a peep into the Golden Age. Or when the mist-rains drifted like companies of ghosts against the ridge of the western hillside as though hunting desperately for their souls and keeping company for very dreariness, they seemed to have come straight from Elysium.

When the rain does come, it is an experience. A Lazarus scene. I have learned that there is no aroma in the world like that of a garden after rain. I would turn up my nose at all the spices of Arabia beside it. It is a Benedicite in terms of scent and appearance. Yet since I methodized my composting, my actual losses from drought have been infinitesimal. The flowers act as though in a film but the produce has never sensibly lessened. In 1943, for instance, the spring drought lasted for three months and the summer one for another three with intervals of only tea-cup rains. But, except for surface-rooters, I never, even in this heart-breaking year for the gardener, used the watering pot. My soil was even fit for light planting at the end of July, 1943, after a drought, broken only by showers, which lasted from mid-February to mid-October. The morning dews helped but the real stay of plant-life was compost. The main damage was caused by birds, who, desperate not so much from thirst as hunger owing to a soil like a pavement, voraciously attacked the hard fruit and many crops.

Contrast this successful resistance to drought with the conditions in the 1943 East Anglian drought, as severe as in my neighbourhood. Complaint was loud among the farmers and the crops suffered acutely from the lack of rain. Why ? For the obvious reason that humus was lacking. The high traditions of East Anglian farming are giving way to the chemical complex. The consequence is that the soil can no longer resist drought as it used to when those traditions were much more active. What the farmers were complaining of was not drought but soil-exhaustion.

I also have a shrewd notion that composted humus regulates the temperature of the soil, making it cooler in summer and warmer in winter, like a roof of thatch on a house. Humus, too, has, as Robert Elliot (see p. 264) pointed out, important properties of binding the soil-particles and preventing them from being blown away as in the dust-bowl areas.

Yet another office the stack performs is as a hot-bed. In 1942, I grew Mammoth Pumpkins on a completed one, while a second was in process of building. Planted from pots at the end of July, they had leaves a foot across by mid-August, flopping in the breeze like elephant's ears and swarming over the whole surface. I banked up the edges with long grasses from the orchard so that the hollow in the centre collected the moisture. When the earth laughed, "ha, ha," like the Biblical steed, after a good rain a few days later, these pumpkins were like tropic plants, and by the end of the month they had thrown a canopy over the whole surface. Compost exercises, too, a transforming effect upon the texture of the soil. Even the colour of my own, naturally reddish, has in course of time turned almost black. No matter how beaten down by heavy autumnal rains, it yields at once to the fork as a flakey crumbled tilth that would warm any gardener's heart and give him as much to look at as a bank of flowers. The compressed clayey patches are loosened and the more sandy areas tightened up. The effect of compost is also to enrich the colouring and add lustre to the flower-heads of plants. Again, it ensures germination. This is particularly noticeable with onions and shallots. In one year and sowing the same amount of seed, I increased the onion crop by a bushel and a half, the shallot by a peck. Lastly, aeration to prevent capillary action in a dry spell can be left for much longer periods than if the soil had been fed with farmyard manure alone.

I will give a few examples collected from outside my own garden of the benefits conferred by compost upon soil and plant and beast and man alike. Mr. Chambers, for instance, of the Cheshire Joint Board Institution for Mental Deficiency, Cranage Hall, declared that he had cured celery of leaf-miner, strawberries of yellow edge, cordon apples of mealy bug and American blight by the use of compost alone. In Barbadoes, sugar canes, once fed by humus and farmed by peasants, were then cultivated on artificials and big business lines. The result was that the canes began to lose the power of vegetative reproduction from the circulation of protein being interrupted. A plan for restoring the old methods by means of mixed farming, animal husbandry, co-operative marketing and a Peasants Loan Bank was reported in the *Times* of December, 1942. Dr. J. W. Scharff reported in September, 1942, that 500 Tamil coolies employed by the Singapore Health Department were granted allotments of 40 acres on condition that they composted and used for themselves the fruit and vegetables grown. All sales were forbidden. At the end of a year, there was "a surprising improvement in stamina and health and sickness was swept away." "My men were capable of and gladly responded to the heavier work demanded by the increasing stress of war."

Instances like these kill the case for large-scale mechanised farming, whose shortage of dung compels it to use artificial fertilisers by the refusal of Government to organise the distribution of town-tips and refuse. They kill the case for thieving instead of borrowing from the soil. When we consider that not one man in ten thousand ever eats fresh food from composted soil and so ever gets properly fed, our modern civilization is seen to be built upon the sand.

In Rhodesia, witchweed is the main obstacle to maize growing and no satisfactory insect control has been found. But if compost is applied to an infested field and maize is then grown, hardly a plant of witchweed is to be seen. Dr. Nicol says:

> "The reason for this astonishingly complete control is not known, but since compost is the product of millions of micro-organisms acting on plant and animal residues, the control of witchweed by means of compost has every right to be included amongst biological methods."

Every right! The *Rhodesian Herald* of September 4, 1942, reported that potatoes dressed with five tons of compost per acre for eelworm were completely rid of it in the second year. In one season, the Greytown District High School increased the potato yield between composted and non-composted ground from 8.2% to 15.58% per acre. A Norfolk head gardener, quoted by Miss Maye Bruce (see p. 104), said: "I had an experiment with outside tomatoes and the plants I treated with compost had easily double the weight of fruit. These two lots were the same seed, set the same day and had the same attention except for the compost."

But the best of all these evidences[1] is a document taken from the U.S.A. Government Journal of "Soil Conservation," issued in the June of 1943. A mere document? Say rather a stick of dynamite, a scientific vindication of all that a few of us have been mocked and derided for urging and of that traditional husbandry which the gardener should practice but is the sport and contempt of scientist, politician and economist alike. For this document is the new science that restores to honour the practices of "obsolete" pre-scientific husbandry and in the end will make scientific orthodoxy as obsolete as the open field system.

World War No. 1, says the text, sent "10,000,000 acres of our topsoil down the rivers of the Midwest." To this must be added

---

[1] When this book was in the press, I hit upon a very striking piece of evidence. Mr. F. Sykes of Chantry Farm, Chute, whom I have met, gave me a detailed account of what his 800 ft. contour farm had achieved by organic means of manuring only. It may be very briefly summed up as follows: (1) he has rid his livestock of all disease (some 80% of our cattle are diseased); (2) he has built up a large herd of home-bred attested dairy cattle tubercle-free and of 100% stamina and constitution; (3) increased the stamina of his young stock; (4) cured a very valuable race-mare of contagious abortion; (5) on a thin, high, neglected soil produced 3 tons of hay per acre; (6) grown heavy corn-crops. His methods have been much the same as those practised by Robert Elliot in the "Clifton Park Experiment" (see p. 264). He uses no artificials at all, and his farm is on high poorish chalk land.

those 250,000,000 acres farmed out in supplying *us* with cheap food
and resulting (I quote from the document) in "the dust bowl and
bankruptcy." Result—"we never have more than 60% enough food
to set an adequate table."[1] Therefore, the future of medical science
is with the new science of nutrition, the only means of building
up resistance and immunity to a host of diseases:

> "The quality of our nutrition depends upon the quality of our
> food. The quality of our food depends primarily upon the
> quality of the soil upon which it is grown."

This is followed by: "Amino-acids are Nature's building stones
out of which are constructed the various proteins." To obtain these
proteins meat and dairy products must be "supplemented by *whole-
grain* cereals, legumes and potatoes." The italics are mine; it is
hardly necessary to point out that this upsets the bread-van of the
white bread fabricators who have controlled the staff of life for half
a century. "We must be prepared to return the minerals which
we borrow, to practise the wise use and conservation of all the vital
elements." Again, "supplemental chemicals are far from being
as efficient as chemicals obtained from a healthy plant" (whose
health depends upon a healthy soil). "Synthetic diets, at best,
leave much to be desired. We must learn to borrow these minerals
and return them again to the soil, *if we are to survive*." "Certainly
the available data do justify accepting a relationship between soil
fertility, plant growth and its nutritive qualities, and animal
growth, resistance to disease, and longevity." In other words,
wholeness is thus scientifically opposed to the separatism of modern
science. We must have vitamins, but they are not food. "Therefore, our vitamins should come in fruits, vegetables, milk, eggs
and meat, *and not from the drug-store*." Once more the italics are
mine. This passage is in direct contradiction to the official (and
commercial) policy before the war of reinforcing the white loaf
with Vitamin B, which was the response to the criticisms directed
against a germless loaf. Against this method of first emasculating
the bread of its nutritious qualities and vitamins and then partially
restoring them by one synthetic vitamin, this Bulletin returns the

[1] This should be juxtaposed beside the fantastic statement of Mr. Peter Cromwell
in the intellectualist journal *Horizon* (August; 1943): "The intensified use of machinery
is one of the three main reasons why America has a higher standard of living than any
other country of the world."

complete answer. First amputate a man's healthy leg and then after protest hand him a pair of crutches. What applies to us applies equally to the soil ("the richer the soils the better the vitamin content have the plants grown thereon.") In other words, what feeds the soil that feeds the plants that feed animals and men comes from humus, *and not from the laboratory of orthodox science.* Recognising these earth-truths, we shall, if we are not too late, cease to manufacture synthetic products and waste the genuine bounty of nature bestowed on us, which is ten times more effective. Good soil, good plants, good food: thus the simple story, the story of wholeness.[1]

Such is the wisdom that bitter experience is teaching America, whose pre-wisdom soil-robbery we are now imitating through orthodox science and the factory-farm. The future is with us "sentimentalists" and a return to a traditional husbandry made conscious by the new science. True, famine will probably come first. For we too must learn by bitter experience.

But personal experience is as good as a feast of examples. I grow three times the amount of food on my holding than of yore, but itself is about thrice as fertile. I have rid it of all but minor ailments without using sprays, fumigants, insecticides, fungicides or any of the paraphernalia of the chemical laboratory. By eating the food so prepared I have cured myself of former afflictions, catarrhs, rheums, colds and the like, with which I used to be beset. Though in the fifties, I recovered from an accident that should reasonably have killed me, and cost me a leg and practically speaking the use of my left arm after four years with intervals in hospital, so effectively that I was able to do twice the amount of intellectual labour I had done before the accident. There were other factors involved, but surely one of them was home-grown food on a soil rich in humus. Perhaps as good evidence as any is the way potato peelings and tomato seeds that happen to lodge on the edge of the stack develop into stout plants with heavy yields. One of these chance-grown tomato-plants produced in 1943 81 tomatoes. If anybody tells me that artificial manures can produce effects like these, I know that he is living in a fool's Hades.

There are two main conclusions to be drawn from the new-old

[1] And so of that health which resists the onset of disease by the self-energy of the organism. *Farming Handbook No. 2* (1934), written by the modern priesthood of machines and chemicals, leads off by describing 30 diseases of cereals alone, smuts, leaf-stripes, rusts, mildews, foot and root rots. Thirty of them!

science of composting. The first is that nature, the greatest of all farmers, wastes nothing. Modern theories of "wastefulness" thus need reversing. Man as he is to-day is the waster, not nature. The second is this. Until we look at nature's science of food-production in an entirely new way, we shall continue to waste instead of husbanding her bounties. The heart of the new science is that fertility is a biological and not a chemical *datum*. Soil is the denudation of rock, the earth's crust, but what gives the plant life is not soil nor its chemical constituents, but the plant itself or rather the live bacterial agents of its " death." The plant is the transformer or translator of the soil, while the animal in its turn translates the plant into a new language. Man is "the paragon of animals," but as a body he is still an animal. Therefore, if he breaks the foreordained sequence or cycle of soil-plant-animal-soil he goes sick and, if he persists, he dies. He is at present sick and, if he is not careful, die he will. His last conquest will be not of nature but himself.

I may sum up the whole issue by referring to the November debate (1943) in the House of Lords upon the relation between the use of artificial manures and what I hand out to our bureaucracy as a nice new word for it, defertilisation. It is a landmark in modern history. It is the first time that any recognition has been given in high places not only to what books, pamphlets, speeches, experiments, whole schools of scientific thought and countrymen's conversations have devoted themselves to for years but to what without a doubt is the major issue of the future, incalculably more important than anything the planners talk about. Barren soil—exit humanity. But because a subject of such high moment has reached the House of Lords, it by no means follows that it percolates to the inner sanctum of authority. What the Lords said was pointed and without any frills. Lord Glentanar:—"We have been walking with a test tube in one hand and a cash-book in the other"; the Earl of Warwick: "Unless we are taught to understand the soil and to love and cherish it, the fate of our civilization will be exactly the same as those of Babylon, Greece and Rome"; Lord Teviot: "There is something wrong with our soil. It has been boosted up with stimulants, and we all know what happens to us when that process is adopted. Disease is increasing. . . . We must plan to put back into the soil those things we take from it"; Lord Portsmouth: "There are serious indications that our treatment of the soil is leading to ill-health in plants, animals and human beings."

The reply of the Government was to "deprecate any suggestion of antagonism between chemical fertilisers and humus. There is no evidence that a balanced use of fertilisers has a harmful effect on soil, crops or man," which is a good example of the art of saying nothing at all. What *is* this "balanced use"? Nobody knows, any more than anybody knows except the drinker and his private doctor what is the balanced use of whisky at your meals. But everybody who is in the know is perfectly well aware that for years the soil has had more whisky than meals, and that this knowledge is "deprecated" by the vested interests in distillery. But though you may put out a deprecating hand to hide the uncomfortable stare of reality, what cannot be hid is the effect of forcible feeding with dope on the soil itself. The knowledge of what happened to the top soil of large areas of Lincolnshire this spring and summer has not been confined within the borders of the county.

Observe the alignment, or, shall I say, battle-array of this gigantic issue. On the one hand, we have the big interests, armed, to paraphrase the image of Lord Glentanar, with a cheque-book in one hand and the law of libel in the other (these are the heavy artillery); we have the supporting columns of orthodox science on one flank and the bureaucracy on the other; we have as light patrols most of the publicists, probably a good half, I regret to say, of the large-scale cash-cropping farmers who are simply industrialists on the land and a motley company of camp-followers among which, I also regret to say, are to be found in spite of themselves the anthroposophists and followers of Rudolf Steiner whose pantheistic eccentricities bring a certain amount of suspicion to bear upon the concrete logical facts of the realists. Nor is the morale of this mighty host to be belittled. This morale has two horns and a tail: one horn is the colossal ignorance of an urban civilization on all matters pertaining to the soil, the other is the predatory philosophy of a century's growth, while the tail is the theory of Progress which bids society not merely to persist in its delusions but to carry them forward into greater and greater excesses and extravagances. Yes, a formidable host. On the other side, we have the new science; the whole weight of tradition which simply means the accumulated experience of our forefathers; we have common sense and observation, and rural opinion as a whole; we have experimental proof, the Dust Bowls of millions upon millions of eroded acres and we have a certain view of the universe which Prof. D. M. S. Watson calls "a curiously mystical attitude," viz.: that love and care of the earth which loathes the methods and attitude of the brigand with it. Lastly, we have the earth, and that is what is going to tip the scales against the big battalions. Such is the assurance of final victory. The question remains—at what cost to humanity in the way of starvation, food-riots, disorder and disease will this victory be achieved? That entirely depends on how long it will take to convince the world that what you take out of the soil you have got to put back again.

II. Season of Fruitfulness

"The valleys also shall stand so thick with
corn, that they shall laugh and sing."

"For out of olde feldes, as men seith,
Cometh al this newe corne froe yeer to yeer."

"To watch the corn grow and the blossoms set; to draw hard breath over
ploughshare or spade; to read, to think, to love, to hope, to pray—these
are the things that make men happy."

JOHN RUSKIN.

I SIT on my terrace blinking like an owl in the westering sun, and
look over the tops of my cone-flowers. The range of the Downs
is a light insubstantial purple, the tree-line below very dark and the
foreground of cornfields almost amber. In some lights and aspects,
the wheat ripe for the harvest is red, in another copper, in others
orange. As the sun dropped to roost, the clouds formed a crescentic
mountain range ramparting a bay of pale blue in which rode one
star like the mast-head light of a fishing smack. The garden, sloping
away below me and melting into the fields as they melted into the
serenity of the sky, seemed, not the portals into some visionary
enchanted land, but a wicket gate into a place of husbandry blest
by the peace of something beyond it. I liked at that moment to
think of my garden as a patch of farming England and of the
expanse of fields beyond it as a cultivated garden, both graced by
fruitfulness.

I remembered a kind of symbolic day of the year before, a July
day when I had gone into the cornfields. From Fawley Top I had
looked down and up again at the multitudinous wheat where, a
few years before, had stood a notice board—"This Land for Sale."
The wind played among the straw, breaking first over an oatfield
and then over wheat, already bleached by the long drought, in a
succession of waves like the waves of the sea. I was reminded of
Perdita whom her creator meant to be in one aspect the spirit of
a happy husbandry, dancing her journey through life. I sat on the
edge of the field and thought of Wordsworth's "Sole sitting by the
shore of old Romance," and surely nothing is more romantic than a
cornfield, so much more so than the empty salt estranging sea.

The bread of life, the Mass, Christ walking through the corn with His disciples on a Sunday, Ruth in tears, Osiris couched like Ariel in the ear of barley, the Highland reaper, Demeter the prototype of so many corn spirits whose icon was plaited of the last sheaf and carried in procession to the farmhouse, is there not more romance in a cornfield than the sea? The spires of Viper's Bugloss were beacons on the edge of the wheat. It has an electric burning blue like no other wild flower, while the shafts are like blue fire, emblematic of that life-giving primal virtue which is the wheat-field. Francis Thompson saw in the wild flower among the corn a symbol of himself:—

> "The sleep-flower sways in the wheat its head,
>   Heavy with dreams, as that with bread;
>   The goodly grain and Time the reaper.
>   I hang 'mid men my needless head
>   And my fruit is dreams, as theirs is bread:
>   The goodly men and the sun-hazed sleeper
>   Time shall reap, but after the reaper
>   The world shall glean of me, me the sleeper."

But to Traherne the field of corn was not fugitive: "the orient and immortal wheat" was where God met man. "'Tis grain, Sir, 'twill endure wind and weather"—what blasts of economic sterility has not the grain endured that I see once more shining in English fields!

As I could see the wind in the corn, so I could hear the corn responding to it, till wind and corn were one in sight and sound. An indescribable unique music, dry but rich, sibilant, the expectant sigh of the labouring earth. There is a greeny-blueness like a mist or thin-spread cloud within the corn which seems to be given off by the arched flag. The blue tint seems distilled from the green, as though the sky had sunk into the corn, a blessing of heaven upon earth. Inside the corn were yet other blues, the pure cobalt of corn-flower and azure of succory so deep that it seemed to soften the splashed scarlet of the poppies. But the corn-flower was best among the silvery oats, mixed with agrimony and yellow mullein, dusky fennel, mealy St. John's wort, mild bedstraw. Their yellows are unlike the harsh insolent yellow of charlock that in the next field had triumphed over the wheat and flaunted the arrogance of the military conqueror. It *looks* "the idle weeds that grow in our sustaining corn" and does not blend with it like the blue flowers and the long black weather-boarded and russet-tiled barns of the region, whose dormers project from the roof-sweep like the flowers among the corn.

The men of letters have neglected the tasselled oat. So far as I know, there is only one reference to it in our literature and that by way of a jape—"A grain, which in England is generally given to horses but in Scotland supports the people." And where, replied Boswell, will you find such horses and such people? Collins's "If aught of oaten stop" (*Ode to Evening*), exquisite as it is, is no more than a conventional classicism, like Milton's "oaten flute." But when the oatfield I saw was bordered by wild roses making embossed Norman arches and by foxgloves and rosebay willowherb standing five feet high in stiff robes of purple and lavender, like Byzantine figures, I was very glad I grew oats myself, and the foxgloves with them. And I have kept records of the last wagon-load of oats that sways and rustles past my hedge early in September. Poetry and fruitfulness, beauty and use, so long as I could keep them together or next door to one another in my garden, I should be true to the landscape.

True also to the English tradition. Outside Cowley, that little industrial hell, I had come upon a vast midden of scrap iron, old tyres, broken up aeroplanes and what not. It was a scene of extraordinary desolation, a kind of surrealist picture of that Industrialism, the corruption of industry, whose apocalypse has been Armageddon with its holocaust of wasted and broken human lives. The contrast was vehement with the glowing cornfields, like a gallery of de Wint water-colours, and the little eighteenth century church of Chislehampton. Undevotional it is and yet so neat, precise, symmetrical, poised beside that litter and disorder. Formal yews fronted the "Gothick"-windowed west door, flanked by floral urns and crowned by a belfry like a Tibetan hat. Within, a tie-beam roof, enclosed box pews, brass chandeliers, a gallery supported by Doric pillars—the church of a faith with no mystery in it, of a sound heavenly government; of a seemly ritual, of a social gathering, not of a congregation; of a rational set of beliefs but not of worship or aspiration. It did not dare the heights nor depths of sin and redemption, but offered comfortable assurance and well-regulated devoirs to a Being who guaranteed earthly prosperity to the right people. The orderly little church was the symbol of a tidied-up cosmos, swept and garnished but empty before it was occupied by the devils of disorder whose activities had culminated in the scrap-iron midden. But though the little church had expelled the soul out of religion, it was still by the quality of its workmanship within the tradition and so at no discord with the immemorial cornfields. For craftsmanship is as timeless as they and, when it was destroyed, the spirit of man was left empty for devils to possess it.

And now out of all the error and destruction, the corn has come back, the emblem of fruitfulness. The pre-war Augusts were always dull and colourless because the dictatorship of urbanism had forced England to become a grassy wilderness. But grass country has become corn country, and the floor of earth has been touched by a magician's wand. It has put off its old Puritan dress and put on the garment of the year's abundance. The heavy greens of the pastures are a screen or backcloth for the rich embroidery of the fields, tawny gold for the wheat, silver for oats, rich red for trifolium and pale gold for the barley. The ripeness is all. In less than two months the field of corn changed from emerald to glaucous-blue and from that to the colour of Blake's lions. In the fields of a smallholding community I know where the old strip measurement is still in being, a parallelogram of wheat is sharply cut off from a slab of beans or potatoes next to it. The wheat thus became a solid block or ingot of gold. Such might have been an offering from the Three Kings to the Lord of the Harvest. More appropriate too than the useless metal or frankincense and myrrh. One's heart quails at the thought of these glowing cornlands going back once more to weedy grass, if or when the international traders prevail. Until the third Great War. . . .

The gaiety and richness of English earth ripe for the harvest could not better be seen in my region than in the miniature Wormsley Valley of the Oxfordshire Chilterns. I climb up from the plain to the crest of the scarp, where the golden fields sweep up to what Leland called "the rotes of the hills," like golden sands up to a seacliff. To drop down from the summit into this flowery hollow is to step back into what seems an inspired scene-painting of husbandry, a fragment of it left over. The open road along the western shelf is lined in August with St. John's wort, wild snapdragon and cushions of marjoram, with succory and scabious, milkwort and tansy. The opposite flank, scalloped into a series of little promontories, jutting out and down from heavy woodlands like dormers under thatch, is streaked and grained with the striations of the shocked corn swinging up the slope. They alternate with splashes of fallow white chalk, dark clover-green, bleached stubble, clear green sward and barley, whose awn, outstretched from the bent heads and suffused with sun, seems to emit filaments of sunlight. The happy valley might have made the scene of one of Calvert's dreams of a rural Renaissance, with his reapers and haymakers dancing the ancient rhythms and celebrating the ancient festivals.

III.   Under the Vine

> "A little saint best fits a little shrine,
> A little prop best fits a little vine,
> As my small cruse best fits my little wine,
> A little stream best fits a little boat,
> A little lead best fits a little float,
> As my small pipe best fits my little note."

"They shall sit every man under his vine and under his fig-tree."

I SIT under my vine and watch the summer sailing by. On one side of it the pale lavender flowers of the clematis, Comtesse de Bouchard, clamber about among its leaves and tendrils. Opposite it, at the corner of the thin metal framework that supports the vine and projects from the south wall of the house, the dangling racemes of the sweet-scented *Clematis flammula* (how few clematises are odorous!) are intertwined among the amber grapes. The French call it L'Argence, and we English "Maiden's Bower." It flings its white spray among the vine-leaves to earn its French name and overhangs them to earn its English. On the other side of the vine, a fig, whose upper branches are festooned with great white flowers of *Clematis Henryi*, spreads its palmated leaves to absorb the shafts of the sun. Close at hand and at the end of the rockery walls which begin just beyond the gadding vine, I can count 14 Tortoiseshells mixed up with the bees and the Red Admirals pulsating their wings on the flat heads of *Sedum spectabile*. Straight down the slope and beyond the orchard, I have many a time from my station under the vine seen the gleaners setting out between the garden and the pastures and arable fields that flow for nine miles as far as the edge of the scarp of the chalk downs. The vine and the gleaners! My mythological vine next to my Biblical fig with the white flowers breaking among their legendary leaves!

Here is the perfect symbol of the shores of the Mediterranean, the cradle of the culture of the West. But English too. The culture of England is Christendom or nothing, and Christendom was born in the land of the fig and the vine. And viticulture has nearly a thousand years behind it in England alone; vineyards are mentioned in Domesday Book, and the Cistercians, the great husbandmen of the Middle Ages, were vine-growers out-of-doors. Their settlements were mainly in the north and west, and the vine did not reach Suffolk until 1553. Cobbett records a whole vineyard of black grapes at Cobham as late as 1828. To sit under my own vine and fig-tree not only brings me into the tradition; it makes me too a kind of symbolic figure. "A man shall eat in safety under his own vine what he plants": I have achieved through my earnings that I should sit under my own vine and fig-tree. It was the wish of Charles II that every good Englishman should. But it has not been fulfilled; indeed it is three centuries further off being fulfilled than it was under the Stuarts. It has not been fulfilled. This is the essential tragedy of progress, the progression away from the free and responsible ownership of the small man, his stake in his native land, to the wage-system of the mass-man. To breed money not to grow crops became the ambition of the Englishman.

My vine is a Royal Muscadine or Muscat which has never failed to bear less than 100 bunches of white grapes for eight years in succession. In 1941, I took 150 and the blackbirds 22. In 1943, I took 200 bunches and the flies and wasps 30. It has never given me any trouble nor shown any sign of disease nor been fed with anything but a few spadefuls of well-rotted humus in the spring. The only disadvantage of it is lateness in ripening, so that the sweetness of the grapes depends to some extent on frequency of sunshine in October. That is of less moment since I started wine-making from it. I prune it lightly and frost in no way affects it. On account of the appalling shortage of stocks of all kinds there will be after the war, I plant out these prunings and nearly all "take." Some I sent away to a friend in the spring of 1943 were five feet high in September.

The fig on the other hand is ripe early in October and if, like Paris, I had to award the palm to one of the kindliest fruits of the earth, the fig, the pear or the greengage, I should find it hard to choose. Midland figs are later than southern figs for the simple reason, not that they take longer to ripen, but that the normal crop of figlings produced in autumn for the following year are usually frozen off and a new crop has to be formed in the spring. The figs that survive ripen in six weeks to two months earlier than the others. Thus, the more northerly fig has the appearance of a double cropper in a mild winter. Actually, the fig produces 3 crops of different sizes on the lower, middle and upper branches. It is

the middle ones that need removing for the largest to ripen and
the embryos to develop the following year. The roots, of course,
must be planted in rubble and confined within little brick court-
yards. With my Brown Turkey, I follow the French practice of
pinching out the leader of every new shoot in the spring to check
woodiness and encourage fruitfulness. But heavy crops I did not
attain until I covered the tree in winter.

What summer skies have I not seen from under the shade of
the vine! Yet my past notes of particular felicities of light and
colour have been nearly always after rain. Then, the washed foliage,
the grateful flowers and the reanimated earth seem to become
one with the incandescence diffused upon them from the evening
skies. Often the stooping sun, tossing off the racing clouds like a
ship's bow cleaving the spray, casts an unearthly effulgence over
the whole landscape that absorbs all earthly hues into its own.
The evening light picks out the varicoloured pastel shades of the
hay aftermath and the oils of the corn and clover crops and crowns
them with a value more than their own. It is the fourth sound
that makes the star. Once in July from Christmas Common nine
miles away, a great leaning tower of soft light, a truncated rainbow,
moved slowly from south-east to south-west, a Christian rather
than a Jehovan pillar, so mild and transfiguring was its splendour.
Falling plumb upon the patchwork of the earth, it gave a tremendous
pictorial aspect to the old philosophical canon of multiplicity in
unity. To achieve that has indeed become my purpose for my
holding. It should be a cell in the multiple and unified body of the
Creation. A garden is a region within a region.

There is a gardener I know who is the perfect regionalist. He
looks after the garden of an Elizabethan yeoman farmstead in the
Tillingbourne Valley where it lies. Though not himself a native
of Surrey, this man seems to have gathered into his own person
the local knowledge of all the vanished Surrey folk. He is a Victorian
History of his adopted region and knows a great deal more than
ever appears in any history. He is an unerring topographer, an
accomplished botanist, an archæologist with a noble collection of
flint arrowheads found by himself, a local historian, a geologist,
a meteorologist, a folklorist, a market gardener, an experienced
horticulturist, a bee-master, a soil expert, a philosopher, a man
with a good working knowledge of farming and a fisherman who
has had a kingfisher perch on his rod. Yet this walking gazetteer

is no University don but just a gardener who looks after somebody else's garden. He knows his region *as a whole*. His knowledge is thus contrary to the principle of modern knowledge, which is specialised knowledge about one thing, or rather one aspect of one thing, or one sub-division of one aspect of one thing, and dense ignorance of the sub-divisions, aspects and things related to it.

But I think of him as the perfect gardener. Often has he held me with his glittering eye (the other like Nelson's has a shade over it), while he discoursed up from the soil on which we stood and the rock that made the soil to everything that grew upon it in the region and the men too who like himself had grown out of it and fitted themselves to it, its masters and its servants. In him their intuitive and traditional knowledge had become conscious and articulate, while he had something else that very few of them have—bookishness. Yet by the standardised standards of modern education he would hardly be called an educated man. For myself, I profess to be in a sense his pupil. He taught me a new method of grafting and he had observed that it is the dumbledore, not the honey bee, which pollinates the bean flower, the hive bees only perforating the petal to get at the nectar. His ecological relation to his chosen region (of which he is not a native) by hand and eye and mind is a mastery I aspire to in my relation to the garden I look out upon from under the vine.

The primary thing about it is the quickthorn hedge which I planted round it ten years ago. This year (1943) it flowered for the first time, a certificate approving that the garden had grown up. For the hedge is the outward and visible sign of the unity; what I have grown in it is the multiplicity. On that account alone I have a high opinion of hedges. I recently attended a " Reclamation Demonstration" in which the bulldozer figured, and a technician present had said to me, " you should just see how it rips up a hedge." I did not want to see how the monster ripped up a hedge; my sympathies would have been entirely with the hedge, and on the way back I reflected about hedges, not the expert way in which bulldozers and prairie busters and gyro-tillers get rid of them.

All over England now, more especially in the Eastern Counties, hedges are being removed with as much aforethought or thought at all as a small boy beheads nettles on a bank. I asked myself why? What is the point of it? Since England is a small country which even bureaucrats and technicians are unable to turn into a big one, hedges play an essential part in our rural economy. The more so as seventy per cent. of our farmers are the owners or renters of small farms under 100 acres. Enormous, monotonous and monocultural areas of arable are as alien to our landscape as to our farming system. It is a great mistake to suppose that the pre-Enclosure farms were hedgeless. The hedges were of mixed growth and all that the Enclosures of capitalist farming did was to add more hedges of single growth, mainly whitethorn. Pfeiffer, the bio-dynamic pioneer, wisely said that one-bush hedgerows are bad for gardens; the more varied the hedge, the better the biological results. This is true of *all* husbandry as I have repeatedly urged, so that here as in many other aspects peasant farming was the best farming.

Hedges were, too, the principal cause for the former abundance of our small birds (I say "former" since the diminution of all small birds except the sparrow and the starling—the most destructive—is generally accepted); they have always been shelter for cattle and horses and sheep both from heat and storm and a beneficently alternative fodder. They are also a kind of citadel for staying the ravages of the flea-bettle or turnip fly that now devastates the crops because it rarely if ever touches shaded ones. They are a cornucopia for supplementary wines and foods; the burnings of the top and lop make potash, as underwood makes charcoal; they supply the material for pea-sticks, hafts for many a metal tool, the thatcher's jack, wimble and spars; their prunings make rick-bottoms and they are of tried service for drainage. Their thorns were once fuel for the cottage bread-oven in that domestic economy which wasted nothing. In laying the hedge, the cottager left the briars standing to bud garden roses on them. The stress of war has revealed the high vitamin content of hips and haws—had we pondered on the birds' relish for them, nature's persuasion rather than man's violence would have converted us. Hedges have also for centuries been a source of supply for the craftsman, second only in importance to the woodland, and of course they have a number of other uses which any countryman could spend half an hour in informing you. But their main value is two-fold: both in themselves and the art of "plushing" them, hedges perfectly illustrate the dual principle of beauty and use, and, secondly, they are the ramparts of the small property. Their destruction to-day, therefore, is one of the most significant signs of the times.

But hedges are no fortress against aeroplanes. If you read old books, you will constantly meet references to "country quiet" and to green nature as a refuge from "the chargeable noise of the great town." Was it once so? A 6th century Collect begins:—"Be present, O merciful God, to protect us through the *silent* hours of the night." This was written in the "Dark Ages"; a darker one might regard it as a copyist's error for "strident," and for modern silence day or night one goes to town. Silence is one of the lost arts, like solitude, and Milton's "Silence was pleased" at the nightingale's song is to us altogether a dream. It is hard for us to hear any bird's song, and indeed to hear out-of-doors one's own or a fellow-being's voice. The Devil's two greatest enemies are music and silence. When quiet comes, it is a hush rather than a silence, a brief suspension and breathing pause before the accustomed harsh uproar. The whole world outside nature is so jangled and out of tune that normality of any kind is "a sweet surprise." How blessed then are the fogs and mists that bring us silence indeed! One sips this quietude like some choice and rare vintage; one listens to the silence as to Bach's "Sheep may safely graze." It is our "balm of hurt minds," a healing power, a gentle dew, a green thought in a green shade, a knitting up of the ravell'd sleeve of care, a benediction like rest after violent exertion, medicinal, restorative.

> "Eternal silence, sing to me,
> And beat upon my whorlèd ear,
> Pipe me to pastures still and be
> The music that I care to hear."

For an analogy to the aeroplane it is necessary to think back into the Jurassic Period when the pterodactyls oared themselves above the steaming swamps. One August day when I sat under the vine, I had the flash of a closer similitude. Is it air which these monsters navigate? No, it is water. This earth is the bed of the deep sea and great devil-fish prowl to and fro above it with rigid fins, blunt snouts and leaden bodies, while high above *them* is the surface of the ocean, broken into dark waves and combing breakers and lit by gleams of the sun above both water and ocean-floor. The tractors crawling over the surface of our undersea world look like squids or enormous crabs, while the huge scrapers that tear the corn off the ground and the top-soil with it to make an aerodrome, are other

T.P.E.   I forms of crustaceans that people our depths. We are deep in the glooms of the abyssal waters, long before Amphioxus got him a four-chambered heart and lungs that the air caressed and sunbeams filled. Our lives too are those of the deep sea creatures; we crawl anxiously about and, when danger threatens from the predators above us, we burrow in the mud like fearful flat-fish. We move in scared shoals and everywhere above our subaqueous depths the armoured ganoids and primeval sharks which rule the abysses prey upon themselves and us.

These marvellous engines of destruction are very brave and brilliant; they perform incredible feats; if some prey on us, others save us. But this whole opaque world in which we live is a world of deepest night, and to find light we must *return to the earth* and what is above and beyond the earth.

I look once more down the garden and try to project myself into it, as Keats projected himself into the sparrow pecking on the gravel. The garden, the fields, the parish that George Russell called "the cradle of the nation," how can we grope our way back to them? Not back into the past since they are only incidentally of the past. They are the permanent conditions of life set out by eternity for our span of temporality. Perhaps we can only readjust ourselves to them by the necessity of chaos, that is to say, by the discovery through a fearful experience that the giant affront to these conditions is failure. For we must grow things or die, and though we are temporarily doing so, the whole weight of urban civilization is against the garden, the fields and the parish. Not the least factor in the disintegration of rural life is the aerodrome which sucks up the village population and drowns its way of life, with hardly less effect than its injury to the soil. Almost as disruptive is the scandal of the casual labourer or the daughter of a landlabourer making more at the aerodrome than he, one of the last survivors of the skilled worker, can make on the land. As an old country-woman of 88 remarked with that profound and unconscious poetry once "in widest commonalty spread," these aerodromes and other works like them are "distressing" to the land.

I have more or less succeeded in keeping the long parallel middle beds between the two larger lawns in continuous and profuse flower from late spring to late autumn.[1] This is very necessary in a

---

[1] Except in 1943, when the long long drought defeated me.

garden like mine. Its site is not susceptible to being partitioned into a number of little gardens, each with its own character and flora. It is a garden of one sweep of the eye, with the niceties to be filled in on more leisured inspection. The centrepiece has not only to be well stocked but with as great variety a as possible both of flowers and colours. The best compliment I ever had paid this general and diversified effect was from a visitor to the garden when it was open in early July for the District Nurses Fund. He said that in its green surround it looked "gemlike."

But I have to be careful that these colours shall be soft and volatile for the reason that I explained in the first chapter (p. 17). The flowers in these beds are numerous—godetias, campanulas, phloxes, annual and perennial scabious, sidalcea, Candidum lilies, medium lemon sunflowers, erigeron, shasta daisy and the fringed white, carmine day lilies, a Florentine willow-herb, a cultivated loosestrife, Canterbury Bells, Santolina and others. Some, too, are impressive—the godetias, for instance, after a mild winter. They grow three feet high and have blooms of great size on laterals freely branching from the main stem. The gallantry of these flowers is partly due to my allowing a certain number to seed themselves. The grass path is double-bordered by white pinks, and all these flowers contribute to the end I had in view for them, especially as they follow the earlier pale irises and a soft-shaded multitude of long-spurred columbines. I head them with a group of *Iris purissima* and white roses.

I have found, indeed, that the judicious use of white flowers in a garden—roses, campanulas, funkia, Regale and Candidum lilies, phlox, the fringed daisy, the Arctotis daisy, Achillea the Pearl, "chaste as unsunn'd snow," pinks, clematis and others—can be very effective. Apart from the lilies, the most beautiful of my white flowers in July is *Romneya Coulteri* or the Californian Poppy. The soft white pleated petals stand out from the central yellow boss in the sunshine like a ballet-dancer in the blaze of the footlights, while the size of the flower is such as the old Dutchmen loved to paint. The resemblance is remarkable when the stuff-like petals flutter in the breeze; each flower on the end of its stem is a poised Pavlova.

Some gardeners have whole beds of white flowers, only varying their qualities and textures. But this seems to me too eclectic, and whites are surely most themselves in relation to the colours of other plants. So with strong colours. Scarlet lychnis, for instance, is wonderful with modulated shades of delphinium, and the same is true of certain of the Riverton Gem group. Thus for these middle beds I have found that to intersperse a chosen few strong colours such as steel-blue bee-busy *Eryngium planum*, vibrant in the sun, rather accentuates than detracts from the main effect. Facing each lawn from top to bottom of the slope is an unbroken line of the polyantha rose called Orange Perfection. It flowers twice in the year and throws out dense trusses of bloom sufficiently bright but not gaudy to form a backcloth to this medley of flowers.

The flanking beds across the two lawns and parallel with this centre-piece I keep on the contrary more uniform. For they frame the flower-garden. Thus, the rose-bed with its pansies and violas across the sunk garden of the smaller of these two lawns has a seamless raised border of catmint which intoxicates the bees. I heard a curious story about bees which to my mind graciously reveals how interlocked into a single whole is the life of the village both with nature and the garden. The bee-mistress of an estate near me told me that the bees no longer swarmed on a Sunday. And why not. "Because the church-bells no longer ring on a Sunday."

Across the largest lawn which runs well behind the house as well as down to the "shrubbery" and has two wide long beds backed by the pillared rose-wall, I also preserve a measure of uniformity. The delphiniums are succeeded by Michaelmas daisy which I break from monotony by growing nearly a score of varieties, large and small, with a border of dwarf white campanulas, clumps of Candidum lilies and a few of the duskier Riverton Gem rudbeckias. Acris that the Peacocks love is first of the Michaelmas daisies, and I have a range of them some 60 feet long, with the Boy Blues, the Pink Ladies, the Barr's Pinks, the King George's, the various Ballards and Climax grouped between and behind them. From under the vine, these daisies make domes and bluffs and spurs and ramps and slopes and rotundities of soft colour that flow into a kind of miniature downland, and in former days there were few miles of our English chalk Downs that I did not travel. I can still see them on their way to Avebury from under the vine, and I have a model of them in the garden.

So I mark the year as it passes, and the grapes swell and the flowers pass in procession before me. It is like turning over the leaves of the Oxford Book of English Verse. But it is well to forget names like Sternbergia, Salpiglossis, that stained glass or Venetian goblet flower, and *Ceratostigma plumbaginoides* as headings to the pages of the weeks. In the earlier section it may be a stanza of Donne's that catches the eye, the wind-music in which he is so cunningly adept interrupted by a trumpet blast—a corner with white perennial candytuft in front, scarlet lychnis behind and above, behind that again and higher still five different shades of delphinium and behind these again the rich clusters of Paul's Scarlet rose. Or it may be a single line that commands the heart, such as you so often find in the minor 17th century poets. I have only one Panther Lily left but it makes up for its solitary state by annually producing fifty blooms from an original single bulb. My bog-garden is sadly neglected from what it once was, chiefly owing to the difficulty of coping with the long series of droughts. The Kaemferi irises in it have all reverted to a magnificent rich dark velvety purple surrounded and pressed upon by a demos of long grasses, like the sansculottes surging into Marie Antoinette's bed-chamber with their long pikes and scythe-blades. I am fond of coral red as a colour and I once discovered a strain of penstemon that possessed it superlatively. I grouped it with phlox of more or less the same tint, but the soil rejected the whole stock of penstemon and I wrote them off as a dead loss. Then in 1942 a superb specimen suddenly appeared on the terrace, self-sown from seed that had lain dormant for five years.

A number of flowers of a single kind and colour in lines or groups or drifts make for happiness if judiciously contrasted either with their opposites or a medley. I have found a mauve petunia and a darker dwarf tobacco plant to be good in bands in front of a mixed herbaceous border—here you may think of a refrain in a ballad. Best of these experiments has been the glazed white of the very handsome South African Arctotis daisy occupying narrow beds on either side of my pair of Irish yews. The dumpling hills in lavender of the Acris Michaelmas daisy; the circles of Golden Gleam nasturtium and autumn crocus round the orchard apples; the Mermaid rose (the latest rose of all), that opens a profusion of its white blooms with their cluster of golden stamens, if trained on wires espalier-fashion, as a background to a bed of mixed chrysanthemum—these are other effects in the same notation. Flowers that stamp a very definite impression on their beholder, as for instance, the white Marcia Stanhope hybrid tea rose with its conical buds and unfolding draperies that still preserve a classical orderliness in form, should, I think, be used singly and as part of the architectural structure of the garden.

But the calendar of deepening summer in the garden is by no means only punctuated by the exits and entrances of the seasonal flowers. There are the first July mushrooms on the lawns and they always appear there. The St. George's mushroom which the village calls champs (champignon), the nation fairy rings and the books' *Trichotoma gambosum*, also rings my lawn. Though it is edible when it has reached the second year, as peasant France has recognised, the thread-like filaments under the soil are as deadly to it as certain unicellular organisms with similar fibrous rootlets are to the human blood. Digging out and replacing the contaminated soil made no difference until I hit upon the idea of dosing the rings with the ashes of my wood and peat fires. This was what purified the dancing floor of Robin Goodfellow.

When the days were too piping hot even for the canopy of vine-leaves to shade me, I camped in the lea of my Hermitage where the very sight of the orchard grasses was a coolness. But I remember these days chiefly for the ritual that took place every evening at the seventh hour. My sheep-dog (aged 91,[1] and my shadow) accompanies me wherever I go, never in her old age moving more than five yards away from me. Except at 7 o'clock; the tropism acts as punctually as Greenwich mean time. She rises, stands by me looking up into my face and when I say, "all right, go and have your supper," off she goes at a sedate trot, at once returning when it is eaten. She is a kind of familiar spirit, moving when I move, stopping when I stop, and this has become for her the perfect journey's end and consummation of her long and devoted life. The tie between man and dog sometimes becomes more intimate than can ever be between man and man, more so than between man and woman, child and parent. For these are conscious relationships, and they allow for and indeed demand temporary separations. Not so in a time-honoured bond between man and dog; Jupiter's moons will as soon be parted from Jupiter as she from me. And when occasion requires a brief disjoining, I become more sensible

[1] You multiply a dog's years by 7 to make them equal to a man's. She died as this book was passing through the press and is buried in the orchard under my Codlin, her tump crowned with daffodils.

of a lacuna in my day than I am of the loss of a limb. The tie between man and dog differs only in degree from the tie between man and land. This sense, now almost lost, is of the very essence of patriotism.

As the grapes swell above my head, there is much I could tell of the garden's slow procession into maturity, of the daily harvests, of the baptism of rain when it came, of reflowerings. I see the flowers pass, the leaves fall, the fields change, the colours come and go. Over in old Crodge's field, I see the elevator against the low stack puffing up straw in the high wind like swirls and eddies of smoke. The year passes before my eyes like the clouds across the sky. But all such passing is the condition of returning, and I finish with an end that is also a beginning. With the first touch of autumn takes place the miracle and mystery of spring. In my salpiglossis beds, the fingers of grape hyacinth forecast the rebirth of the year. The medlar loaded with its green starfish-headed fruit (from which we make a *purée* almost as good as that of chestnut) bursts into flower once more. Fulfilment is fused with promise, decay with renewal, ripeness with infancy. Nothing comes to an end in life or in a garden, for the new is instantly born out of it. At this time of fruition, I sow the China Rose Winter Radish. For the gardener as for nature there is no end.

So, in mid-September, as I string the onions and tie up the pears in their muslin bags, past, present and future are all concerned in what I do. This is husbandry and craftsmanship, to act by tradition, to prepare for the future, to perform the present need, three in one and one in three. Only modern folly boxes them up apart. And in stringing the onions I learn the village way. The stick method has the advantage of the string because then the onions can be either hung or leaned against a wall. For the first, you loop the end with string, tighten it, place the necks of three or sometimes four onions on the stick, wind the string over them and on and down the length of the stick. For the second, you take two onions, twist their necks together and then band them round the string with a knotted end just as the binders following the scythe-men used to band the corn into sheaves. In both methods, the snouts of the bulbs face outwards.

CHAPTER FOUR

THE EVENING OF THE YEAR
(October—November—December)

I. My Livestock

> "'Tis bad enough in man or woman
> To steal a goose from off a common;
> But surely he's without excuse
> Who steals a common from the goose."

THE GARDENER's punctilious evening walk to examine his crops, fruit and flowers is like the Sunday one of the farmer whose "foot fats the soil." It is something between a survey, a diurnal stock-taking, a strategical campaign, an examination paper and a ritual. His emotions, too, are a blend of satisfaction, anxiety, speculation, disappointment and pleased surprise. He is at once a paterfamilias, a purging dictator, a doctor going his rounds and a silent psalmist. Not only does he never dream of doubting that every plant enjoys the air it breathes, but it is his office to take good care that it should.

Yet if he has a grazing herbage (as the kind of gardener I am trying to body forth most emphatically should have), his prevailing mood will be one of perplexity. How *do* you get a really good sward? If a man like the mythical cat had nine lives, one of them could not be better spent than in making an ecological study of vegetation, with particular attention to the grasses. He is something of a hero in my eyes if he can identify the commoner grasses on the British list. I recognise all or most of mine in the orchard at the beginning of the year. But I forget them at the end of it and have to learn them all over again.

Thus, a walk I took at the beginning of the summer of 1943 with that great husbandman I have alluded to more than once in the course of this book made a profound impression on me. We were walking through a greensand pasture in North Wiltshire. Ahead of us was a magnificent field of wheat that before the war had been part of the pasture; beyond it lay a group of black, weatherboarded and thatched barns and above them "the decent church that tops the neighbouring hill." But it was more than decent: the disposition of the wheat-field, the barns and the church, the whole cupped in the enormous ramp of the Downs, had a deeply symbolic meaning. It was not only a pictorial representation of the roots of the English culture as contrasted with her mercantile civilization, but of how Adam, short of Paradise, could make a demi-Eden of this earth.

As we walked, my friend the husbandman was noting the sleek and well-conditioned aspect of the cows and gathering from their pasture a particularly happy association of grasses at our feet. He pointed out the differences between the two rye-grasses, the perennial with the long ligule or tooth, the Italian with the short, and the two poas, the one with the broad and the other with the twisted leaflet. Indeed, this man never misses anything. He had recently discovered that that commonest and insignificant poa grass that colonizes every mean waste, backyard or dumping ground is packed with protein. For years he had kept a pasture of his own constant to 25% white clover by never grazing it in winter and punctuating the spring and summer grazings to a fine art. He had found out too that the over-stimulation of clover crops with nitrogenous manures had turned the clover from a producer to a consumer of nitrogen.

I love knowledge like this; it is utterly different from the over-specialization of the laboratory. It is seeing in little how the macrocosm of organic nature works as a whole and so justifying Hamlet's "what a piece of work is man!" For all his mechanical dreams, man can never master nature. But he can become her manager and husband through love, meditation and observation. In my very much smaller way, I have pondered my lawn and orchard grasses. I study how to encourage the tenderer and richer leafage at the expense of the coarser and in the latter how to make a sward out of rough grazing land. It was partly this factor, together with consideration for the general self-supporting economy of the garden, that led me to try feeding down the orchard with geese. This was after weighing the pros and cons of a tethered Dexter cow, chickens, runner ducks and even sheep. What finally made me decide on geese was my profound regard for the husbandry of the peasant. It was not for nothing that the open-field villager kept geese on the common for at least two and probably three millennia. Folklore would not be what it is without the goose on the common. One of the least noticed effects of the Enclosures was the decline of goose-keeping as a consequence of the theft of the poor man's common. They stole the "common from the goose." Thus, to bring the goose back to the garden or small holding is an important step in the cause of the restoration of a self-sufficient husbandry.

I justified it, and at the end of six months was only confirmed in a view I have held for many years—that excess urbanism has except among about 1 per cent. of the population destroyed the arts of husbandry. Otherwise, there would not be throughout the kingdom a single paddock, orchard, common or rough pasture lonely for lack of geese. They are no trouble; they sleep out rough all spring and summer (my pair were housed only twice up to the end of the year, and then only for fear of foxes); they cost next to nothing to feed and will regenerate a pasture within a single season. What they accomplished for my orchard in that season might have caused the directing staff of I.C.I. to turn pale. They shaved it down almost to the smoothness, resilience and close texture of a Downland turf, with islets and tufts of hassock grass rising out of it. In October, by a judicious sparseness of their supplementary diet, they tackled even this and the loathsome squitch with it.

It must not be inferred that I half-starved them; there can be no mistaking when geese are hungry. They can make themselves heard even above a low-flying aeroplane. Perhaps their most brilliant performance was to bring total annihilation to that scourge of all sweet grasses, the creeping buttercup. This diminutive monster among the ranunculi throws out new births from each joint. By travelling yards underground it smothers out everything weaker than dock, squitch or hassocks. But such a delicacy did the pair find its original corms that the next year not one appeared above ground. Under their toothed bills the orchard became a refinery. Next spring the earth turned sweet with poas, cocksfoot, rye-grass, fescue, rough-stalked meadow grass and other of the more nutritious grasses that the year before had been the paupers and submerged tenth of the orchard community. It was now the turn of previous dominants like Yorkshire fog and sorrel to become recessive.

But the renovation of pasture was only one of the services rendered by my pair of benefactors. They showed me the way of becoming independent even of neighbouring farmers, if I so chose, in keeping the fertility of the garden at high pitch. They did more than manure the whole ground and so incidentally the fruit trees. From their conservative habit of retiring nightly to the same bedchamber under an arching rose, they provided me with three or four daily spadefuls of highly concentrated fuel for the compost stack. Their own feeding consisted of no more than the emptying of a daily pail of kitchen waste in which nothing came amiss to them except the cores, peelings and etceteras of tomatoes. Though I now grow oats partly for fattening future geese, my first year with them cost me nothing whatever over and beyond the original outlay of the price for themselves, a couple of sheep hurdles from my local hurdler to keep them out of the garden proper, and some wire netting to fence them out of the arable ground in the orchard. I resold what I took to be the goose for the sake of my orchard daffodils and devoured what I took to be the gander (as I confess with some qualms of soul rather than flesh) for my Christmas dinner. This goose, though only what Dr. Grant in *Mansfield Park* calls a "grass goose" (viz.: not corn-fattened), weighed 12 lbs. I consider then that the enterprise was as economical and the profit as handsome as to have earned the approval not only of the peasant but his antithesis, the dealer. I mean economy in Ruskin's sense of "stewardship," not in the modern sense which as often as not is a euphemism for waste. The entertainment and company these "amusive" birds (as Gilbert White spoke of his "*hirundines*") afforded me may be considered as a psychological compound interest on the transaction.

Geese, besides their intelligence and independence (watch how they will crane their necks and greet a skein of their wild brethren clanging across the sky and it will be seen that the captivity has not mortgaged the pride of anserine Israel), do undoubtedly possess a sense of humour. A domestic scene in the orchard of a local labourer was of the dog lying down and licking a couple of young rabbits, a pig lying down and licking the dog. Enter a goose who steals up and tweaks the dog's tail, whereupon the dog rises and hustles the goose off stage. My English Bob-Tail, Friday, has no tail to be sported with and so they used to stalk and harry her buttocks. She never resented these gross witticisms, always tried to give them a wide berth but instantly chased them off without touching them if I gave the word.

The tamest of geese—and the gander used to feed from my

hand—never make the pure surrender to man of the dog. When I fed Daphnis and Chloe with household scraps which they consumed with extraordinary speed and greed, she looked wistfully on. Not that she coveted apple and potato peelings, but she was out of the play. When she was a trifle pernicketty about her own food, as her great age sometimes made her, I used to let her come in to the feast. All three, diverting ancestral antagonisms into a cut-price competition for markets, would shovel down food in great gobbets, the heads of the pair occasionally touching her expansive muzzle. My even tamer second pair, Harold Logic and Anne Fallacy, used to walk, like circus geese, under her belly. Except on these occasions and when I set her to drive them off from forcing their company upon us, she never so much as glanced at them.

When they first arrived, they spent the first day marching about in a stately manner (as Gilbert White said of his hoopoes) from one hurdle to the other at each entrance to the main garden. They were seeking a way out. Each followed and imitated the actions of the other. Indeed they carried their matehood to ludicrous lengths, not only as two minds but two bodies with but a single thought. If one opened his or her wings to wave, the other immediately plagiarized. If one stared, the other stared, if one preened, the other preened, if one neck-rubbed, the other neck-rubbed, if one fed, the other fed, if one took a drink from the pail, the other took a drink from the pail, if one went to sleep, the other went to sleep. As they usually kept the same distance apart, my orchard became a drill-yard. There was only one exception to such laborious devotedness; if one stood on one leg, the other did not invariably follow suit. Consequently, when these uxorious birds took to following me about, stopping when I stopped, going on when I went on, seating themselves on either side of me when I sat down, I began to feel that I was under military escort or even arrest. Indeed they drove me in the end out of one of my favoured orchard work-sites. I liked all four of us to be in sociable proximity but not that two of the company should converse across me. For geese are birds of incredible volubility. They possess an astonishing variety of syllables in tone and inflection, from musical twitterings to staccato exclamations. These in their turn are suddenly broken— geese have acute hearing—by harsh and raucous greetings to a flock of geese unfortunately overheard from the field on the other side of the lane. Once, the goose flew over the hedge and was recaught in the ditch, Dickory and I subsequently cutting the flight feathers with the garden secateurs. The uproar made by the gander prancing round us on outspread wings, hissing, cackling, trumpeting, screaming and even snorting, made it easy to understand how the Gauls were baffled before Rome.

Not only the appetites of these birds but their manners of obtaining food were as varied as their conversation. Accomplished graziers, they also fed abundantly on grubs, worms, insects, crane-flies, leather-jackets and wireworms. They dibbled under the grass like ducks, probed the soil like waders, snatched up woodlice and other small fry like woodpeckers among ants and ringed plover among sand-flies. They loved wet weather; it enabled them to eat and drink at the same time. If their bucket was late in being refilled, they set up a clamour that could be heard in the village a quarter of a mile away. The tough white core of cabbage ringed with leaflets they devoured like carnivores. They shook it like a dog a rat, hammered it, drove the bill through it and tore slices off it with their bone-like teeth. If I spoke to them before feeding them, they cocked their heads on one side like terriers to listen. If a morsel was invulnerable even to them, they ran full tilt for the bucket in a parody of the fantastically parading Teuton soldier, plunged in the sinuous neck, shook the head till the water spilled over and then gulped it down. Damaged potatoes they ate not at all in the pastoral manner, but sideways like a dog chewing gristle. Often they impatiently swallowed it whole, and made frantic efforts to force it home along the channel of the distended gullet.

Mouldy potatoes excited them to such gluttony that they often displayed a clever stupidity. Each would seize upon a hunk, turn its back upon the other and with lowered extended neck and the most elaborate doublings, twistings and manoeuvrings retreat further and further away from the other with every appearance of being pursued by the other. For once in a way "goose" was no misnomer. In these quick-food contests which momentarily marred the unanimity of their lives, the goose as the most engrossed in greed usually came off worse than the gander. When she picked up a sizeable crust, she wasted much time shambling and shuffling off at a rapid trot to keep it to herself while he was disposing of the board as though head and neck were a suction pipe. They were almost too human when, accompanying me down to the compost stack, they would stare at me with the superior gaze of a bland and wise inanity.

It was remarkable how they managed to combine dignity with absurdity. When I called them for scraps, they came sprinting across the orchard grass like the old dames in the potato race at the pre-war Flower Show. Their way of opening their wings and taking a few mincing dancing steps was more like Mr. Pickwick on the ice than the jacana wing-tripping across a leaf-pad. But Mr. Pickwick had dignity too, and so had they. When standing on one leg with head tucked into the scapulars in a "drowsy numbness," their bodies swaying like a boat in the swell, my geese were swans and might have been the originals of a Brjeska bronze or a Dürer wood-engraving. They are beautiful too in the rain and every feather lifts to receive it. Rain clothes them in a richer vitality partly because it freshens and greens the autumn grass, and partly because they are by inheritance water-birds. They are beautiful, too, in sleet and snow when their droppings are frozen and their drinking water is ice before I break it. The ancient grandeur of these birds of Boreas then returns. But for danger from foxes, they would have required no night-shelter and were as plump as ever.

Something too there is of the incalculable and even mysterious about the goose. Why does it fall so ready a victim to the fox, this hardy, bold and sagacious bird? The country people all believe that the fox "mesmerises" his prey, as the weasel does rabbits and, as Hudson relates, birds in hedge or tree. One good backyarder told me that the fox stares at a hen roosting in a tree until the bird flutters down. The gander can be a dangerous bird in the breeding season and has all the secrecy of the wild state about its tactics. Yet to the fox it goes as a lamb to the slaughter. Its affectionate nature is, I think, a legacy from the wild the remnants of which the goose hoards above all domesticated fowl. I heard of a devoted friendship between a goose and a lamb, both of whom accompanied their master to the post-box and back, and the attachment of my pair to one another and in a very much lesser degree to me was not unusual. But unlike the ignoble turkey and the mechanized hen, their self-respect has not been depraved by captivity. They welcome familiarity but thus far and no further. Though the gander fed from my hand (with fearful-ferocious lunges), he and his mate had to be caught before they would enter their shelter.

Their intelligence is incomparably superior to that of any farm-yard fowl—they used to tread a watery porridge I gave them in the winter to make an even consistency—but they sometimes behaved like imbeciles.[1]

Came the time of parting in December and even a year later I feel compunctious about it. How could I have celebrated Christmas Day by cold-bloodedly devouring the bird that had fed from my hand? What cannibals we men are! But, though the husbandman loves his animals, he does not keep them for pets. If I had spared this bird, I should have dislocated my whole economy on which feeding off my pasture for six months in the year depended. Only thus could I save winter keep, the daffodils and the inaffordable labours of the breeding season, a trickier business with geese than with poultry. Yet I still wonder how I could have brought myself to eat this particular gander. Or what I took to be the gander. I think it was carrying the benefits I derived from him a little too far. Especially when, the day before he died, he became a mysterious bird. In a sense I paid for the deed, since, with the geese away and my Friday undergoing a serious operation, the orchard became as empty as a dust bowl.

I have always held that one of the merciful dispensations of nature is that animals have no fore-knowledge or anticipation of death, and that fear is a passing emotion in wild nature, strictly utilitarian in its operation. And I have in the past collected a formidable array of evidence to that effect. But is this universally true, at any rate of domestic animals? The tale is thus. The small farmer who was to help me catch the gander and wring his neck—he was a very handsome bird with a belly band of dark grey like the sheldrake's similar chestnut one, dark grey head and all the rest brilliant white—did not come into action until the evening. So I had the whole day for observation. What I first noticed was that, though the goose was feeding as usual, the gander never took a single bite. On the contrary, he held his head nigh, turning it nervously from side to side and moving restlessly to and fro across the orchard. This was so unwonted, indeed unique, in his behaviour that I watched him for a long time, keeping at a distance from him.

[1] I mysteriously lost the gander of my second pair. Perhaps I was indiscreet in feeding him. He was a bird of fine appearance, of shining health and vitality and exceptional friendliness. After his death, the goose, though I replaced her mate, became a changed character. She developed a slightly malicious technique, grew suspicious and a hisser, and was always making covert attacks on my sheep dog's buttocks.

The goose as usual followed me about but, for the first time since our acquaintance, not the gander. He would not come near me, though the pair were always imitating one another. He ate nothing all day, for, when I was absent, I had him observed, and when I appeared with the lunch-pail, he failed to come running to the gate-hurdle where I used to feed them both. He still held his neck rigid, made hurried steps one way and another and glanced about him as sense as well as anthropomorphism would have called distractedly. If I made but a few steps in his direction, he darted off with flapping wings. He still would not feed, though he had had no food other than grass the day before, to keep his crop clear. He had suddenly changed from the confiding familiar to the apprehensive stranger.

At last the farmer arrived and we advanced to commit our fell work. Long before we could reach him or attempt to cut off his range, he flung himself, squarking wildly and beating his wings, with such force into the hedge that he imprisoned himself in it half-way. The goose, infected by his panic, followed him into the gap, where she was easily caught and shut away, making no agitation. But before we could reach her mate, he had forced his way right through the hedge, climbed the ditch with wings and feet, crossed the lane and crawled under a farm-gate into a cow-pasture. We set out on his pursuit and, flapping along with trailing feet and harsh screams of alarm and rage, he plunged into the new hedge where we caught him just as he was emerging into the road. He struck like an adder at the farmer, lunged at me, beat madly with his wings and in the end it took three of us to hold him. The gallant creature was as indomitable in his way as the little cow being unshipped in Tomlinson's *The Sea and the Jungle*. How could I have brought myself to eat him?

The actual chase and capture might have been no oddity if his dash for liberty and ferocity had not been in total contradiction with his previous conduct on other occasions when he had been caught. Normally he was a tranquil bird and, if anything, the goose had in penning and clipping been the more troublesome of the two. When he had first arrived, he had twice escaped and been recaptured without undue fuss or resentment by strangers. Putting this beside his attitude during the whole day and correlating all the phenomena together, how can one explain them except by his anticipation and indeed prevision of danger? His environment had undergone no disconcerting change during the day; no change of routine, nor shift of circumstance out of customary perspective, no whisper of nature to her imperilled creature had betrayed my design. Yet his suspicion and avoidance of me had been such as to give me some inkling of the feelings of the Ancient Mariner.

Thus, the only explanation that explains all the facts is the one impossible one. For how can we suppose that any creature but man can "look before and after"? After, yes, since animals certainly have memory. But before? The unfortunate prerogative of man must surely remain his. Animals do, of course, dread the future by being brought into contact with associational factors; horses seem to see ghosts, while sheep and birds and many other animals anticipate changes in weather conditions. But how can an animal apprehend a boding peril to itself alone by which its mate is not affected; how can it sense the invisible sword of Damocles suspended over its head? Obviously not. *Credo quia impossibile*, and believe it I do. I will not pervert nor misinterpret the facts to fit them into any theory of scientific dogmatism.

The career of science is strewn with discarded theories and exploded dogmas; the scientific faith is as riddled with superstition as any other faith. More so indeed, since no other faith has quite so blindly credited its own infallibility. The first scientists were modest men; they advanced postulates with diffidence and a respect for truth that recognised they could only touch the hem of her garment. But the modern scientist is rarely distinguished for either. I accept the plain and single inference from what I have seen, and no scientist shall bully me out of it.

But how this thing can be, and whether or no some animals possess a supersensory faculty that enables them in certain conditions to achieve a premonitory awareness of the future without evidential guidance I do not profess to answer. It seems to me that I came out of this adventure with little enough credit: but at least I have opened up a new area for speculation or research in natural history.

There was yet another sequel to the whole affair, and that was that the goose turned out to be the gander. Whether the gander was after all a goose, so that I committed the unpardonable sin against good husbandry of killing the goose with the golden eggs, I shall never know. The discovery was made because the sham goose which I sold was always fighting with the other gander in her (his) new home. Yet this goose-gander took veteran countrymen in as well as me; "she" was more sedate, incurious and less adventurous; "she" was more feminine and she looked more feminine, while nobody could have mistaken the gander-goose for other than a male. He-she was quite definitely the master-mistress of her-him. At any rate, in this inverted world of female dominance, the genuine goose would seem to have been myself.

My next pair of geese in the following year I was happier with, for the simple reason that I resolved that I would sell, but not eat them. Partly because I had no idea which was Jack and which Jill and partly because they were even more confiding and engaging than their predecessors. One can eat the members of other families, but not of one's own.

II. *Ripeness is All*

"Who soweth too lateward hath seldom good seed
Who soweth too soon little better shall speed."
                                                THOMAS TUSSER.

"The fig-tree ripeneth her green figs."

OCTOBER sails over the horizon bringing the Indian Summer in
its year-long voyage round the world. The glowing weather it
brings, with their infantile clouds like cherubs, might be Cleopatra's
barge on the Cidnus. At sundown, the sky is flecked with and fretted
into golden streaks, eddies, swirls, freshets and whirlpools as
though in visual representation of the great flowing River of Life
along which comes sailing this princeliest month of all the year.
It brings in its train grape-ripening, fig-ripening, tomato-ripening
days, days of melancholy and joy, of fulfilment and deceptive
promise, days of autumn big with spring, days like the culture of
the 17th century before the hard frost of the Puritan Revolution.
Some are George Herbert days, cool, calm and bright. They are
days only to be described in monosyllables, clear, warm and blue,
as Gilbert White describes birds and days in his *Journal*, so unlike
his polysyllabic Letters. Days of sunsets of old gold and morns of
gossamer. Nights when the Hunter's moon hangs like an apple
on the Tree of Life.

But the tartness in the air, like the first bite of the first orchard
apple, are a leave-taking of summer. The wind strikes different
notes from every different kind of tree, and my balsam poplars
render into their music the sharpness and the sweetness of these
apple-like days. They have a double sound; a whispering, but also
what at first seems a tapping but then a crackling as of a distant
fire. It might be the crackling of their own yellow flames, for
my poplars are the first of my trees to burn themselves out. The
pomps of autumn are so rich, that leaves are no longer leaves but
flowers. The whole landscape becomes an orchard of fruit, pink,
crimson, scarlet, red, mahogany and black, and the bloom of the
purple grape rests on the very hills. I am forced to choose out of
all this superabundance a single symbol of the ripened year. Let

it be the apple, the wild apple of the woods and hedgerows, the domesticated apple of the orchard.

I have an odd memory of the crab-apple which grows plentifully in our Chiltern woods. I relate this memory here because it is pertinent to the theme of this book, the theme of *il faut cultiver notre jardin*. It happened that I ran across a commercial traveller, a species with which I am but little acquainted. There did not seem to be any point of contact until he mentioned that he had once been a seller of hats. Hats, yes, I knew something about them, or rather the straw-plaiters who used to supply the material for hats. I told him about them. Nearly every cottager for fifty miles in circumference round my home used to grow a special plot of corn, the straw of which was plaited by the cottagers' wives and sold to an emissary from Luton. Yes, he had himself seen them just before Great War No. 1 sitting before their cottage doors of an evening. So Shakespeare had seen the lace-makers and made a song about them.

This was promising: here was a business man who actually knew something about the business on which his business lived. So I asked him where he got his straw from before Great War No. 2, by which time home-grown straw for a home industry had become obsolete in the march of progress. Oh, he said, from all over the world. And why? said I. He regarded this question as puerile. Because it was cheaper, of course. Well, I said, one of the reasons why straw-plaiting went the way of nearly every other country industry was because the cottagers made about 2/- a week at it, working for the whole of their leisure time. Ah, said he, but in Japan they could work even harder for less money.

The conversation rather languished after this. Then he happened to mention to somebody else that he knew a hedge in Bedfordshire which grew seven different kinds of crab-apple. He described each kind minutely and said that his wife had made a hundred pounds of jelly out of these crabs. But he himself preferred them raw when you could tell the difference in taste by the difference in colour and size. I told him that some old husbandman must have cultivated this hedge. Then it came out that, after the first war in which he had been a soldier, he went into a textile factory, but left it to become a traveller in hats because he had somehow to get out into the open air. He was in fact a countryman *manqué*, like tens of thousands of others who could not become countrymen because there was no livelihood in the land. Finance had seen to that. I was "disillusioned," he said, "after the first war, and now I worry that it will be even worse after this one." Evidently he had not been impressed by the paper-Paradises of the planners. He foresaw chaos, unemployment, the fight for markets, the same dreary hopeless business all over again, ultimately leading to Great War No. 3. What he would have liked was a job in the open air which gave him enough peace and means to be able to go off and pick crab-apples.

Here was your "common man." A man blind to the tragedy of those straw-plaiters *both* in England and abroad, blind to the unholy fetichism of cheapness. Yet he himself was a victim to the same system that had dispossessed and ruined our peasants. It had given the land over to the thistle and thought of nothing but fitting man into an industrialism he loathes without understanding why or how he is to find a way out of it. It would have been cruel to suggest to this man that he should cast his eye over an article in *The Times* called "Exports and the Future" that had appeared on the very day of our conversation. It would have confirmed his worst fears. Dealing with the alternative between the "expansion of trade" and home-production, it said:—

"In the interests of world prosperity and international co-operation, we ought most certainly to exhaust the possibilities of the first alternative before turning to the second. British policy after the war must and will strive for the greatest scope and volume of international exchange."

I feared that the prospects of this traveller peacefully picking his crab-apples in the future were about as roseate as those of reconciling cut-throat competition for foreign markets and world-exploitation of raw materials with international peace.

When I go down to pick my own apples in the orchard, I feel it is a solid raft among the estranging seas of "world-policy." I had already taken 51 lbs. from my three short rows of tomatoes. I had gathered the carrot harvest, more than 2 bushels in 6 rows, the early Scarlet Horn with the blunt nose and the Intermediate with the tapering one, both the colour of the local roof-tiling. But picking apples and still more so pears is a much more ticklish business than lifting carrots. Your small-holder is confronted with no more vexing problem than when to pick, where to store and how to preserve his autumn hard fruit. There is so exquisitely a right time for pears (all true husbandry is doing the right thing at the right time in the right place with the right touch) that you have to choose not merely the month and the week but the very hour: I know no other method of how to lift the yellowing pear in its muslin bag than to see whether it comes away in the hand.

Apples are nearly always plucked too early. Bramley's Seedling,[1] for instance, being the best of keepers, should always be preceded by James Grieve and Cox (October apples), the Codlins, Warner's King, and dual purpose apples like Blenheim and Allington Pippin. That painted deceiver, that shop-window syren, Worcester Pearmain, is an exception and makes quite a respectable dessert apple if plucked green. But these seasonal calculations were all upset by the North African weather of 1943, when I was picking Allingtons before the end of August and walking over a carpet of dead leaves to reach them. The apple-picking season was enormously complicated during this year by three factors: the attacks of the blackbirds, the precocity of the season and the damnable iteration of the winds. These last strewed the grass with windfalls and tempted the distracted gardener to pluck his harvest unripe to forestall the greedy gales.

Perhaps the most difficult apple of all to gauge aright is the Spice Apple or East Anglian Spice Pippin. If caught at the flood-tide of mellow maturity, taken, one might say, at that superb moment of ripeness when Andrew Marvell at Appleton House found the fruit on the trees melting into his mouth, it makes a dessert apple that some countrymen call "the pearl." Other fine late dessert apples that seem rarely if ever grown to-day are Askeard's Kernel, the Pine Golden Pippin and the Rusbock Pippin. There can be no doubt that the number of kinds of apples grown has declined. Mascal himself introduced the Pippins in 1572 and Parkinson enumerates 57, while Hartlib (1650) mentions one orchardist as cultivating 200 sorts out of a total for the kingdom of 500. When I was well acquainted with the orchard country between the Malverns and the Cotswold scarp, I was amazed at the bewildering variety of traditional apples grown for cider and of pears for perry. In this particular as in all things, quality and

[1] Stewed apples can be a lodging-house nightmare. But Bramley windfalls, stewed the same day as they are picked up in an earthenware pot with *Les Battus*, the cores and peelings placed on top, with syrup, honey and a little sugar to sweeten and vanilla and cloves to flavour, are a delicacy few of us deserve.

variety have been replaced by quantity and sameness. Progress has made for a dulled and undistinguishing palate.

In my own orchard, I do not neglect my solitary Medlar. I have an affection for the medlar tree not only for its own sake but an association it brings. It is an affection also for Bemerton as George Herbert's parish, and in the rectory he planted a medlar tree. I harvest mine in the second week of October, taking on an average a bushel and a half year by year. Every year it turns the colour of the hunter's moon with its large leaves and closely-knit umbrella-like growth, a moon that fails to rise. Its fellow in the east throws heavy blue shadows across the white lane, pearls the hedge, elongates the trees and makes the landscape dreamlike and yet hard and clear as a drypoint. For our *purée* the medlars are skinned and put through a sieve so that no stones, like round shot, pass it. On this some creamy top milk and a sprinkling of sugar complete a dish that is the essence of this beautiful little tree, whose structure is so shapely. Its blossom is larger than that of any other fruit-tree, nor does it ever fail to bear and put on a radiance in October as though Pomona had touched it in passing.

As the year ripens and moves towards its end, so the signs of spring accumulate. Apple buds are clothed in silver fir, clematis buds appear close to the terracotta button chrysanthemums, fretted and scalloped with rime like a Tudor Rose. Some days are as though spring and autumn were fused, bright and cold. The shadows are sharply etched and the hills on the horizon deeply incised. Clouds have clear edges, leaves gleam and flutter as though cut in glass, petals are glazed, every twig, stem, shoot, blade, head picked out as though wrought in metal. I am in tune with the season by harvesting the haricots. One is coloured a deep indigo and lavender with indigo splashes, another half white and half a delicate pinkish red and all are in harmony with a time as gaudy as a gipsy. On the same day as I plant six rows of cabbages on the newly composted onion bed, Sternbergia, the great yellow crocus of autumn, unfolds as a symbol of this mating of opposite seasons and so of the inter-dependence between life and death.

Yet all the time this complex month is making husbandly pro-vision for the winter: my Chicory, invaluable as a triple-purpose plant—for its leaves which are very rich in minerals, for its deep roots to break up the subsoil pan and for use as a winter salad, has formed good lettuce-like crowns and the broad-leaved Endive and broad-leaved Cress are ready. At the same time, autumn is a memoried summer. Many roses are reflowering, a few for the third time; I am still picking runner beans and in the middle of the month ate a dish of Alpine strawberries. The Pumpkins, "swelling wisibly" all summer, are for the pot, baked in casserole in the oven with a little fat and garnished with parsley, marjoram or sweet basil. On All Hallowe'en, I always take an inventory of the summer flowers still blooming, and usually can bring it into just the right side or the wrong side of the fifties. But not in 1943, whose summer brought autumn in August and drove the very cattle to break out of the parched fields into the corn—and through my fence to devour my haricot beans.

Under my grapes I look out on the autumn fields, once of corn so far as the eye could see, then of summer-worn pasture, and now again in fallow and stubble. The bleached corn-ricks (rounded with an apex prolonged unto a short finial like an upright finger and the long or short rectangular type with end-gables) lend warmth, companionableness and purpose to a somewhat Quakerish landscape. Its emptiness comes almost as a shock. Thirty years ago, this same land, over which the long rays of the sun and the long blue shadows of the hedgerow elms now fall, was arable under a thousand folded sheep with three shepherds. After 1920, the sheep were sold, the shepherds dismissed, the hurdles burned and the dogs destroyed. And still, though by some magic crops are sown and reaped, it is as empty as the moon. The sweat of man and the dung of beast in the home-field have given place to the distant by-products of the alliance between chemistry and big business. The only dung-cart left in the neighbourhood was in 1942 up to auction in the market-town and fetched no bid to reach the reserve price. To be making my own wine from my own grapes, my own porridge from my own oats,[1] as my forefathers did before me, sends echoing to me across the ocean Whitman's (though hardly in the sense he intended) "Pioneers, O Pioneers!"

November is to me one of the dearest of months. It is rarely cold; the fogs drive the aeroplanes away; the nobler splendour of the trees replaces the more garish splendour of the now veiled and diaphanous hedgerows; the soft rains, the mild sunshine and the musing clouds distil a poignancy that is free of *aliquid amari*.

---

[1] This proved impossible in 1943, when the starved birds fell on my fine crop and more than halved it.

Light frosts crisp the celery and tighten up the Brussels sprouts. What was once a mere garage is now heady with apple-scent like a cider-mill, while from the rafters hang tufts of flageolet beans, bunches of amber grapes, fasces of carrots and ropes of onions. Chrysanthemums, pink, yellow, bronze, purple, white and terra-cotta, gladden my northern bed. The last roses possess the joyful enhancement of rarity and brevity, and nothing becomes the year so well as its dying. In the absurdly mild November of 1943 I had 35 different kinds of plants in flower, most of them summer ones. The first authentic day of winter comes about the middle of the month, though the air is soft, the sun shines and buds and shoots and seedlings crowd the earth. It is subtly caught, the sense that the winter has stolen on the scene, a communication rather than evidence. It seems to be a message from the earth itself, neither climatic nor barometric. A quality is exuded into the air, a sense of something far more deeply interfused than the testimony of leafless bough, poached cattle-ways, steaming cow-breath and sodden or frosted flowers.

A heavy frost brings the sudden dismantling of autumn finery. Showers of gold dribble down upon the silver ground, and the blue sky is repeated in a lighter silvery blue from the sun-shadows and in the lea of the hedgerow. The fall of the leaf is of rich variety not only in colour but in motion. Sometimes single spies like early birds leave the dense foliage; then a small company comes briskly down like a flight of finches from stack to cow-yard; sometimes there is a confused drifting like a migration of butterflies; sometimes a clot of leaves falls with almost a thud as though a burden were shouldered off; or the tree drops a few tears as our first parents did on leaving Paradise. But the brightness does not fade; it but falls to a lower place and in the spinney a netted blue sky overhangs a burnished floor. In the act of leaf-shedding, the tree is renewing its life; it is a disembarrassment and first stage in the transformation of waste into use. So leaf-showers, flittings, driftings, sudden flights, sidling falls of solitary leaves, nature's gentlest change of the year, are not melancholy. They are a prudent husbanding, an exercise of thrift over superfluity, a falling back upon inward resources, and all gardeners with me follow the teaching of the tree. We pile leaves (which I never burn), cut out ash-roots from the pear-beds, dig, fork, build up the sacrificial waste-products, garrison and fortify the plot against the dark days. I do for my garden what the two copses I see from my terrace have already done in changing from green and gold to smoky blue and lustrous black.

The light frosts bring us as copious a horn of plenty as did the sunshine of July. All roots, especially swedes, benefit from them. I refuse to believe that anybody who has eaten compost-grown celery within a few hours of morning frost could be other than a convert to self-sufficiency. And humus by its retention of moisture is particularly valuable for celery, which quickly bolts if it gets at all dry. Marketed celery grown with artificials and transported some distance is as inferior to home-grown celery grown from humus and eaten soon after digging from a frosty ground as Japanese red tinned salmon is to Severn fresh salmon. Argument is futile; the evidence of the senses is final.

As the shadows grow longer and leaner, the wind gallops over the earth like a stallion released into pasture and the wild felties launch from the yet unplushed hedgerows into the wild wind. The earth itself, full-fed with the summer's sun, is stretched in repose and the corn-stacks on the crest of the rise stand out like carbuncles in the coronet of the declining sun. In the evening of the year, I reflect upon the year's blessings with which the heavens have endowed this earth. The dew, the rain, the frost, the mist and the light, the warmth, the kindling power of the sun, the very storms and the night, all these the earth patiently receives and turns to good and for the nourishment of her children. Man cannot interfere with the cycle of this ordinance nor control its revolutions. He can only turn it to fruitfulness, as the earth does, the fruitfulness of a kind and perceptive management from which proceed all his larger creative enterprises. Like the ancient Titans, he has attempted to free himself from the wheel of life and now makes war both on heaven and earth to, as he must now begin to see, his confusion. He must recognise his finiteness and in so doing he transcends it. Such is the paradox of his being, the self-pride that comes to dust, the humility that inherits the earth. He must reknit the ancient partnership between man and the earth, he must bow once more before the heavens. These prerequisites of his mortal existence he can only accomplish by building up once more from the foundations—the family, the plot, the village, the market town and the region. Otherwise, he will perish from the earth.

At Christmas, the Great Dance of the earth with the seasons pauses, and the figures are grouped together without motion, a vast statuary of the Creation, such as even Michael Angelo could hardly conceive. Almost my last act of the year is depodding the flageolet bean called Little Green Gem which emerges in five colours, white, green, pink, brown and mottled, the best and largest being the brown. On Christmas Eve, I take my usual tally of what flowers are still blooming. Even in so balmy a winter as that of 1942, it is never in my cold and exposed garden one to write to the papers about, much less in a book. I found more buds than flowers, not only of late-flowering roses and early flowering Lenten roses[1] but of wallflower, cherry and snapdragon. Grape hyacinth grass was full-grown, the figs were still swelling, the iris blades full of fresh green points, the pale fat delphinium shoots had shouldered off the soil. The corn promised to be winter-proud and so to need the sheep on it more even than usual. The goldfinches flitted through the apple-boughs, either very late or very prematurely and dunnock, song-thrush and mistle-thrush were all in song. For days we went without fires which we were to light the following June. There was no mockery in the chaplet of winter jessamine and *Viburnum fragrans* set about the bald crown of old Hiems. Both were in richest flower, each at its own corner of the west wall.

Our Christmas dinner, including dessert of walnuts, cob-nuts, pears and apples, together with all the vegetables, the apple-sauce and the sage and onion stuffing, not to mention the goose which I would prefer not to mention, was entirely the harvest of the neighbourhood. We owed nothing whatever to the chain store, the emporium, the metropolis, the whole vast organisation of keeping people away from their food and the food away from those who were to eat it. Thus it was a true celebration of Galilee, the little peasant community surrounded by the *latifundia* of the centralised and overblown Romano-Syriac civilization.

We knew the history of everything on our plates; through the window we could see the fields that had produced this goodness. Though the bounty was nature's, it had been vain without the co-operation of our own diligence and husbandry. No combine, nor middleman nor processor nor salesman had come between us and our cheer; no animal had been maltreated for it (again that

[1] In the un-English summer of 1943, these reflowered in August, mistaking it for late autumn, and small blame to them.

uneasy qualm about my goose); no predatory passions had been
exercised on our account. No over-reaching, no buying cheap to
sell dear had tainted our feast, and as we ate, so had our forefathers eaten before us. We were beholden to none except in
the way of neighbourliness and willing service, and we partook
of the fruits of our own earth with a good conscience. What we
had taken we had rendered back and had kindly entreated the earth
for what we had kindly received. Was not then our feast a sacramental one, feeding the spirit no less than the body?

Surely this wholeness was part of the holiness of the day. For
a day and a night no aeroplane rammed a roaring nose into its
serenity. The sun came out of the eastern sky

> "as a bridegroom out of his chamber, and rejoiceth as a giant
> to run his course. It goeth forth from the uttermost part of
> the heaven and runneth about unto the end of it again. . . .
> The law of the Lord is an undefiled law, converting the soul."

This day the heavens were undefiled and one could look up as the
shepherds did and see the same sky arching over the world in an
unbroken peace. And with the peace came a strange timelessness.
As I walked up the village street, the bells rang out as those who
slept under the grey tombstones of the churchyard had heard them;
a gig drawn by a spanking cob passed me and out of a side-street
jingled the milk-float with a good pony in the shafts. For a stretch
the cottages were as men had seen them for three hundred years.
Some are cream-washed on a plinth of black or grey Portland stone,
others laced with timber with leaded panes and green shutters to
the windows, others of soft Tudor brick, oak-timbered, with here
and there a course of herring-boning or a proper inn-sign or a
wrought-iron vane or a strapped door. There was nothing to show
me that this peace and comeliness, this deliverance from time,
this perfect adaptation of nature to man and man to nature was
an illusion. Nothing to show that the whole world outside was a
witch's cauldron, bubbling and seething with evil.

All I saw and heard was compatible with the idea of Christmas,
not only as the birthday of the Prince of Peace but as a rustic festival.
Heaven was married to earth, the light was returning, the year
had reawakened. The earth-festival was faithfully reflected in the
Manger, the Shepherds, the Carpenter's Shop, the village Messiah,

the Saviour of the Parables of Husbandry. But it was immeasurably transfigured into a rebirth of the soul and symbolised in the day when the organic was fused with the spiritual and the temporal met with the eternal. I dared to think it compatible too with my own small plot, with all small plots wheresoever they be. For the Christian God differs fundamentally from the pantheon of Olympian and other mythological oligarchies who may be said to represent the earthly government "in another sphere." The Christian God, on the other hand, depicted in wayside churches of the Middle Ages as the "Christ of the Trades," is sacredly associated with cows and carpenters or, in other words, with the craftsman who possesses a small holding. It seems to me the supreme and unique merit of Christianity that it has always favoured the small man, not "the common man," who is simply the proletarian mass-man, but the men of little properties, especially in the country, the corner-stone of every civilization. Indeed, the more heathen modern civilization became, the more it turned its powers against the small man. Industrialism, "large-scale economic units," financial powers and commercial combines, together with State-Socialistic despotism of whatever brand in whatever country, have proved to be inveterately hostile to the small man.

But this small man built the cathedrals, not the architect with a couple of thousands a year. Thus smallness may contain sublimity. For the fourth year in succession I heard the Gregorian Plain Chant of the Midnight Mass, and each time I hear it, it shakes me to the core. Why is this? Partly, I think, because it is so primitive; it has a profound affinity with the grander, more elemental aspects of wild nature. The sea, the mountain, the rock, the firmament. Partly, too, because it was composed in another Dark Age, so that what it communicates reaches us more nearly. Partly, of course, its solemnity and order have a majesty of their own, but partly it moves us for its sheer holiness. We hardly know what that means nowadays but, when we hear the Gregorian Plain Chant and Handel's Messiah and Bach's Nativity, we *do* know what it means. There is too its ineffable sadness; it is the very voice of the whole world in supplication. But I see in it also the dignity and grandeur of man, the finite being who is infinite in the perception of how finite he is. De Quincey has expressed part of this in the piece he wrote about Compline:—

"The ordinary physical rhabdomanist, who undertakes to evoke from the dark chambers of our earth wells of water lying far below its surface, and more rarely to evoke minerals, or hidden deposits of jewels and gold, by some magnetic sympathy between his rod and the occult object of his divination, is able to indicate the spot at which this object can be hopefully sought for. Not otherwise has the marvellous magnetism of Christianity called up from darkness sentiments the most august, previously inconceivable, formless, without life; but also at the same time by incarnating these sentiments in images of corresponding grandeur, it has so exalted their character as to lodge them eternally in human hearts."

Plain Chant is not the redemption of the primitive but the perception of the primitive as the new-minted creation, the generative source of life, the new-born child of the divine idea. It is then true to Christmas.

The year ends with a fierce wind-frost—the most dangerous of all the numerous frosts for pipe-freezing—followed by what the Cotswold hill-men used to call a "peffle" of snow. Welcome as is a mild winter, a cold spell confers a triple boon. It pulverises the soil; it prevents the plants from becoming too "frim" and also rests them, while snow is a natural fertilizer in mineral salts. In the fields, tree-creepers consort with buntings and finches (among them a few bramblings) about the corn-stacks. But on the last days of the year summer peered out at winter again when a Peacock climbed up my bookcase and the "felties" in the fields were chak-chaking from tree-top to tree-top.

CHAPTER FIVE

(January—February—March)

I. *The Turn of the Year*

> "I, singularly moved
> To love the lovely that are not beloved,
> Of all the Seasons, most
> Love Winter."
>
> COVENTRY PATMORE.

> "March dust to be sold
> Worth ransom of gold.
>
> . . . . .
>
> Good tilth brings seeds,
> Ill tilture, weeds."
>
> THOMAS TUSSER.

"That poetry which . . . is inseparable from such a condition of life as the countryman's lies in his absolute dependence on the moods of air, earth and sky. Sun, rain, snow, wind, dawn, darkness, are to him, now as ever, personal assistants and instructors, masters and acquaintances with whom he comes directly into contact, whose varying tempers must be well considered before he can act with effect."

> THOMAS HARDY.

NEW YEAR'S DAY in 1943 was a pre-natal spring. It was so soft and mild that it would have perfectly matched the purpose of the pre-industrial celebrations of Plough Monday. Vast rain-clouds swooped down and dyed the day a smoky blue. Downy ones followed as though floating across a Fragonard canvas, to be blotted out by the sooty wing of another cloud-bank, itself routed by yet another painted Arcadia of the skies. In the too forward fields, the daisies were out in troops, though I believed them to be poultry droppings.

> "If the grass grows green in Janeveer,
> It grows the worse for it all the year."

159

A rural saw that came true. Marigolds and wallflowers were blooming in the cottage gardens, though only the day before the hanging woods of the Chilterns had long white beards. Throughout the month the temperature was seldom below 50 degrees, and well before the middle of it the rooks had assembled in vociferous planning committees at their nesting trees. A morning chorus of dunnock, robin, starling, song and mistle-thrush became wonted and called out buds on vine, clematis, pear, plum and rose; blue-bottles mounted the window-panes and aconite and dandelion had seeded before month's end.

In mid-month a party of gnats was gyrating and interweaving its figures above my compost stack. In sheltered places sprays of my quick-hedge were in full leaf, the tender shoots draped like a figured muslin over the dense network of twigs. January 19 was the earliest date I had ever heard the blackbird singing in my region. He had snowdrops and primroses to back him up and must have seen me sticking the orchard daffodils to prevent them being trodden on six weeks earlier than of yore. *Daphne Mezereum* was in flower two miles away. My own *Daphne laureola*, with its cluster of apple-green trumpets under tents of polished leaves was scenting the evening air like honey only a few days earlier than the flowering of the Lenten Roses.

How many green flowers are scented? Jason Hill in *The Curious Gardener* mentions the Musk Orchid "whose intensity recalls the musky fragrance of a ripe William pear." But the only flower to be compared with my Daphne's "sweet odour" is the Columbine (*Aquilegia viridifolia*). My Lenten Roses make up for lack of scent by flowering in three colours, first a delicate green, then pure white, while some are what the modern milliner calls "clover" but used to be called "old rose." This is not *Helleborus niger* but *olympicus*, though some of its blooms resemble *H. colchicum* which flowers a little earlier. Here were Lent flowers ablow in a January as mild as butter. The most promising and penetrating of all spring scents, the intoxicating earth-scent of *Cladothrix odorifera*, the primal odour of that great body that sustains all life, disclosed itself two months before the equinox.

Many of my daffodils were in bud in January and wall-flowers, crocuses, stocks, polyanthus and aconite in bloom while the gibbering "felties" were riding its blast. Horace's child brought him a starling's egg dropped on the grass on the last day of the month.

Bees were swarming, and larks singing between Alpine skies and
quilted winter-proud cornfields, and the black buds of the ash and
the pennons of the hazels arched over leafing hedge-bottoms. But
it must not be thought that we countrymen went "piping down
the valleys wild." On the contrary, we were full of misgivings
about this proto- or pseudo-spring, expecting the iron hand to be
sheathed in and unseasonably withdrawn from this velvet glove.
Would there not be "ruination weather" to come?[1] A time so
milky that the blue periwinkle trailed its wreath over my wattled
hurdles was debilitating to plant-life. Growth, lacking the discipline of frost, became sappy and enervated. The farmers liked
it less even than we gardeners, for there were no arable and few
enough grasssheep to eat down the winter-proud corn. As the days
of warmth and humidity passed, frost became a potential peril
rather than a "secret ministry" performing prodigies of cultivation
for a spring tilth. The generative wetness made plants too "frim,"
leached out the minerals from the top soil, found out the weak
spots in drainage and encouraged the growth of mosses and horsetails which spell acidity. Days of languor when spring is impatient
and the bald crown of Hiems wears a chaplet of buds communicate
themselves to the salsify and celery to which a touch of frost brings
an astringent virtue.

The prevalence of the south-west winds brought us hurricane
on the last day of an unnatural month. The giant wind and bolting
rain beat on the house with hammer blows that shook it to its
foundations and snapped every pole of the rose-walk. The awful
fury of man was for once matched by the ungovernable passion
of the gale. A King Lear storm—one could imagine his "I tax
not you, you elements with unkindness" and "Blow winds, crack
your cheeks" being torn out of his mouth and borne down the
blast like the skeins of rain across the hillside. The mad dogs of
the wind had a thin high baying note which was uncanny. Even
my turreted Irish yews, bent under the pounding of the gusts as
though they were each a rod of withy.

But the heavens were kinder than man and, as dusk was falling,
relented. The rain ceased, the wind fell to a sigh. Flung across the
zenith appeared a vast Norman chancel arch, the apparition of a
rainbow, clearly defined for all its translucence. One pillar rested

---

[1] There was a drought that lasted from February 10th to August 23rd, with only
brief thunder-showers between, at once made impotent by the incessant gales.

on the western slope of the hill where the old village and the new lie scattered like a flock of sheep. Its amber light settled on the grass, the roofs and gables, the raw new houses, the tops of the trees in the coppice. Everything was transfigured; the grass to emerald, the old cottages to a David Cox water-colour, the new into trolls and witches as in a fairy story.

I turned to look at the crest of the opposite hill where old Crodge takes his daily walk. Between the hedges of the saddle-back, a marvellous flaming light was streaming, a waving curtain of fire that drew me to the summit. As I walked, the soft air was full of the sound of many waters racing in brown tumescence down the field ditches. When I reached the crest, such a splendour of the heavens was spread before me as I had never seen before. Though the sun was invisible, there shone in the west a rose of fire with the myriad veinings of the petals of spun gold. All round this boss of flame, the foliage of the rose was a tangle not so much of leaves as of fronds, all running with active fire, molten fountains of flame. My awed sight shifted to the north and here was displayed a bay of delicatest aquamarine on which floated snowy little sailing-boats. Round this enchanted bay, mountain-ranges were piled of the softest Payne's grey, downy mountains not of fantastic angular shapes, not of peaks and pinnacles and canyons, but rounded, flowing with col and bluff and spur and slope. They reminded me of Gilbert White's description of the South Downs as "a chain of majestical mountains." Beneath these celestial heights, the earth lay spread an imperial purple upon which in every direction lay a complex system of lagoons, channels, meres and creeks of the flood-water, all of a pearly silver. I looked west again and the rose had changed into a kind of whirlwind of fire, such a whirlwind as Job had seen, with tossing manes and streaming locks of gold at its margins:—

"heaven's cherubim, horsed
Upon the sightless couriers of the air."

. . . for a few minutes, the fiery edge of another world than ours had impinged upon our own that had itself caught a reflection from the presence of the Lord of Light.

In this apocalyptic manner gentle January went out. Then I, after the damage in the garden had been repaired, the orchard strewn with twigs and branches, the wattled hurdles levelled to the ground, climbers torn from their moorings and post after post snapped off, made my own fire ceremony of the year. All the toppings, loppings and trimmings not rottable on the compost stack went to the building of the pyre for my Samhain, in which the sun's rays were quickened by the feeding of the beacon. At first the struggle goes against the fiery element and the inertia of cold dead matter muffles and subdues the flame. It creeps underground, like the Christian in the catacombs, extinguished here, blindly seeking a hold there. Suddenly it leaps out bold and strong, seizes on its prey, bursts into sparks, throws out flickering tongues and roars like a demon. The smoke ascends in great sweet-scented whorls and folds and scrolls and clouds of blue and white, until the insubstantial pageant of intertwining forms dissolves "into thin air" and leaves not a wrack behind.

You watch the flames again. They pounce upon the reluctant woods and transport them into their own pure essence; the dross is refined out in hissings and cracklings by the indomitable energy of the fire. The cruel but liberating embrace reaches its climax and the marriage of earth and flame is consummated. The spirit of these fierce nuptials pours heavenward and becomes part of the invisible world. There is craftsmanship in piling, feeding, timing, weighting and evening a bonfire till all is consumed, as there is in all dealings with the earth. But there is always too that something more that attends a careful husbandry. It participates in the purposes of nature and the universe, as the little flame in my plot reflected that enormous conflagration in the heavens.

February masqueraded as April and in its first week the whitethorn was budded on every shoot and the sloe beaded with tiny points and globules of green. The evening chorus of the rooks took on the drowsy contentment of spring, an almost languishing response to the landscape drawing its dusky veil and to the slow sliding of day into night. The blackbird now spoke out loud and bold; he had got into good heart, as we say of the fields. As the soft days went by, he worked out his theme with less faltering and ellipse, like a composer no longer crossing out his crotchets and quavers. The song of the thrush was so full of bravura that it must have reached the rooks circling and planing in the upper blue and slanting down in pairs to the elm-tops. The two long lines of my polyantha rose, Orange Perfection, whose trusses are so gay in

June, had come into full leaf more than a month too early and over its heads I saw a landscape as firmly graved as a drypoint. The Scots pines above Lopemead Farm were indigo, the stacks buffish, the pastures and cornfields green and emerald, the tops of the trees in the spinney glaucous and the ramparts of the Downs a blueish purple. Pollen from the catkins of my nuttery drifted upon the red female "buds," and half-way through the month I was both feeding and protecting my delphinium shoots with little piles of wood-ash. The late February crocus, *C. susianus*, flowered simultaneously with the early *C. Imperati*—my soil is too heavy for the beautiful *C. Tomassianus*—and the snowflake overpeered the snowdrop as though the one were the mother of the other.

In January, a village dame dug up her new potatoes she had sown in September, as though for a wager. I was contented with turnip tops in February and with planting early Laxtonian peas, intermediate carrots and a second crop of broad beans. It was a great time for self-seeded vegetables. I usually leave some few of my stock to run to seed, nature's planting fetching up seedlings twice as strong and healthy as man's. In this way I got a hundred lusty calabresse plants from one old winter matron and had nothing to do but set them in rows when the time came. I did the same with seakale beet, than which no food-plant is more valuable in a small holding. It was originally a hybrid of perennial spinach beet and sugar beet, and it was a friend of mine who first sent it to Reading with the recommendation that it was probably the best fodder crop in existence. In France he used to keep cattle and sheep on it all winter and the cattle he fed it to gave as much winter as summer milk. From the point of view of nutrition there is only one other garden vegetable to touch it—the shallott, which contains more iron, phosphates and protein than either onion or spinach, partly because the bulb ripens better and contains less water and so the minerals are less diluted. The old gardeners appreciated its properties so highly that they gave it dried blood. But compost, containing nitrogen for growth, potash for flavour and humus, is the best of all. On a heavy soil, too, coal-ashes come in handy for the shallott which prefers a light one.

The sense of continuity in a more or less self-sufficient garden is not the least of its satisfactions. Thus, in the early planting months of the year I am consuming the stored capital of the year before. I enjoy autumn and spring at one and the same time, and link what has been with what is to be. In the winter and spring, we have an almost daily meal of peasant soups out of the celery, celeriac, sprouts, artichokes, cabbage, leeks, potatoes and other herbal and vegetable produce of the garden in an endless variety of blend and concoction. Mr. F. C. King in *The Compost Gardener* (he is the head gardener of Levens Hall in the north) recommends that leeks should be eaten once a week in spring for their special blood-purifying properties. I know of nothing more replenishing than such a midday meal, followed by whole-wheat bread, raw celery, a cream cheese with chives, cress (rich in iodine) or endive and an apple or a pear. For almost half the year I repeat this meal daily. So far from wearying of it, I prefer it to any other that could be put before me in the most Utopian of a potential "age of plenty." Such a soup, grown with husbandry and cooked with art from the resources of one's own home, with no deception, no adulteration, no thimble-rigging nor profit-making imposed by the world without sends a man away from the table with a sense of gratitude. He knows the meaning of wholesomeness in its sense not of gentility but unity and completeness. Especially if he draws a mug of Somerset home-made cider from the barrel, as I did for my midday meal in 1943, soft, medium-sweet, apple-of-concord cider made by a yeoman friend of mine. Only a Cotswold-Cardew cider-jar was lacking for perfection. But no man nowadays can achieve such wholesomeness without sooner or later being dropped on by some money interest. My little watermill in Sussex that for years had supplied me with the most palatable and nutritious whole-wheat bread was spied out by the milling combine and so was ordered to fall in with the standardized loaf by the Ministry of Food. One hardly knows which is the Ministry of Food and which the Combine. But we made such a fuss about the mill, almost the last of the stone-grinding, whole-grain country mills, that we saved it from the jaws of the combineaucracy.

Our evening meal would follow no pleasing formula. I take two casually out of February. One was Scotch salmon with sprouting broccoli tops of the spring's growth that had failed to turn in, the tenderest of winter-spring vegetables, followed by a summer pudding of the raspberries bottled from the last year's crop. Another was home-bred boiled bacon with plum-and-onion chutney, carrots and potatoes all from the garden, together with Comtesse de Chambord flageolet beans, with mixed raspberries and rhubarb and Les

Battus from local fresh milk, sweetened by honey bought from the Vicar, to follow. As I consumed this milk from the neighbouring fields, I wondered how our urban masters are going to deal with the problem of pasteurizing milk from the human mother's breast. I ate this meal after a heavy day with fork and pen, and, as I ate, I listened to Beethoven's Second Symphony. Such a meal brings the word *pietas* to me. It confers beauty on the spirit, virtue on the body. After toil meat, after labour in the earth, wings above it. Feet on earth, head in the stars. Body and spirit are we and not without reason is the imagery of Christianity, that most realistic of religions, so concerned with the earth and its fruits.

It happened to be the day (February 26) when the first daffodils were out in the orchard. *Saxifraga apiculata* was flowering on the rockery walls and I had caught a breath of the violet scent from the Netted Iris, standing on them like mediaeval Italian soldiers with upright lances. I was meditating the pruning of the fruit-trees in a year which promised (but, as I suspected, would not and owing to the drought did not fulfil a very heavy cropping). What I have read in books about pruning left my mind in such utter confusion that I have deserted all absolute book-rules, prescriptions and criteria for purely relative measures in the field. My own empirical way is to choose a mild period whether in autumn or early spring for light pruning but to summer-prune drastically in July against those irritating three-inch growths gardeners are so apt to leave but which almost invariably put out those sappy lengths in autumn no good to man or tree. If I miss any, out they come in autumn but of course too late for fruit-buds to form until the following year. My spring pruning is in consequence always very light. Taking the whole year, I believe it to be sound counsel either to prune severely (except on the plums and gooseberries), or not to prune at all. But don't play with the knife if you use it. On my heavy soil which constantly needs liming, I go at it boldly. The text of the pruner, I have found, should be—let there be light. To the quick-growing trees like Bramley Seedling, Newton Wonder, Codlins, etc., in which there is a massing of twigs, which, as Shakespeare said of his pleached honeysuckle alley, "prevent the sun to enter," one should, I believe, apply the same principle as to walnuts. This is to drive the fruit outwards into the sun's embrace.

Spring pruning should be a kind of window-opening, a simplification of twig-pattern, a centrifugal process, a method of decentralization such as our sick society so sorely needs. But above all and to sum up all, it should be a letting-in of light, which our society needs most of all. Therefore, the pruner should not be too chary of cutting away those short fruit-bud spurs in the centre of a tree whose promise it seems a surgical sin to amputate. And let the orchardist in whose operations production and prediction should be twin, be careful to clean the surrounds of each trunk from future encroachment of grasses. Nothing does more hurt to a fruit-tree than for its root-fibres to have their free absorption of humus interfered with by grass. The same for the cordon pears, wrapped up in their mottled protective sheaths, like pieces of snake-skin.

The February of 1943 was notable for the flowering of my almond. It was its first appearance on the stage of spring since I planted it ten years ago. Year by year I have said to it, "you shall be cut down and cast into the oven," and spared it for the next. Because it is not its own fault but that of the nurseryman I was fool enough to let plant it, or rather to ball up its roots and drop it in a hole. The sensibility of Giles Winterbourne in planting a tree was that of a poet who projects himself into his object, and that passage in *The Woodlanders* is one of the unanswerable briefs for peasant husbandry.

The close of the month was celebrated by the flowering of the wild bullace in the hedgerows. This subspecies of *Prunus spinosa* is uncommon but not rare and little known, in spite of its slender grace among ranker growths. Perhaps the only reference to this aristocrat of the hedgerow in literature is by Alfred Williams ("the rich ripe bullace") in *Poems in Wiltshire*. The wild plum, the handsomest of the tribe, which we call "skegs" hereabouts, did not flower until April 1st, simultaneously with the sloe (here called "slan-bush"), the original of the family. The fruit of the earlier bullace is thin-skinned, juicy and with a very small stone, while the large flowers of skegs, borne on delicate long sprays, form a fruit twice as large as and less sharp than that of the sloe.[1] What little use we make nowadays of our wild fruits and wild foods! Arum and black bryony and dropwort for flour, the yellow goat's beard as a substitute for salsify and asparagus, the pignuts that Caliban, wiser in food-values than we, dug up with his long nails, the seeds of the

[1] On Little Hampden Common, one of the wildest places in the Midlands, though little distant from High Wycombe, all three can be seen fruiting together.

yellow flag as a substitute for coffee, ivy and soapwort for cleansings, borage, broom and dandelion for salads and many, many others for food, drink and industry too obvious to name.

Such are weeds for peasants who need to be improved out of their old ways of life and for whom tinned salmon from Japan or tinned peas in summer all ready for the tin-opener will introduce to "a proper standard of living." Food, you must know, has no virtue any longer unless it be a globe-trotter, and the further it travels, the better it is. That is why tinned salmon is so estimable: it comes or came all the way from Japan. How can these peasants be taught civilization? Only, I fear, by repeating the Enclosures on a yet larger scale and robbing them of their land to make slot-machine factories. How, for instance, cope with the backwardness of my Dickory who, on the year of his marriage 33 years ago, received a present of 6 Sunrise Early potatoes? He is still using the progeny of those 6 every year both for seed and cropping potatoes. So long as men like these (and there are 170 million of them in Europe) have a fork and a spit of land, they will go on growing things and saving things and keeping themselves. There is only one way of making them unemployed or a fluid labour force and that is to take the spit and the spade away from them.

But I, alas, am often uncomfortably conscious that I am not backward enough. If I had only known William Lawson, that old orchardist, sooner, I should have taken his advice and planted "filberts, plummes, damsons, cherries and such-like" not in the orchard but its hedge, partly to save ground for trees of more value and partly "to abide the blasts of Aeolus." He suggests planting herbs between the trees and that the larger trees should stand in the north of the orchard so as not to hide the sun from trees of lower stature. I am too much of a modern not to have to learn my lessons of economy and husbandry through many a trial and many an error.

It was the greenest March I can remember, the month of chlorophyll, what Sir William Beach Thomas calls its "ichor." Many March flowers are green—dog's mercury, epipactis, hellebore, wood sanicle, moschatel—and in this "flowery green bird-singing land" my weeping willow, whose leaves are as yellow as its flowers, bright as crocus and even forsythia, stood out like a fountain of fire. In spite of all man's endeavours to plunge the world into a dateless winter, like the dateless darkness of the oceanic depths, the earth will have her spring and give her pledge of the inviolability of the natural order. I have the absolute assurance year by year that my weeping willow will be yellow and the tufted flowers of my weeping wych elm green. Here is law, not chaos, rhythm, not regimentation. Though the rooks "come home in scramble sort," home they always come at the close of the day.

March is always memorable for me for the leafing of my northern screen of balsam poplars. These trees are a bit of a nuisance, since their surface roots are greedy and incorrigible travellers. But what Sir Thomas Browne called "the handsomenesse of the same," their invaluable service as a wind-break and their powers of drenching the whole garden with their aromatic essences overtrump any such disadvantage. Their March leaves have not only the magic but the scent of flowers. They are leaves so richly green and highly polished that *viridissima* is the right word for them. Their scent is so penetrating that it can be wafted 200 yards away from the parent trees. To approach them and the sweet briar below them is like sailing through an odorous sea of enchantment. Rub the nose in a leaf and the fragrance remains for hours afterwards, whether indoors or outdoors. Through a magnifying glass the scent-glands can be discerned as minute bubbles on the shiny glutinous surface of the lanceolate leaflet which is as adhesive as a moist postage stamp. Its "glad light grene" and voluptuous spikenardy smell remind me, when I rub my nose in a cluster of the leaves, of the passage in W. H. Hudson describing how sweet gale so intoxicated him that he wrapped himself up in it. It is interesting that the quality of the feeling in this passage is identical with that of Marvell in the self-forgetful transport of the senses in *Appleton House*. In March, too, the central spires of each tree are tasselled with the long red catkins. To these swaying pennons pour the bees, especially old Bombus, the dumbledore, bumbling and blundering along like a brown wherry scudding a Norfolk waterway. Such is my home guard against the north winds of dusty March.[1]

In that pregnant dust the self-seeded annuals freely germinate and for years, too, I have been self-supporting in my potting soil. It is old compost mixed with friable earth thrown up by the moles and the black mould crumbled out of my peat-stack for the winter

[1] In August of this same year, I nearly lost these poplars, which are shallow-rooted, from the fixity of the drought.

hearth. This compound makes a soil as runnable as sand but very potent and in my opinion a superior seed-bed to the burned, sterilized or made-up substances of the laboratory or large-scale nursery. In this soil I sowed in 1943 among others a few seeds of a plant which I think must be very rare in gardens. Nobody at any rate who has seen it in full flower in my garden has ever recognized it. This was a sad indication of how completely even country people have broken with the traditions that made England what she was before the financial interests got hold of her. For it was certainly cultivated in England for ceremonial purposes long before the Romans exploited our wheat-lands to feed their garrisons and the Roman proletariat. A number of our villages and smaller market towns (Watchett, for instance) were named from the extensive cultivation of this plant in their neighbourhood. When I was in-vestigating the relations between social custom and festival and seasonal husbandry in an Oxfordshire village,[1] I discovered that this same plant had a whole nexus of social observances and rites still associated with it in living memory.

The plant is, of course, woad (Dyer's Woad—*Isatis tinctoria*). Bentham and Hooker say it is possibly indigenous only at Tewkes-bury. Mary Roberts in *Annals of my Village* (1831) has an account of its cultivation and processing in Bedfordshire:—

"It is sown about the beginning of March, and gathered in May or June; if the weather is fair and dry, it is best in quality; if showery, more abundant. When cut, the whole plant is ground, and made up into balls. The balls are then laid on hurdles to dry, they are afterwards reduced to powder, spread over a floor and watered, which operation is called couching. In this state the powder remains to smoke and heat, and is turned every day until perfectly dry and mouldy. It is then weighed by the hundred, put into bags, and sent for sale to the dyers. . . . It yields a colour equal to the best Spanish indigo, and is mentioned by Caesar, Vitruvius and Pliny under the name of *vitrum*."

Yet this famous plant of a once self-supporting England has been so utterly forgotten by the parasitic one that not even expert horticulturists and men of historical knowledge in our rural

[1]The village of Yarnton. See my *Men of Earth*.

history recognize it growing in my garden. I sowed my seeds[1] "about the beginning of March," but, being old seed, only one germinated. I gave it a place of its own in the borders of my kitchen garden with sage, sweet cecily, chives and other herbs in its neighbourhood. Before the end of May it had grown five feet high, with a score of lateral shoots forking into short spurs, each with a soft flowering head or raceme of golden yellow. With its toothed, lanceolate and "obovate" leaves, its glaucous stem, architectural growth and all-over masses of these yellow flowers, it is one of the handsomest and most striking garden plants I know. In June and July, the top was still flowering but the lower part was densely hung with flat ribbed pods of a rich indigo, each containing one seed.

I grow this woad for decorative and what would be called "sentimental" reasons. But I have another reason as well. This illustrious dye-plant, not less so than the acanthus which was the original of the Corinthian capital and the yellow asphodel among which the shade of Agamemnon strode, once ministered to the arts, the culture and the prosperity of an England who depended on the virtues of her own earth. "Woadsmen" were appointed to be its wardens; mills were set up near the fields and villages where it was grown and small woad-towns grew out of them. It is certain that this vegetable dye had great value among weavers of fabrics and among people of taste who bought them. When William Morris was trying to stem the flood of industrial ugliness drowning the true England and was experimenting with vegetable dyes for silk, wool and cotton fabrics, did he use woad in his abortive revival of indigo? But the new England got rid of woad and flax and country mills and many another crop and industry for the sake of what it calls "cheapness." She exchanged the Sword of St. George for the tin-opener. For this she has had to pay a cost very dear indeed in comparison with the superficial gain. So I store the seeds of the woad plant in the hope that a truer England, linked up once more with her traditional self, will throw off the burden of the moneychanger. This England will find her own land the source, not merely in war but a true peace that is not merely a trade-war, of her riches.

In March, I have found it a good thing to correlate my plantings with the foliation of my trees, according, that is to say, to a natural calendar. It is a practice that peasants instinctively observe and that

[1] I obtained them from my friend, E. W. Hendy, the naturalist.

Linnaeus recommended. But we, divorced from earth, have forgotten it. It varies, of course, from year to year, but I have noticed that the leafing of my trees, omitting late ones like walnut, usually corresponds with the flowering of my squat little purple *Pumila* iris. That is when I plant my oats, reaping them by the convenient and old-fashioned method of beheading them. This burgeoning, the condition of the soil's temperature, the strengthening of the neaptide of bird-migration and other quickenings of the pulse of life are much more important promptings to the planter than the mechanical progression of the calendar.

I see and hear little enough of the great spring surges of bird-life through or over my South Midlands garden. But in the March of 1943 I saw the golden plover and heard the curlew passing across the firmament. Even above the uproar of the aeroplanes, hardly ever lulling and worse by night than by day, I heard the wild and liquid pipings of the curlew. Infinitely high and remote, it might have been the choirings of "the young-eyed cherubim" or the singing of the stars looking down on our man-fouled world. The plover went over in a shifting, undulating line, a shining serpent cleaving the blue. I took them for lapwing until the pure dissyllabic travel-whistle floated down like a melodious dew. "Balm of hurt minds" indeed, a fluted reassurance that the appointed courses of nature are uninhibited by the explosive decadence of our human world.

The hot rainless weeks hurried one flower after another across the stage. The crocuses were all over in the third week and the blackthorn blossomed before the little hoop-petticoat daffodil (Bulbocodium) had played its brief and modest part. With the flowering of the vernal squill and the true-blue Chionodoxa, pear, peach and plum blossom appeared simultaneously. In the droughty springs of recent years, we often get the Oriental effect of plum-blossom against a blue sky. But I like it best dancing against one of full-sailed purple clouds. Its beauty is not only pictorial against the sky as a mere background but also because the bough, lifting into a stormy sky, reflects from the cloud-tumult the tension of its emergence into blossom. The bough was drawn against its cloud like a bowstring across a violin and music came from it. I have never been able to understand why the most defenceless fruit-flowers, those of plum, peach and pear, unprotected by their leaves like apples, should be the first to appear.

One of the most conspicuous of my March flowers is the blue

anemone (*blanda*), with *appenina* the only ones to survive my once abundant "lilies of the field." It flowers with the rosemary and both are bee-beloved. I often wish I could find the time to keep bees, so that I could supplement the exiguous ration of sugar we have to buy and use it for sweetening. For, though I say it, I have a garden much frequented by bees and Narbonne rosemary honey is the finest in the world. In March, I have an abundance of blue, purple and yellow flowers which bees mostly frequent, being colour-blind to reds to which the vision of birds is highly responsive. *Blanda* is the Greek anemone with very large flowers so that the bees have no troublesome search. Why blanda? Because the flowers open so confidingly to a sun and a climate which is becoming as little humid as that of Greece? In these springs of hot days and cold nights, the spring flowers that are the more sensitive to variations of temperature—crocus, anemone, aconite—have seldom to withdraw into themselves any more than "bright Phoebus in his strength" into the clouds.

The March of 1943 gathered into itself far more than others I remember winter with spring and spring with summer. Thomson's "Come, gentle spring! ethereal mildness, come!" would rapidly alternate with "The blessed sun himself a fair hot wench in flame-coloured taffeta." Summer-painted Brimstone, Peacock and Tortoise-shell butterflies were fluttering about the 25 different kinds of spring flowers I took an inventory of on the first day of the month. But the peculiar light among the blades of *Iris ochroleuca* had that spiritual quality which is of spring and autumn alone. By the middle of the month they were some three feet high, their tips level with the grey drystone retaining wall behind them. The sun shining on them turned them to a greenish-yellow shade with olive-green tops against a wall whose surface was mantled with fronds and leaves of sea-grey and glaucous. The light reflected from the wall to the blades and from the blades to the grass beneath them, "mingling and opposed," had the same unearthly quality as when on autumn evenings the sun shines on my wattled hurdles. This light draws all earthly variety and incident into its unity, as Prospero's "our revels now are ended" does those of the play. The rooks, populous and clamorous at their elm-tops thick with nests, made a din perfectly in tune with that rural silence that is now so rare among us countrymen. They were in measure with an orthodox spring.

Not so the hedgers plushing hedges with the twigs in full leaf, usually, inexpertly except in one small area near Oxford. Here a beautiful localism in hedging technique survives. Every ten yards one rod is laid the contrary diagonal to its fellows. The particular rod is chosen for its "long tails," that is to say, its whippy pliant growth from stool to tip. This is crooked and plaited between the stakes as in the normal "heathering" process, performed with hazel or stripped bramble. The rod is thus live wood and this enables the hedge to regenerate itself and bush out much quicker than when the heathering is of dead wood. But this type of plushing is only possible with a much overgrown hedge. Hedging is a craft of winter and early spring. But so early was the spring of 1943 and so scanty the labour (the key-men having been taken off into the mines with that beautiful economy of labour characteristic of our times) that winter and summer met in the plying of the billhook.

The corn-stacks have returned to redeem and enliven what a few years ago was a flat and featureless landscape of monotonous grass. They were so bleached by the premature sun that they were exactly the colour of my summer cephalaria, a scabious-like flower, itself the colour of flaxen hair. It was strange to see a long line of these stacks stretching and diminishing in perspective down a gentle slope to the willows at right angles to them along the river bank and brilliant in spring. Stranger still to see these evidences of human skill and labour upon the labouring earth and the fields themselves almost as solitary as when this same slope was a wilderness of grass. We sow and till and reap an empty land, studded with the sprawling formicaria of the "wens."

March ends with my early peas and carrots well above their beds.

II. Bygones?

"Five decades hardly modified the cut of a gaiter, the embroidery of a smock-frock, by the breadth of a hair. Ten generations failed to alter the turn of a single phrase. In these Wessex nooks the busy outsider's ancient times are only old; his old times are still new; his present is futurity."
THOMAS HARDY, *Far from the Madding Crowd.*

"If those philosophers are right who hold that beauty is an attribute of the Deity, and that ugliness of every kind is displeasing in His sight, our modern civilization is a blatant blasphemy."
DEAN INGE, *Outspoken Essays.*

IN the middle of the orchard I built some years ago a thatched almshouse. It might be called a hibernaculum for my collection of implements of husbandry, old kitchen ware, specimens of country crafts and the like in the winter of their discontent. As they continued to pour in, I had to erect an annexe to the original "Hermitage" (after Gilbert White's). It was thatched by a mastercraftsman, now retired, whose performance was a fitting *requiescat* upon the workmanship of the dead masters that had found a resting place within. Upon these rural relics I wrote, with the powerful aid of Tom Hennell's draughtsmanship, a book which sought to resuscitate in mere description the lives these tools and crafts had once led and the kind of rural pattern and economy they represented.

What I did not do was to relate these antiquities to the garden in which they have found a home. This desideratum I now intend to fulfil. According to the interpretation of the term "garden" I have followed throughout, this would take another book in itself. I shall confine myself, therefore, to a selection from those objects of country virtue which have enriched my collection since I wrote *Country Relics* and explore their bearing upon my general theme. It is well that I should do so. Since the "Hermitage" was built and has weathered itself down to grass and trees and flowers and crops, it has become an inseparable part of the garden.

But not only in appearance. For the modern age the attraction of a museum is that it is a mortuary; the thing has to be dead before anybody will take any interest in it. This is an inevitable consequence of the theory of automatic progress which is only concerned with the past so far as it *is* dead and so acquires an antiquarian value. The past is ornament; something to be admired from the distance of the superior present. Its treasures are objects of a *virtu* which is obsolete, not of a virtue which by its very nature is not subject to time, though time may re-interpret it. This is well illustrated by the artefacts of my friends, Samuel Rockall, the woodmaster of the Chilterns. For his chair-legs by the gross he received thirty shillings a week, a price for the betrayal of craftsmanship. But when the dealer faked them up to look like antiques, a very easy matter with the timeless craftsman, one of them could be sold for the price of the whole gross. The past of our countryside, whatever its faults, was based upon husbandry and craftsmanship, virtues necessary to the life of man. The present, therefore, in breaking with the continuity of creative work, has as good as abolished husbandry and craftsmanship. It can only look at them in a museum instead of using them in its daily life. But the combination of use and beauty is part of what used to be called "the natural law" and is indispensable for human self-preservation. Therefore great trouble has come upon the world, and it is perishing, though it does not yet know it.

I have been at pains to show that the principle of a holding rests upon the twin pillars of use and beauty. If it fails to do so, it becomes something quite different, a pleasure resort, an exploitable mechanism for gain. How then could I keep a museum in mine? The answer is that I do not and never have done so. My Hermitage serves a triple purpose. In the first, I actually use many of its contents, both in the garden and the house, and for the very good reason that they are an asset to both. In the second, these contents are a telling history and memorial of man in a right relation to the earth. Man cannot reach contentment nor exercise his functions harmoniously nor express his natural skill-hunger nor preserve his individuality nor conduct his society without this right relation. The "exhibits" in my "museum" will thus be of service to a future which has discovered these truths for itself through the experience of what happens when they are violated.

Already the contemporary world is grimly suffering that experience and the nemesis it brings. In rediscovering the meaning of skill and pleasure in work, posterity will need my collection and those of others, public or private. Through them, it will be

able to examine the kinds of things man made before his work
had ceased to have anything to do either with his hand or his eye,
his pleasure or his skill. Value and quality belong to the past only
because in our present stage we have abandoned them. In the third
place, certain of these objects have memories for me which are
not nostalgic and so merely in the air. They have been part of my
education and have enabled me to come into touch with certain
realities that should be communicated to others. These are all
realistic, not sentimental, purposes.

I am constantly finding horticultural uses for my museum pieces.
The hedge-maul pulverises stubborn stems; the fagging hook
cuts the oats and long grass; the basketry is for picked legumes
and pulled brassicas; the smaller sheep-bells are useful for the
yearly geese when they first arrive[1] and attempt to escape, and the
crooks for catching them; the sheep-shears trim odd corners; the
paddle downs stray thistles; the bill elve punches holes; the sickles
sever marrows, cabbages, broccoli; the fromard splits wood; the
steelyard weighs; the bird-clappers frighten off bird-thieves; the
very light malting shovel scatters lime and wood-ash; and other
tools perform other functions. The turnip-pecker, the dock-weeder,
the butter-balancers, the fine turf-cutter with its long curved
wings, and others are all handy implements for garden use, while
the long, wrought-iron rushlight-holders make decorative candle-
stands.

Many I have transferred from what, from the "picturesque"
point of view, might be called their tomb to my living-room and
so have raised them from the dead. The framed specimens of straw-
plait wrought by Hannah Firman of Essex in her ninety-first year

[1] As an example of the sensibilities of shepherds and their attunement to the finest
tones of sheep-bells, I quote the following letter sent to me by an ex-magistrate of Cyprus:

"In Cyprus I was trying a case where a man was charged with stealing goats' bells.
. . . Each of the bells in possession of the accused man was stated by the shpeherd to
have been worn by a goat which was the leader of a particular band of animals in the
flock. One bell he said was that of the black-sheeted goat, another of one with flat horns,
etc. Counsel for the defence asked him if there was any distinctive mark on any of the
bells. "None." Were they different in size or shape? "No, but they are my bells off my
goats," and the counsel sat down in triumph. I then asked if the bells all gave the same
sound, and he said "No." Accordingly, other similar bells were sent for and arranged
with the bells in question . . . and all were rung in chance succession. To myself and
every one else in Court they all sounded alike, but in every case he picked out his own
bell, allotting it to the particular goat that he had already described as wearing it. Lying
out on the hills night after night, he had heard the quiet tinkle of a bell and mentally
said to himself, "The black-sheeted goats lot are feeding undisturbed," or, hearing a
quick jangle, would have to go and see what was worrying them, and so on, till the finest
shades of tone were ingrained into his hearing."

T.P.E.   M accommodate themselves aptly with the Staffordshire figures, the Chinese bowl with the ears of barley and the plaster horses from the Parthenon frieze on my mantelpiece. The rare gravy-glass takes my spills; the lead tobacco-box holds too moist tobacco; the wonderful picture of sheep under a tree, all in coloured sands, takes its place among my pictures; the box of spillikins,[1] nearly a century old, would adorn the most fastidious room; the elm-bowl made by George Lailey of Bucklebury Common and the great oaken bowl from Shere of the colour of old brown sherry hold letters, fruit or oddments. These and other comely pieces add grace to habitation, are happy with books and chairs. They blend perfectly with the furniture which various craftsmen have made for me at various times and so bring that continuity of tradition which is true culture right into the home. They are bygones that have ceased to be so because they have become integral with the mind and personal life of their owner.

The modern world despises memory which is unprogressive, but it is the nourishment of the countryman's social and individual life. I mind me of a day in November (1942) when, coming in from the fields, I found awaiting me a sturdy, stockish, spectacled old lady who had brought me three offerings for my "Hermitage." One was the gravy-glass. Another was a very fine copper muller or hooter or shipton with a curved handle for heating, as Dickens records, the ale in the fire. The third was a rose with foliage and stem all in wrought iron, the leaves being veined and the flower half-open and slightly pendulous. This is one of the most curious and splendid examples of country smith's work I have ever seen. To crown all, the smith who made it still lives. I value that rose the more for its contemporary date than if the maker had been that William Faber who held ten acres of land in the mediæval village of Yarnton where I discovered many interesting things about the traditional parcelling out of the lot-meadows.[2]   That such workmanship can still exist is ground for hope, ground for hope.   Nor could there be a choicer symbol and, as it were, coat-of-arms for a garden whose sun is the midsummer rose, than one wrought of the element that is for all time.

There are many records of men having fairy godmothers when they open their eyes to the world. There can be few who possess

[1] I have described this unique specimen in my *Men of Earth*.
[2] See my *Men of Earth*.

one after fifty. I am one of those few. A few weeks later she re-
appeared in the same mysterious manner, bearing yet more out-
of-dates. The first was a cream-skimmer that came from the kitchen
of Shandy House at Coxwold, near the great Cistercian abbey of
Rievaulx, and the rectory where Sterne wrote part of *Tristram
Shandy*. It may be as old as that now immortal event and so one
of his household utensils. The wood is of white ash, sycamore or
lime and a sensuous experience to handle. The ladle, whose holes
from the roughness of their edges were probably pierced by a
bradawl, is curved like the keel of a boat. The Welsh turners in the
Teifi Valley from which came that great craftsman, William Rees,
used to turn these skimmers as thin as cardboard. Next was a
gingerbread or spiced bread press, a panel of wood (beech?) 14
inches long by 5 wide carved on one side with a lady of fashion
of the late 18th century. She has an elaborate coiffured wig, fan
and necklace, while the folds of the dress, the strands of the hair,
the bracelets and the minutest details of the frills and garniture
of the dress are faithfully executed. On the reverse side are nine
figures, three soldiers in 18th century dress, three women in bonnets
carrying a water-can, a sheaf of corn and a basket of flowers and three
musicians, playing respectively a clarinet, a harp and a violin.
Perhaps Sue Bridehead pressed her cakes on just such a board as
this, and some such press was known at Dawlish:—

> "Where gingerbread wives have a scanty sale,
> And gingerbread nuts are smallish."

Next, half a dozen large lace-bobbins (of which I have a large
collection), the darkest in box-wood (called the plum-pudding
bobbin), the others in pear, plum and cherry wood, one being
bi-coloured, with pewter rings and all with "jingles." These bobbins
belonged to a Mrs. Newall of Bovingdon Green, an old lace-maker
who with her mother made a hundred yards of Bucks Point Lace
for Queen Mary's trousseau. Her brother used to turn her bobbins
on his lathe in the evening after his day's work was done. I do not
regard these details as trivial. On the contrary, they are an initiation
into the true meaning of folk-art, the communal art of our former
rural culture, killed by the Industrial Revolution, the Enclosures
and the Machine Age that followed them. That meaning will appear
more clearly in the fourth and last gift.

This was a smock, the second I have ever been able to acquire. The first was worn by a shepherd for forty years and brings back to me the intoxicating smell of apples being crushed in the cider-mill. The cottage of the shepherd's daughter who made this smock and gave it me, was a few yards from the mill. As I talked to her, I could hear the horse clopping round the mill. The second one, brought by my fairy godmother, brings me into touch with fairy-land, so remote is the world of peasant art from our own. The smock is descended from the workaday dress of my Saxon ancestry. "Smic" means chemise or shift and in Saxon times was a cross between a tunic and a shirt. The gathering later at front and back was for freer movement. The "smocking" was exactly like bobbin-making, a purely peasant art without money value. Smocks, like bobbins, were rarely if ever sold in shops, as the mis-spellings of the inscriptions on some of my more elaborate bobbins reveals. ("I love you, my dere, it is true."). They were the art of illiterate people, part of the profound culture of a people who wrote crosses for signatures. We have yet to learn that reading and writing are by no means synonymous with wisdom and understanding, as the failure of State education sufficiently demonstrates.

My second smock, perhaps a century old, was made by the wife of a woodsman who lived in a cottage in the wood (again that touch of fairyland) on the estate of Lord Hollanden, near Tunbridge. The cloth was woven by her from home-grown flax, all handspun linen coming either from flax or hemp ("hempen homespuns"), and, like rush-baskets, lasting virtually for ever. It is almost certainly the oldest smock in my county. It is evidently a Sunday smock because the embroidery (quite different from the "smocking" front and back, at the wrists and on the upper arms) indicates no particular trade. The traditional workaday smock was embroidered for a purpose, namely to identify the occupation of the wearer. His trade-mark was placed just below and on either side of the lapels of the collar. At the old Hiring Fairs the farmers looked at the embroidery of the men and women's smocks. Stylised cart-wheels, whip-lashes, reins and bits showed the man was a carter; trees and leaves spelt woodman; crooks, sheep-pens, hurdles and sheep advertised a shepherd; flowers and leaves expressed the gardener; crosses pictured a grave-digger; churns, butter-pats, hearts, etc., meant the woman was a milkmaid.

Modern embroidery on sham smocks is worthless, while the

curving of the cut is quite contrary to the traditional style. This followed the same method as that of the Celtic decorators. All the measurement was done by eye, and the richness of these conventionalized designs has to be seen to be believed. There is a succinct account of them in "English Smocks" by the Handicrafts Organizer of the Women's Institutes, Alice Armes, to whom I owe many bobbins and an elegant lace-pillow horse in my "Hermitage." The Sunday smock was always handspun into white linen, while the week-day smock was by no means always white. In the Midlands, it was usually blue, in East Anglia olive green, in Surrey black and sometimes grey or drab, and in Dorset the drab smock was worked in blue and white.

I will say no more about my own smock except that it is one of the finest I have ever seen. Though so old, it looks as though it had never been worn. It allows for complete freedom of movement, and the delicacy and elasticity of the smocking are beyond praise. Being traditional, it was cut out of squares and oblongs by folding with gussets under the armpits. It has a collar, French knots at the shoulder-straps but no pockets. If then a smock lasts for ever, keeps out the rain, is light and yet warm and combines serviceableness and simplicity with such beauty of decoration, why do you never see a countryman in one? Think, for instance, of its utility in the clean milk campaign, just at a time when the utmost attention to clean milk is necessary if we are to be saved from the compulsory pasteurization which our urban rulers are meditating to the ruin of the small producer-retailer. The reason why the smock became obsolete was, of course, "the march of progress." In other words, the power-loom and its cheap, ephemeral and more often than not ugly and shoddy clothing replaced the old beauty-and-utility of country wear made by countrymen for themselves.

Bobbins in all their bewildering diversity of form and exuberance of decoration were keepsakes, love-tokens, birthday gifts, neighbourly services and so never commercialised. So the smock, with its imaginative variety of designs in embroidery, escaped the uniformity and mediocrity of the mass-produced article. It is a variety common to all peasant handicrafts: in one region of Ireland for instance, there are 150 different kinds of spade. The smock is a perfect example of the combination of use with decoration, of poetry with practice, because its patterned poetry sprang out of its

very utility.[1] This, of course, is true of all country crafts and of
all peasant art, as it is true of nature herself and so presumably of
the whole universe. Rarely if ever in nature does ornament appear
for its own sake. It nearly always serves a purpose as did the peasant
arts. But though they were in a right relation with the universe,
they were in a wrong with the age which has disintegrated what
is "pretty" from what is serviceable.

The smock has survived only by mention in local charities.
There is one such three miles from my garden. A piece of land was
bought by Thomas Phillips, and the yearly rent in it gave in
November three old women and three old men certain gifts—for
the men a pair of shoes, a shirt, a blue overcoat with T.P. marked
in red on it and a smock. The only requirement was that the old
men should appear in church on Christmas Day in their new smocks.
Now the rent has declined and there are no smocks to be given.

Almost daily I expect a further visit from my fairy godmother.
She has herself a passion for the beauty and excellence of these
"bygones," for wild flowers and for the old country life of self-
sufficiency and peasant art such as I have rarely met. She seems to
embody all their graces, qualities and endurances. When she last
left me to walk three miles to catch her bus, she burst into song.
She is hardly real to me in our present world. Bearing gifts she
comes, singing she goes, like some allegorical figure with a horn of
plenty come to life. Full of grief for what has gone and full of joy
in herself, she talks as in a dream of the days when she found *Tulipa
sylvestris*, our solitary native tulip, and of the life-histories of the
old folk who have left behind these memorials of a rural and
domestic art all but utterly vanished from the land.

I have in my Hermitage a pair of clogs, quite different from
my pattens which everybody in the country used to wear. This pair
reminds me of a man who, when the demand for clogs was insistent
during the last war, migrated with his whole family to Anglesey
which is rich in alders, alders being the best wood for clogs, willow
and birch coming second and third. In the summer, the whole
family moved into the woods for felling, sawing and preparing
the timber; in the winter they made the clogs at home. He thus
reversed the guiding principle of modernism, which is to take

---

[1] I think I understand through the humblest of my "bygones," from which beauty
peers shyly and undemonstratively, why the greatest poetry is always a kind of divine
speech, as F. R. Leavis has shown in *Revaluation*.

the food or raw material to the people not the people to them, the only condition of stability.

This false principle has brought its nemesis by paralysing man's creative and self-helping powers, well illustrated by the disuse of craftsmanship in the purple, Tyrian or royal dye industry at Braintree. Of recent years two power-looms were set up but some handlooms were still left in operation. They ceased to be so simply because nobody, no matter how high the wages offered, could be persuaded or knew how to work them. Being unique, this very special industry was in a position to offer the highest of wages. The shying away from the hand-looms was, that is to say, not a matter of economics at all. It was what can only be called the obsession with or infection of mechanism.

Among the more recent acquisitions to my collection is a great oaken bowl from the village of Shere in Surrey. It is flat-rimmed and some forty inches in circumference. The outside is delicately moulded and a kind of patina of blackish brown has been superimposed from long use upon the natural colour of the wood. When I look into it I see as in a crystal myself standing on the crest of Holmbury Hill, contemplating one of the most magnificent views in all England. I know many of the views of southern England, the Vale of the White Horse from Uffington Hill, the Vale of Blackmore from Shillingstone Hill, the Vale of the Kennet from Inkpen Beacon, the Vale of Pewsey from Martinsell, the Vale of the Severn from Harewood Beacon and Cleeve Hill, the Vale of the Parrett and the Somerset flats from Lodge Hill and Camelot and Glastonbury Tor, Dartmoor from Brown Willy and the Cheesewring, the Vale of Marshwood from Pilsdon Pen, the Sussex littoral from Mount Caburn and Firle Beacon and many others from Butser, Quarley, Eggardun and other high places of the chalk, the limestone, the granite and the Old Red Sandstone. Each has grandeur after its own kind but none more so than that seen from the summit of Holmbury.

I was on the apex of one of those turrets of the Lower Greensand range which throws a bridge across the enormous basin of the wealden clay and the gault. These in their turn are enclosed by the yet vaster oval of the North and South Downs. I could take in the whole tremendous conformation within a few steps: first, the horizon ramp of the chalk downland from the Betchworth Quarry to the north-east and west to Box Hill, Dorking, Ranmore Common (where I used to hear the woodlark), White Down, St. Martha's, St. Catherine's by Guildford and along the Hog's Back to Cobbett's Farnham. Thence, my eye travelled round the western bend past Cissbury and Chanctonbury, whose topknots of beeches were plainly visible, to the Shoreham Gap away in the south-east. Within this shallow basin and looking towards Winchester, the promontories beyond the purple cone of Pitch Hill with its bell-heather clothing the summit, Hambledon, Hindhead and Black Down, pushed their long lean necks like animals drinking at a water-hole into the blue Weald. The blue Weald, the Roman Anderida Silva, the Saxon Andredsweald, Cobbett's country of the oak, lay within the pupil of my eye.

The whole point of a great view is that the place where you stand, the hub and core of the immense surround, should be in perfect harmony with all that can be seen from it. And this was so; what I saw Cobbett had seen:—

"Here are hill and dale in endless variety. Here are the chalk and the sand, vieing with each other in making beautiful scenes. Here is a navigable river and fine meadows. Here are woods and downs. Here is something of everything but fat marshes and their skeleton-making agues."

From where I stood, I could see nothing of the ammunition dumps on Leith Hill, the highest hill, being only 40 feet short of a mountain, in England. The dumps squatted there among the glades and commons and woodlands and now this wild hill resembles the cemetery where the elephants come to die. But I could not see them. What I could see was the long and clean line of the downland and the blueish-purple sheen of the oaken Weald. Primitive and yet luxuriant in its hollows was Holmbury itself, my Darien peak. Its peat-bogs were as thickly clustered with foxgloves as though they were willow-herb ; its pine-groves and commons of scrub-oak, scrub-birch, bracken and hurts, spread about my feet. Beyond them the varied woodlands extended from Tanhurst on Leith Hill far over John Evelyn's Wotton Estate where the curving boles and branches of the sweet chestnuts give these noble trees the air of arrested motion and intense vitality. From my feet to the horizon all was undefiled as when our rural ancestors possessed them.

It was appropriate too, that this country should be the shrine of Cobbett's birthplace, Cobbett the great representative of the peasantry he saw being robbed of their lands. The fact that so many of the Surrey commons are still unenclosed is the reason why this part of Surrey has not been degraded into a London dormitory. There was nothing to show from my height that the modern age has actually been over this great scene outside its commons, felling the woods, suburbanising the valleys and slopes, poisoning the rivers, making speed-ways, driving out the natives, upsetting the whole rural economy and occupying the land without roots in it or understanding of it.

We have come indeed to think of Surrey as London's playground, and as happy hunting for the speculative builder. But the country of the greensand is so wild on its thinner and less fertile soils, so exuberant on its richer, so diversified along its narrow serpentine river-valleys and on its irregular heights, that the suburbanism only becomes apparent on a near view. The villas and bungalows are more or less hidden in dense screens of greenery. It is only when you are in the villages that you realize the full extent of what has happened—namely, the expulsion of their rural communities by economic pressure and re-occupation by their urban conquerors.

You see it clearly enough in the village of Shere, Cobbett's Sheer, at the foot of the Merrow Downs over which passes the great Bronze Age Drove Road, the Hoarway or Harroway from Cornish Marazion to Dover. This village, from which I obtained my great bowl, once responded to the beautiful diversity of its green setting by the truly astonishing variety in structure and materials of its cottages. Some are grouped about the little church with its pepper-pot shingled spire, the navel of the village, and others along the Tillingbourne with its little fleets of Aylesbury Ducks. There are flint in square timber panels (rare this anywhere), half-timbering in a number of patterns, tile-hanging both square and fish-tail, brick rosy, white and colour-washed with "Shere yellow," gabling, garnet-jointing with ironstone studs, stone-walls of Leith Hill and other local stones with rounded copings, shingling, thatching, slatting with the rippled Horsham stone, overhangs, oriels, brackets, porches. The very steep pitch of the roofs is a local mannerism in itself. Into this expressive and individual medley, so true to the variety in scene and strata of its neighbourhood, have intruded solid Victorian and flimsy modern atrocities built of bilious brick, Welsh slates and sham timbering, the outposts of Urbs's conquest.

Nor was Shere an exceptional village. Turville, for instance, in the Oxfordshire Chilterns, is a hamlet only about 100 yards long and stretched in two rows along a byroad. Yet it handled flint, brick, stone, tiles, timber and colour-wash with the utmost freedom of difference. But the very squat, very square flint tower of the church draws all this diversity and multiformity into a unified whole.

I think I discovered the main source of this desolating change at the stone-grinding water-mill of Gomshall, mentioned in Domesday Book. Up to the last war, this mill ground the local corn for wholewheat flour of local consumption. There are many disused bread-ovens projecting from the cottages in the neighbourhood to reveal how this stone-ground flour was used. Now the rumble of the giant stones, the rhythmic thunder of the giant wheel threshing the waters into a furnace of energy, the creaking and shuddering of the giant timbers, the cheerful chatter of the gearing, the ingenious and purposive harnessing of the elements to the service of man's daily bread, all these titanic and friendly forces are directed only to grinding grist for the cattle. The spaces between the grooves of the harp-like patterns on the millstone are still called "lands" and the grooves themselves "furrows." By the pressure upon them of the upper millstone, the nut of the wheat-germ is so pulverised and coated over that it cannot be separated from the flour. These names are symbols of an association between this stone and the cornfields round the mill as intimate as the hand's to the mouth. Yet the farmers are not *allowed* to bring their sacks of corn to the mill and the miller is not *allowed* to grind them.

Who, coming from a region where honesty and sanity were an integral part of men's lives, would believe it? He would call out in a loud voice, " *Why* are the miller and the farmer not *allowed* to benefit one another and all the neighbours who eat bread?" The answer would be because it is more profitable to separate the wheat-germ from the flour, more profitable for the great milling combine, more profitable for the proprietors of special foods and medicines who resell the wheat-germ at fancy prices. The answer is given in the words of the Parliamentary Secretary to the Ministry of Food (May 13, 1943):—"I divide the Department into bureaucrats and magnates." The government of a great country is compelled to compel the farmers to send their corn to the combine roller-mills. It compels the very few millers left who use the traditionally honest method of grinding in the wheat-germ between the stones to grind cattle-meal only. Hopkins and Freese in *The English Wind-mill* say that these stone mills ground "the very best flour obtainable, and it is a thousand pities they are not in use to-day." But they are, perhaps one per cent. of them, since 26,000 of them have been put out of action by the combine in this century, and they do grind the very best, not for men but cattle.[1]

The threshing and thudding of the giant wheel was the beating heart of the whole rural culture and economy. It pumped the life-blood into all the arteries of country communications and inter-dependences. The image is just, since these water-mills also regulated the flow and level of the rivers and prevented them from silting up, accumulating weeds and so flooding. When, therefore, the wheel was stilled—"and all that mighty heart is lying still"—that culture and economy died. The linch-pin fell out of the self-support-ing rural structure, and the country became what it is to-day, the chattel of the town, bullied and exploited when it is needed, as in war, neglected and ignored when it is not, as in peace. The character, the meaning, the beauty and individuality of rural England, both natural and man-made, became a bygone. No longer were great oaken bowls made like the one I have from Shere; they were collected and put into museums for one per cent. of the population to stare at and for ninety-nine per cent. to do without them.

---

[1] The latest official bulletin of soil-conservation in the United States (June, 1943) declares that for a proper nutritional standard cereals must have the "whole grain." Thus traditional practice is at one with the most advanced science. This is a reaffirmation of traditional self-sufficiency. Mr. David Smith in *No Rain in Those Clouds* (1943), a chronicle of his father, an Essex yeoman, says that there was nothing to touch the cottage loaves baked in the bread-ovens by the labourers' wives from local wholewheat ground at the local mill. Another point. If these local mills had been working during the war, the saving in steam, oil and petrol would have been enormous. But even if, in the interests of nutrition, these country mills were reconditioned and reinstated, half their good work would be dissipated, unless the grain came from a healthy soil, organically manured.

Part Two

CHAPTER SIX

WORK AND PLAY

"When you sing
I'ld have you buy and sell so; so give alms;
Pray so; and for the ord'ring your affairs,
To sing them too."

The Winter's Tale.

THROUGHOUT, I have maintained that a garden is not only a piece of but contains the world. For the rest of the book I propose to develop these implications first by way of criticism and then by way of hope and affirmation. Earlier in the book, I have looked upon the garden as a thing both of use and beauty which demands work that is a kind of play. I gave the hedge as an example of this use in union with beauty (p. 127), and now hedges over wide areas of England are being rooted out. Since then experience proves their utility and not even an economist could deny their beauty, what is the point of grubbing them up? The answer is that it is more "economical" to do so, and the question is—what the devil does "economical" mean? I use the word devil advisedly, since, if a certain policy is advocated in defiance of common sense, of reason, of utility and of emotional experience, it plainly comes from the devil. In America, for instance, *they* are planting hedges in imitation of our old-fashioned husbandry, while *we* are modelling our hedge-policy on the dust-bowl economics of the America whose folly caused *them* to imitate the policy *we* have repudiated. What irony! In 1939, an able book was written by Dr. Drucker, called *The End of Economic Man*, the object of which was to prove "that the teachings of economic science have ceased to correspond to social reality." One might add—or any other kind of reality. And that economics have bedevilled the world is such a platitude that nobody except an expert in them could fail to see it. Dr. Drucker's theme is that Fascism was intrinsically a revolt of despair against the concept of the "Economic Man." But in as much as

188

that revolt substituted for that concept the idea of the autocratic
State organized as a pure war-machine, seven devils as Scripture
informs us took the place of the one devil. His book resolves itself
into this question—how are we to exorcise not only the seven devils
but the one devil that preceded and dry-nursed them? One answer—
by not grubbing up our hedges on the abstract plea of economics.

The question, of course, goes far beyond hedges. But hedges
are very convenient to it because they exemplify the inter-relationship between beauty and use. If our own country is not to introduce
the seven devils as a remedy for the one devil (namely to go totalitarian), it must restore the beauty-cum-use principle. Otherwise,
if it traffics with devils, it will go to the devil. The importance of
the garden is, then, paramount, since the order has not yet gone
out to destroy our garden hedges, the citadels of our traditional
freedom and independence. When, therefore, I look down the
garden, the hedge that surrounds it is the background of my observa-
tions.

The laying or "plushing" of a hedge shows us work that, however hard, is play because it is accompanied by skill and art and so
pleasure. It serves a useful purpose and the result has beauty. I
will look a little more closely into this idea of pleasure associated
with work for two reasons—it is of the first importance for our
life upon earth and it is of the first relevance to a garden. A Land-
Girl once passed me driving a horse-rake. She had shorts on and her
legs were those of a statue in copper. Her straw-coloured hair
was blown back by the wind and her blue eyes looked over the
nodding head of her black horse as though she saw something in
the open swinging lines of the multicoloured field-quilt others
did not. Her shirt was open at the throat and the arms of her
limber body grasped the rein with the nonchalance of perfect
familiarity. Chloe—Audrey—Celia—Corinna—Daphne—the heiress
of countless classical and Renaissance and Augustan shepherdesses
and milkmaids. The rightful one of all their airs and graces, since
what turned her from Staffordshire china into Oxfordshire flesh
and blood was that she worked, not played. She had become the
adopted child of the fields not of the mantelpiece. She made
ridiculous the doctrinaire decree of that great townsman, Dr.
Johnson, that there could not be "a poetry of serges and druggets."
Not so long ago she had been perhaps a typist or a cashier or a
packer, and now she milked cows, built ricks, drove carts, fed

stock, drilled corn and harnessed horses. She had come not only out of the office but the prison of time, since, in joining the fields, she had entered the dateless age of husbandry.

The flower of that age appears in the lines:—

"The ploughman near at hand
   Whistles o'er the furrowed land,
And the milkmaid singeth blithe,
   And the mower whets his scythe."

Because in them play and work are regarded as parts of one whole. The progressive who drifts down the flux of time and calls his fatalism[1] automatic betterment, regards such essentials and realities as these as the trinkets of a picturesque past. This is the central flaw of modernism by which it has delivered itself over to the total bondage of time and lost its hold upon the eternities as they are set forth by religion and the permanences as they are set forth by husbandry. Change, yes, but within, not outside the law. The whistling ploughman and the singing milkmaid can never be *vieux jeu*, never be thrust back arbitrarily into the past. They are part of the inviolable law of work-in-play and play-in-work, the expressions of a due and fit adjustment to the laws of husbandry that cannot be broken. Here is the Great Illusion of the modern world—that these irrefragable laws can and shall be broken in the cause of automatic progress. But because they cannot be broken, catastrophe is the judgment, and the modern has been mastered and enslaved and all his ambitions are being ground down into the dust by his own machines, by his own machinery of government. He cannot escape unless he changes his mind, and he cannot deliver himself from his own fantasies until he does. I think he is beginning to change it, but that change has not yet penetrated into the political and economic spheres. Not until the tares of this illusion have come to the harvest and been burned in the oven will the ploughman whistle and the milkmaid sing once more. It will evaporate into thin air when it is realised that to whistle at the plough makes for better ploughmanship and that the singing milkmaid makes the truer countrywoman than the silent.

But once the ploughman whistled, yet only because he was a

---

[1]As an intellectual puts it: "The forces of economic and political progress are ineluctable and cannot be stemmed." (Peter Cromwell: *Horizon*; August, 1943).

master-man and husband to the earth. Or, as Charles Marson has written in his and Cecil Sharp's collection of Somerset Folk Songs:

"It (the folk song) is the last lingering remnant of the old village life: a survival of the times when the village had more or less an independent existence, built its own church, hanged its rogues, made its own boots, shirts and wedding rings, and chanted its own tunes. All the rest is gone. We cannot call our souls our own now. We create nothing. The people are going away fast, and in a couple of generations of such progress, there will be neither songs nor singers in the silent fields."

This was written in 1914: it is doubly true in our generation. The songs themselves in the book are all obviously much older, centuries older than was the generation still singing them; they are not new songs but echoes, blurred memories, faint undertones of old songs. They are half-remembered songs; the full tragedy was yet to come, when the ploughman whistled no more, not even his forefathers' airs.

But there is one song I know which has, I must think, survived intact, and so gives us some measure of what we have lost. It is the *Sowers' Song* in Alfred Williams's *Folk Songs of the Upper Thames*:—[1]

"Now hands to seed-sheet, boys,
We step and we cast, Old Time's on wing;
And would you partake of Harvest's joys,
The corn must be sown in spring.

Fall gently and still, good corn,
Lie warm in your earthy bed,
And stand so yellow some morn,
For beast and man must be fed.

Old earth is a pleasure to see
In sunshiney cloak of red and green;
The furrow lies fresh and this year will be
As years that are past have been.

Old mother, receive this corn,
The son of six thousand golden sires;
All these on thy kindly breast were born,
One more thy poor child requires.

[1] Sent me by my friend, Mr. L. T. C. Rolt.

> Now, steady and sure again,
> And measure of stroke and step we keep:
> Then up and down we cast our grain,
> Sow well, and you shall gladly reap."

This is no careless whistle; it is the ritual of the English people going forth to sow their corn. The land of England was still theirs, their mother to receive the corn; the days ahead when no man sings and no man sows were still to come. Once too the milkmaid sang, she who said to Florizel, "I'll go milk my ewes." The blend between country realism and country symbolism is subtle in *The Winter's Tale*. Hardly any of the Shakespearean critics have seen the significance of Shakespeare's country-mindedness, but Dr. E. M. W. Tillyard is one of them. He finds a particular profundity of meaning in the character of Perdita, nearly always misconstrued on the stage:—

> "The play has been far too much the property of vague young women doing eurhythmics on Speech Days or on vicarage lawns; and, when it is acted professionally, the part of Perdita is usually taken by some pretty little fool or pert suburban charmer."—
>
> (Shakespeare's Last Plays).

On the contrary, he says, she is "one of Shakespeare's richest characters; at once a symbol[1] and a human being," a judgment pleasing to me personally, since I would give a dozen Imogens for this adorable creature. The Doctor with fine sensitiveness proceeds to demolish the notion of Perdita's famous flower-speech as merely idyllic and so escapist. There is a distinct element of fertility symbolism in it; she is a "symbol of the creative powers of nature, physical fertility, and of healing and recreation of the mind." At the same time, she is a human being full of good country sense and playfulness and feminine sweetness, as well (so Florizel calls her) as

> "no shepherdess but Flora
> Peering in April's front."

---

[1] "Symbol" has been defined by Coleridge as (1) existing in itself, (2) derived from something greater than itself, and (3) representing in itself the greatness from which it comes. Yet, as a complete human being in herself, Perdita is greater than this greatness.

I would go even further than this. I see in her a personification, without any sacrifice of humanity, of the English countryside itself, its landscape but also its people. Before the Industrial Revolution brought it such grief and persecution, it was a people which uniquely combined its work with its play and its play with its work. There it is in Perdita, "the queen of curds and cream," when Florizel declares that all her work about the farm and indeed her whole life were a singing and a dancing. There it is in the illustrious Sheep Shearing Feast. The Feast is a celebration of the countryman's *daily work*. It could not be more realistic—Autolycus who sings all the best songs is stark realism. But it also has a queer kind of magic and enchantment about it, as though this frank and jolly festival and this exquisite milkmaid and shepherdess were ideally acting man's primary basic function in this mortal world, the cultivation of the earth with joy and thanksgiving, with content and praise. This is the creative source of all human activities, the play seems to say, the background of all sane and healthy living; it is the sanctification through an act of intense imagination of the ploughman who whistles and the milkmaid who sings.

We have got so far away from Shakespeare's conception of the art of true living, both realistically and symbolically figured, that we now look upon *The Winter's Tale* as a bit of pure fairyland. But it is not; it is the great poet's perception of a final and immutable truth about human life. And in our hearts, we countrymen know that it is truth.

The adjustment between men and the fields has been lost. There is conflict and dislocation between the smiling corn of fruitfulness and the ways and means of cultivating it. The fields are no longer *gardened*, and the meaning of this is that the knowledgeable as well as the happy husbandman is out of date. Not the machine as machine is the source of the tragedy of maladjustment, but the machine that has escaped the harness of husbandry and so has been its Juggernaut. We tamed the horse but the machine as yet has escaped all human discipline.

In the old days, the work of the field-labourer was play, however hard and ill-requited, because it was a patterned and a social function in key with nature and the law of man's own being. By its very nature, that work was a form of play and the festival, the drama, the cricket match, the village choir were a flowering from it. To have lost these is no trifle; it is to be at discord with the meaning of existence. It is only another way of saying that modern man has gained the whole world and lost his own soul.

To-day this play-in-work principle is a heresy against the orthodox economics of work and the accepted irresponsibility of leisure so radical that modern industrial and financial civilization could not possibly survive its adoption. The actual separation of work from pleasure and of leisure from work was set in motion by the Industrial Revolution by which utility became sordid and recreation was dissociated from work. What was "beautiful" became "picturesque" (viz., removed from its context of utility) and what was "useful" ceased to be so by the motive of profit displacing that of service. The tests were monetary wealth, salesmanship, competition for commodities first in the home and then in the international market, mass-production as an end in itself, though the bulk of the population had not the wherewithal to buy the mass-products. As the last century unfolded its legacy to the next, the whole process, with some alleviations that helped to conceal its harms and perils, became hardened and stereotyped. Play became an escape mechanism from the deadly drudgery of irresponsible work on the office-chair or at the assembly-line and yet as mechanised as what it escaped from. The mechanical dream-world of the cinema is the release from the automatism of the factory. The divorce between work and play could not be more absolute than it is to-day. Yet the automaton-worker of the one is the automaton-player of the other, and from this joyless and lifeless servitude to the machines was conceived the Utopia of the Leisure State. From both work and leisure have been withdrawn that personal interest in and control of what is done, that exercise of talent and skill, which is the pleasure and play-element of work. So play itself, in ceasing to be associated with work of any kind, deprived the player of his own choice and initiative in it, the very sources of its reality as play. "God forbid," said the old labourer in Fred Kitchen's *The Farming Front*, "as we should be drawn into line wi' a lot o' poor beggars whose on'y idea of a spree is a dog race, and whose on'y notion of a fine seet is in watchin' Blackpool illuminations."

It can occasion no surprise, therefore, that "employment" came to be regarded either as an end in itself for mere existence' sake or as a means for getting as much out of it in payment or profit and at the expense of the neighbour and the work as guile or manipulation could secure. To this end, the osier beds, the brick-kilns, the pottery works, the tanneries, the little breweries, the wind and water mills, the quarries of roof-stone and wall-stone and a hundred other rural industries fell derelict in thousands. Consequently, to train many of the soldiers home from the war[1] for those and other industries depending upon agriculture, would solve a great deal more than "the problem of unemployment." To make keeping a garden part of that training would teach them more than how to grow cabbages and roses. It would satisfy their craving for a new life on the land. It would fulfil their profound need for fruitful and responsible work and help to reknit the broken rural fabric.[2] Garden and craft are at one in that both pay heed to the traditional meaning of work and play, of use and beauty, and so guard against the violent reactions which agitate a frustrated human nature.

[1] From lectures I have given, letters I have received and reports I have heard, I have come to believe that one hope for the future of the real England will come from the men in the Forces.

[2] It is significant that Sir John Russell, recently made Chairman of the Committee of Management for the estate bought by *Country Life*, makes strong points of the need for village crafts to accompany the estate and an arable flock for the light land to be properly cultivated.

CHAPTER SEVEN

THE DECLINE OF SKILLED LABOUR

"·You talk about making this article cheaper by reducing its price in
the market from 8d. to 6d. But suppose in so doing you have rendered
your country weaker against a foreign foe ; suppose you have demor-
alized thousands of your fellow-countrymen and have sown discontent
between one class of society and another, your article is tolerably dear,
I take it, after all."

S. T. COLERIDGE.

IN Chapter V, I described some specimens of a collection in my
orchard Hermitage which is a monument of man's skilled labour.
The importance of this is universal—here is a world-stage of
immense implications gathered, as Shakespeare said of his theatre,
within "this wooden O." Man became man by the exercise of
skilled labour; would it not be true to say that his hand and his
eye became what they are by their gradual correlation in acts of
craftsmanship? The supreme schoolmaster of man has been the
flint nodule of the chalk downland.

What is happening to-day but the abandonment of this primary
human activity of a million years of education ? They have produced a world-treasury of works of hand and eye, the infinitesimal
fragments of which have been hoarded into museums. I do not
exaggerate: man's skilled labour is becoming as obsolete as are
the things that he made by it. His industry in cities is becoming
more and more vested into the "hands" of a very small body of
highly specialised technicians who, by virtue of that overwhelming
fact, are bound to be technocrats, the high priesthood of the machine.
The rest of the workers can be nothing but parts themselves of the
machine, automatons executing automatic and repetitive move-
ments.

More slowly but pervasively the same thing is happening to
agriculture. Machines have been substituted for men in "large-
scale economic units"; the State and the Corporation for the
personal owner. Skill-less gangs, what is called a "fluid labour
force," replace the agricultural labourer and the craftsman whose

work is always manifold. Such is the inevitable consequence of regarding agriculture as an industry rather than a craft and so applying to it the methods of and mentality of industrialism. Modern farming by machines, one or two mechanics and gangs at the peak periods means, writes A. G. Street in *Hitler's Whistle* (1943), "the end of farm and country life as I have loved and known it all my life." We are rapidly approaching a time when the only skilled labour throughout the whole world will be done by a handful of technicians and artisans, a scattering of hothouse or lackey artists, and a tiny percentage of the peasants, agricultural labourers, working farmers and craftsmen who chance to escape by being unnoticed in the industrialisation of the globe. Only the extinction of the human race could be a greater tragedy. I quote from a letter I recently (1943) received from a friend of mine who is a highly skilled engineer:

"I have recently been engaged on a survey of labour in several engineering works with a view to finding out how increased production demands would best be met. The results were revealing in that they confirmed even beyond my gloomiest anticipation the extent to which the process of eliminating skill has been carried. In one plant employing over 1500 people the proportion of skilled labour employed worked out at less than 10%. You may imagine the organization, the tools and mechanical equipment that enables a tremendous rate of production to be maintained under these conditions, a production far greater than pre-war. This plant will not be scrapped simply to provide jobs for the skilled men who come back after the war without a fundamental change in the whole basis of industry. What will happen?"

This independent private judgment was sensationally and publicly corroborated by a statement of Sir Frank Spriggs, managing director of the largest aircraft building organization in the Empire. He said: "Most of us in the industry marvel at the fact that the overwhelming bulk of our output is achieved by unskilled labour." Lastly, Sir Stafford Cripps, dancing like a dervish round the funeral pyre of skilled workmanship, extolled the diminution of it to 2 per cent as "a magnificent achievement in labour dilution." These words only bear out Dean Inge's in *Outspoken Essays:*—" The majority of workmen are parasites on the machine which has ousted them from natural human occupations." The more then do I treasure my "museum" examples of folk-art and husbandry which once evoked a man's full capabilities and ministered to a common need, practical and spiritual in one. My garden protects these examples in the hope that one day man, at last perceiving whither his madness leads, will come to his senses.

Being "parasitic" on the machine, these unskilled workers have also become mobile—that is to say, homeless—in order to serve the far-flung demands of mass-production and industrialism. Here, again, the contrast is with the craftsmen who were attached to one place. They belonged to the days crystallized by Flora Thompson in *Candleford Green* :—

> "The community was largely self-supporting. Every household grew its own vegetables, produced its new-laid eggs and cured its own bacon. Most gardens had a row of beehives. In the houses of the well-to-do there was an abundance of such foods, and even the poor enjoyed a rough plenty."

They belonged to their own place—this is the fitting epitaph of the old countrymen. I once asked a tractor-driver, who did the land he was ploughing belong to? He did not know. I asked what it was to be sown to. He did not know. In desperation I asked him some questions about the actual ploughing. Not only was he more ignorant about the particular land he was ploughing than I was, though I did not know the field, but he, a ploughman, took not the faintest interest in ploughing. Contrast this up-to-date attitude with that of Tom Bell, the labourer of 50 years ago, as described in David Smith's *No Rain in Those Clouds* (1943). He took the deepest pride in his horses, waggons, plough, and the straightness of his furrows. His work was not only ploughing but hedging, ditching, cartering, threshing, draining, rabbiting, drilling, carpentering, broadcasting seed, gardening, singling roots, sheep-shearing, mowing, cocking, loading, stacking, thatching and acting foreman to the pea-pickets, all performed with the rhythm and economy of a loving craftsmanship.

The completely impersonal attitude of this ploughman struck me as desolating. The work was simply a job to be done at so much the hour. The only interest in the field being ploughed was how big it was and how long it would take to plough it. The W.A.E.C.

hired the contractor and the contractor hired the man. When he had done this job, he would go on somewhere else and plough another field; somebody else would come along and do the sowing. There might or might not be further cultivations by imported labour and in the end the crop would be harvested by an influx of expediency workers. These might enjoy it, might for a day or two experience the integrating bond of working for a common purpose. But after that they would be dissipated "into thin air" for all the field and the farmer and the place knew about it. Then the same or another tractor-ploughman could come and chug across the field and go away again.

Nothing has any hold on such a man except the pay and the hours and the smooth running of the machine. No roots, no home, no pleasure nor interest in the job nor in its results. No belongingness anywhere, though everything on earth belongs to its own soil. Even the mobile and volatile birds are attached to particular soils and vegetation, and the face of England was moulded into its supreme beauty by the Englishmen who responded to the genius of place. What this ploughman was expounding was the brand-new doctrine of the fluidity of labour. The economists and politicians who propound it, that is to say, think it is new. But it is not; the fluidity of labour was one of the causes for the Captain Swing Revolt and the Luddite Riots of 1812. The peasants, having become a Poor Law proletariat by being jockeyed out of their lands, were organized into gangs who moved about the country singling turnips, harvesting, threshing, etc., under the supervision of overseers (with whips). At night they were herded into temporary shelters just as degrading as the permanent *ergastula* or slave-quarters on the *latifundia* of the Roman villas. Because they had once been free men, they revolted and the story of how that revolt was put down and what was done to the revolters even the conventional historians were unable to cover up.

This first instalment of the principle of the fluidity of labour in our country[1] was as old as the erection of the Pyramids. It was a failure for the very good reason that the opposing principle of private property distributed among the mass of the people was still strong in the Englishman. He felt that he still *belonged* to the land, what was left of him after the drift to the towns. So Flora Thompson was able to describe her village in the 'eighties as still

[1] Except under the Roman slave-farms or *latifundia*.

being self-supporting and so free and so averse to being moved about from place to place and job to job like a pawn on a chess-board. Since the 'eighties, however, the world has made considerable progress in the abolition of private property or rather its con-centration into the hands of the few who no longer admit or exercise personal responsibility for it. The final result has been the combine on the one hand and a bureaucratic paternalism which is only another term for absentee landlordism, on the other The further consequence is that the principle of the fluidity of labour has become once more a leading political motive. Unhappily, the principle of responsible private property without which the principle of freedom cannot be maintained, is much less virile and tenacious than it was during and immediately after the Enclosures. People who want to deprive others of their private property and so of their liberties are considered idealists.

If these conditions were regarded as a temporary war-measure, let them pass. But they have become ingrained and are posited as inevitable both now and in the future. We live in an era which step by step and with cumulative force from the Enclosures and the Industrial Revolution onwards has undermined the status and stifled the social expression of the small independent master, whether in industry, in the rural crafts or on the land. In innumerable direc-tions it has destroyed his livelihood, and in so doing has razed the foundations of that liberty and democracy to which it still acknow-ledges a lip-service. So much is self-confessed out of its own mouth. What is put in the place of the Craft-Guild, the village community and the small business is the ultra-modern concept of the Common Man. Not merely a foolish but an evil thing. What is this Common Man but a dehumanised abstraction, a chemical synthesis? He is a heresy against the variety of human nature. To accept man as number and quantity is to deny him as the unique and qualitative being that religion considers him.

> "They forget that man was born to be loved or hated, to plough a field or write a poem, to win a battle or lose it, to take a risk, to make his soul; he is not on this earth to be counted as though he were one of a million beads on the adding-machine of some gargantuan and idiot child."

It is not the soul of the Common Man that is in question, but

THE FALL OF THE FISHERMEN 201

his body only and his capacity to be employed in terms of the market-place. He is to be saved from downright destitution by a State charity. His "standard of living" is to be raised by a system of international trading monopolies financed by an international bank. By providing cheap goods and so (it is assumed) high wages, the system will secure the support of the Socialists. By these means, profit and usury will be reconciled with proletarian welfare, the State (as in Germany) can be merged with private self-interest, and "people's cars" finally take the place of people's cows. But the widened and deepened gulf between production and consumption such centralised monopolies must entail, the complexity of parasitic distribution and the total tyranny of a fictitious wealth are ignored. The predatory powers that manipulate him, the vast machine of pointless production, the Economic State that has no ends but only a means in the economic expansion of itself, these remain in the Utopia of the Common Man. There is no way out of this but the restoration of the principle of responsible property, and of this return to the true traditions of the Englishman the garden as a more or less self-sufficient unit is one and not the least of what modern means are open to us. The feeling back to this tradi-tional conception of property, that has received the sanction of religion for 2000 years, is the work of the true pioneer. It releases men from the horns of the dilemma on which faulty thinking has placed them: the choice between "private enterprise" and State control. But the choice is not really that at all; it is between a bureaucracy acting on behalf of monopoly and a revaluation of the meaning of property and responsibility.

I take a vivid example of the destruction of this traditional principle from a book published a dozen or more years ago and called *Cornish Seafarers*. It is a description of how the small Cornish share-fisherman has been driven off his fishing grounds and degraded from being his own master to becoming a proletarian wage-earner in the service of the big trawling and drifting interests which have destroyed his craft. This is a common enough tale in all industries. It is particularly relevant here because of the effect of what the author of the book calls "the natural trend of the times" upon the fisheries themselves. The reduction of the sailing fleet of Brixham from 250 to less than 50 within a period of fifteen years was paralleled by the impoverishment of the fishing grounds through the annihilation of all the immature fish that came within reach of the trawling nets. The disparity between the prices paid to producers in comparison with those paid to distributors was so great that out of every £1's worth of herring consumed the fisherman got half a crown, the middleman 15/6, while the 2/- left went for freight charges. The drift from a traditional and highly skilled calling and the loss of their little properties by the fishermen went hand in hand with the decline of the great inshore seine fishery, the falling off of pilchard fishing and the destruction of the fry by bottom trawling.

What has this to do with my ideas about gardening? A great deal. The story of the Cornish fisheries offers a precise analogy in miniature with the application of large-scale industrial methods to agriculture throughout the world. The master-men of both industries fell victim to the creation and destruction of money by the Bank of England and to the manipulation of prices by the financial corporations and interests. As the fisherman lost his independent status, so the peasant and the small-owner were forced to sell out or saddled with debt or degraded to a mechanical milk-producer by speculation, cheap imports and bank interest. As the trawler eliminates the spawn, so the large-scale mechanised farm managed by big business methods breaks down the structure of the soil. As trawling destroys long-line fishing, so factory farming a long-term agriculture. The emptying of the seas keeps pace with the erosion of the earth. The poverty of the real producer is the result of the obsolescence of his traditional crafts and pattern of life; the loss of his status and independence enforces the drift to the town, while the waste of natural riches and the falling away of natural fecundity are both of the sea and the land.

Thus loss of property,[1] fluidity of labour, and unskilled work are three in one and one in three. It is obvious that if anything belongs to a man, he is likely to take interest in it, and if he takes interest in it, he will devote pains and skill to it. He will, that is to say, take pleasure in it and, once he does so, his work becomes play. Was my tractor-driver a skilled man when all he thought about was getting from one end of the field to the other, regardless of all the factors involved in his mechanical motion? The most skilful man

---

[1] The modern antipathy to the holding of property is not, of course, confined to the small man. The attack is upon responsibly held property, whether large or small. Mr. Geoffrey Faber has pointed out that the Excess Profits Tax discriminates between "proprietary" and "non-proprietary" principals. The man who puts his money in the business he works himself is the more penalised.

in the world is the craftsman who is at the same time free and the holder of private property. If the principle of the fluidity of labour becomes established after the war, the last of English liberties will vanish. The force resisting this tendency is no longer traditional but based on a reaction against the ineptitude and pettifogging interference of the new bureaucracy. Once it is seen that it and the combine work hand in hand, then there are hopes that this force will become a power. But it will not become so until it is recognised that this evil and other evils allied to it proceed from the great assumption that industrialism is the norm of civilization. To it the countryside, whose true norm and base are the garden in the sense I have tried to make clear, must, whether by force or propaganda, conform. Hence, the ideas of the factory-farm, cinemas for land-workers, bureaucratic "control," no "sentiment" and the "fluidity of labour." Hence, too, the inability to understand that the revolt against this delusion is the revolt of the human being frustrated of his human rights.

There are other rural consequences of modern labour having become largely fluid, mechanical and propertyless. Since machines can do mechanical work more "efficiently" than men, they tend to replace men both in war *and* peace. This in its turn means that land is no longer properly cultivated. It produces by way of machines and chemicals and these methods react in their turn upon the quality of our food. Here is an illustration completely relevant to the economy of a garden. In the spring of 1943, the Minister of Agriculture made a speech in which he said, "The output of food per man in Britain is probably the highest in the world." Fine, but what does it mean? As it obviously means nothing as it stands, I hazard the guess that the Minister was handed this statement by one of the economists who think of farming in terms of figures and, as it sounded impressive, out it was trotted. The obvious reply by anybody taught by bitter experience to be sceptical of slogans is, "It all depends on how many men there are to produce the food." Supposing, for example, there were only ten men in every county who were producing many tons of food per man, the total amount of food produced in all the counties would certainly not be impressive.

In Sir John Russell's *English Farming* (1942), a table of figures was given from seven European nations classifying among other statistics the acres per worker and the output per acre in 1937.

In the first, Great Britain headed the list with 33.8, more than double the figure of the country that came next to it (Denmark) and treble that of the country next to Denmark (France). In the second, Great Britain was at the bottom of the list, averaging less than half the output per acre of Belgium, Denmark, Switzerland and the Netherlands. Now these figures do mean something; they mean that in the displacement of men by machines on the land Great Britain outdistanced the other six European countries which were "also rans," while these countries made her an "also ran" in the actual yield of crops per acre. Those that headed the list in this output per acre—Denmark, Switzerland, Holland and Belgium—are all peasant countries, countries which cultivate their land mainly by human and very little by mechanical labour. What is more, they are countries which still practice husbandry, and by methods intensive (viz., garden cultivation) rather than extensive. They return at least some of their wastes to the soil on organic principles and so the less exploit and exhaust their lands. The same is true of our own country in all instances where few are broken up into many farms. Thus, an estate of 1000 acres under four farms in Lincolnshire was subdivided into 90 ten-acre farms. The results were (1) an increase of population from 40 to 180, and (2) a triple increase of yield per acre. I have proved in my own region that the yield per acre fifty years ago was double what it is now under modern conditions.[1] Mr. Wentworth Day in *Farming Adventure* obtained from Mr. Gunston, the estate agent, the wheat-yield per acre of the celebrated Holkham Estate. In 1813, it was 56 bushels; the average yield per acre for Great Britain between 1928 and 1937 was 32. Holkham land is, too, some of the lightest in the kingdom, barley not wheat land.

Thus, we do not need to go outside our own land to prove that, *where it is not starved or unduly handicapped by financial pressure from without,*[2] small-scale beats large-scale farming every time. It wins not only in quality, which no economist nor politician ever bothers about, but in *quantity*—viz., output per acre. In the light

[1] See my *Men of Earth*. It is probable that successes in plant-breeding have helped to conceal the bad farming of modern industrial methods applied to the land.

[2] Such pressure was responsible for the wretched grassland farming of small-holders between 1920-39, "teat-pulling," as Lord Portsmouth has called it. The cow-keeper depended on cow-sick pasture and imported feed to run his farm, was usually in debt, was put to all manner of shifts to make both ends meet, and lost all the arts of husbandry. He was a victim of the depression engineered by finance.

of these data, which is the best thing to achieve, the highest output per man (that is to say, the most acres per worker) or the highest yield per acre? No man in his senses could hesitate as to the answer, but unhappily the modern world is not in its senses. Imagining, however, that reason still has a voice, what is there to boast about in the fewness of our population on the land? That is all that these grandiose figures mean about output per man. We are proud of ourselves because there is only one man working 33 acres of food-producing land. Nor is this shortage of labour only the effect of war; these figures I have quoted are pre-war. First, we drain the land of its best blood, brain and sinew; then we invent machines to do the work of men and so save us from starvation and lastly we consider a process due to our own fantasies and malpractices as an end desirable in itself.[1] Is it not an inversion of values that something we ought to be heartily ashamed of is an occasion of vainglory? We empty and ruin our own land and then have the effrontery to pat ourselves on the back.

When peace comes, are we to cry from the housetops to a listening world that, whereas one worked 33 acres before the war, he now works 50 after it? The only remedy, of course, is to get as many men back on the land as it will hold and to educate them in good husbandry, not in land-banditry. It is to encourage farms and families to be self-supporting and to use machines as servants to that end, not to offer ourselves up to the Juju of automatism. The business of the gardener is to adopt the same principles and pursue the same methods as those which, aiming at quality, achieve the greater productivity. But the illusion of the Age of Plenty, which has sacrificed quality to quantity as an end in itself, is the same illusion as that of Tantalus whose cup was always beyond his reach, and of Alice whose bulrushes withered in her hand. No improved methods nor ingenious contrivances can circumvent this fundamental fallacy; what alone can draw its poison is to replace it with the truth. The truth is that the quality of the soil conditions the quality of the food derived from it and the quality of nutrition depends upon the quality of the food. All these qualities depend upon an adequate supply of skilled labour.

It seems, then, that rural unemployment and soil-depletion are two facets of one problem. The many unskilled but higher

[1] In Denmark, 1000 acres supported 70 people; in England they support 30. Between 1918-39, there were half a million fewer allotments and between 1921-39, 300,000 labourers left the land.

paid serve the machines at the conveyor belt and assembly line, the few skilled but lower paid serve the land. It thus becomes clear that the economy of the gardener is to use as much skilled labour as he possibly can and of the kind which will nurse, not exploit, the land.

The history of all nations has demonstrated that the technique and the way of life of the peasant or the small proprietor are by nature those of conservation. Nor is it possible to achieve self-sufficiency whether in a garden or on a farm or from the land-surface of a nation except by that love and care of the natural wealth which are the principle of husbandry. Were not the famous Arran potatoes bred on a 30-acre plot? Self-sufficiency is the guarantee of such husbandry. You must cherish, not conquer, nature if you wish or have to live on her, and you cannot live in harmony with the laws of nature without understanding them and translating them into your own methods and principles. There is no other way of so doing except by the mixed farm, the balanced rotation and the return of all wastes. The interdependence of stock, crop and pasture and the exercise of a craftsmanly labour are a human rendering of nature's own immutable laws of health and organic equilibrium. Her wholeness must be yours, since soil-fertility and nutrition, direct personal responsibility and conservation, are parts of one whole. My own process of self-education was the developing realisation that my own garden could and must become a unit of husbandry.

Thus the gardener is completely in accord with intensive peasant cultivation all over the world. He is as inevitably out of harmony with all urban civilizations which apply their quantitative and industrial methods to agriculture to the destruction of craftsmanship, the depopulation of the country and the ruin of the land.

Here is another aspect of the same issue, and I take this example from an advertisement of a tractor-plough:—

"In the year 1727, Jonathan Swift wanted 2 blades of grass where one grew before. To-day, the demand is for 3 furrows where 2 were ploughed before and 4 where formerly 3 seemed good going."

Here is the root of our contemporary confusion, namely the assumption that double the number of plough-shares means double the blades in the field. What the advertisement really means is that more ground can be covered in a shorter time and with less labour with a multiple than with a single plough. But so far from this meaning that more blades can be grown with 4 shares than with 1, in actual practice it usually means exactly the opposite, namely, that fewer blades will appear on more ground. The fallacy consists in the assumption that more elaborate mechanical contrivance implies a heavier yield.[1] If it were true that the earth were not a finite but a limitless surface, one can imagine this boundless area sprinkled over with enough blades to outnumber those grown, however intensively, over the actual available surface of the earth. But it is not true: on the contrary, the spread of urbanism, suburbanism and industrialism together with the creep of the desert and the growth of the population since the Industrial Revolution has contracted the dimensions of soil-surface on which blades can be grown. Military and industrial works since the war began have, for instance, taken more land than have agriculture and reclamation.

How dangerously unrealistic, then, this quantitative habit of mind! Only more labour, greater skill and better husbandry can make 2 blades grow where only 1 grew before. People who think like this belong to the same camp as those who talk of keeping 2,000,000 unemployed in the towns as a potential war-reserve for the third Armageddon, instead of training them for employment in agriculture and its attendant industries and so to resettle the empty spaces of our native land. The strangest part of all this muddled economics is that this latter life is, if one may judge from the feeling among the soldiers, the one that this two million would prefer.

Every day old Crodge, the retired farmer (73), walks over a mile from his cottage in the village to the crest of the ridge. There he draws great draughts of air into his lungs and can look over to the Oxford Heights and the Berkshire Downs.

> "To the top of the hill
> Where the sky grows wide
> And where the sun grows red."

[1] "Machinery has been subsidised from soils which are now eroded, destroyed or in course of losing their food-producing value. Very little of this subsidy has yet appeared in the cost of the machines. The argument that food from a mechanised farm is cheaper than from a mixed farm is without foundation. Its roots lie in the deserts of the world." H. R. Broadbent. Letter in the *Farmer's Weekly* of May 14, 1942.

Rain or shine, heat or chill, he always takes the same saunter at the same pace. Only in the lane past my house he pauses in April to sniff up the Oriental aroma of my balsam poplars and, a little further on, to gaze through the just greening hedge at my orchard daffodils. Because he would be surprised if you called him a nature-lover, he is the more so. And he takes in what the nature-lover usually misses, the condition of the fields, the growth of the corn, the "plushing" of the hedges, the look of the soil. He is thus a true son of Cobbett. He notices too what the view-gazer would rejoice in. The emptiness of the land. But that does not rejoice him. For he sees further back and further ahead than the appraiser of landscape. When he looks into his memories, he sees full and populous fields; when into the future, it is with a somewhat mournful and sardonic eye.

From what he has told me, the land-population of the view we can see both from my terrace and the top of the ridge, the goal of his daily walk, has been reduced by 90% from what it was some fifty years before the production of home-grown food became a matter of life or death. The oat-field at which we would often gaze together, leaning over a broken-down field-gate, is harvested by four men, a tractor-driver, a man on the self-binder and two stookers. In old Crodge's young days it took 40, and produced exactly double the yield it does now. Yet no planner ever dreams of mentioning the re-settlement of the land in discussing the "problems" of post-war employment.

A glance, then, at some of the new inventions which are saving the world from work.

The displacement of labour by machinery has become so omnivorous that no government can cope with it. It used to take a craftsman $5\frac{1}{2}$ days to make one pair of boots; modern plant turns out 595,000 pairs of boots in $5\frac{1}{2}$ days. Before the era of indiscriminate and uncontrolled mechanical power, a man would lay 450 bricks a day; now a brick plant can produce 400,000 per man per day.

A manless plough has been proved so efficient that it guided itself along the furrow and turned at the headland without even a tractor-driver. Lord Northbourne tells the true story of a neighbour of his who bought a new self-propelled 12 ft. Combine Harvester. One of his men asked how many acres it would deal with in a season. The answer was 450. The old man asked how many people were needed to work it: the answer was one. The old man replied: "Then I suppose there will soon be nothing left for any of us to do except to stand about wondering why we were born." If, being a progressive, you looked into the future, you might picture a time when the machine had "released" man from the burden of Adam altogether, so that he could enter the Utopia of the Leisure State with nothing whatever to do in it. How grossly uneconomic, then, were our fathers who were in the habit of employing 40 men in one field! Empty fields and empty machine-shops. What labour-saving felicity! True, there might well be no food to eat. But soon another mechanical marvel would be invented which, with one man operating 10,000 slot-machines, each producing 1,000,000 synthetic pillules (called "foodax") made up in the laboratory, would solve the problem of nourishment. But mankind is so unregenerate and unprogressive by nature that it is quite certain he will abandon the heaven of industrialism promised him and return once more to the earth and repopulate it, if it is only for the sake of getting his teeth into a hunk of bread and cheese. "2 men do the work of 50" was a heading I read in a farming paper, and our post-war planners, mistaking present emergency for a state of affairs desirable in itself, applaud. Yet if a man will not work, he shall not eat, and if he does not eat he dies. And serve him right if he is such a fool as to lend his ear to the modern heresy that the craftsman's work of hand and eye, which is the gardener's and the husbandman's, is obsolete, a mere drudgery, a loss of status.

CHAPTER EIGHT

THE SACRIFICE OF SELF-HELP

"Those who own no part of the means of production, who are economically unfree, who cannot stand on their own feet and look after themselves and their families if they are discharged, are always subject to having their wills coerced. They have no effective power except the final power of revolution. They have been denied the blessings of liberty even if the State gives them a dole or a job after they have become unemployed; for it is a delusion to suppose that the State is more gentle a master than the private employer, if the State gets complete control over a man's support. The delusion, which is widespread in our world, comes from ignoring the first of the maxims : All power corrupts and absolute power corrupts absolutely."

HERBERT AGAR, *A Time for Greatness.*

HEALTH is closely interlocked with all these issues. It is needless to labour the point that the machinery of the modern economic system has been and is promised to be based upon distance, upon transport, upon quantity, upon size and upon speed. These from means to a vaguely defined end have become ends in themselves. We have come to believe in dumping things in and out of ships and lorries as a kind of national self-preservation. The inevitable consequence has been that the great aggregations of modern populations have become almost wholly parasitic in the necessities of life. So much so that parasitism as near as may be lost us the war and deeply compromised the soul of our people. The war of exchanges and the cut-price competition for foreign markets resulted in the exhaustion of virgin soils and the beggaring of the primary producer. The enormous powers vested in the secondary interests of distribution and the dominance of finance over industry in their turn built up a colossal mechanism in the expert processing and adulteration of foods and the removal of their vital elements to be resold for larger profits. The cost of food-distribution was £850 millions as compared with £650 millions for food-production. These effects all hinged upon this parasitism. Thus self-sufficiency, nutrition and health are seen to be tripartite divisions of one whole.

The moment the war came, the whole policy was reversed and the nation was ordered to become self-supporting. But the bureaucratic control which regimented the producer stretched a protective wing over the vested interests in distribution and identified itself more and more closely with the self-interested combines. Once learn the habits of waste and to undo them under existing mechanisms is too hard a lesson to learn. With changes only towards more centralization,[1] the smaller businesses were swallowed up and the larger ones extended their powers, in spite of their cumbrous machinery and the inefficiency of their costliness. In the country itself, every obstacle was placed in the path of regional self-support; the stone-grinding mills continued to be "liquidated" by the milling combine and the egg that the countryman cracked was hardly lawful unless it came from Canada. The W.A.E.C. have done much hard and useful work through their local connections but were also forced to be arbitrary and to adopt urban methods of soil-exploitation by this rapidly growing centralization. It is impossible not to be dubious of their husbandry when they claim the credit for the bumper crops obtained from newly reclaimed land—and so withhold it from nature when her stored-up fertility, not they, achieved such crops. They have, again, acted merely as the agents of Whitehall and not in the interests of food-production nor the farmers responsible for it when they ordered extensive wheat-growing in those regions of the south-west, west and north-west where the rainfall is heavy. The unhappy results of such arbitrary misgovernment speak for themselves. Lastly, the representation on the Committees has only a tiny minority of yeomen and small farmers, still the predominant class numerically in the countryside. These are only a fraction of the evils of centralization.

In the capital, the House of Commons indulged in community-singing on behalf of the post-war export trade, the word "export" being chanted in the spirit of Owen Glendower calling up spirits from the vasty deep. "And will they come when you call," when

[1] "In recent years, it must be admitted, the democratic façade of local government has shown serious cracks . . . public apathy, the complexity of local government machinery, the development of local party politics, the pressure of extraneous interests and increasing intervention of Government departments have combined to lead . . . to control by agencies outside the elected representative or by Government departments and officials. This is a dangarous development."—*Interim Report of the Reconstruction Committee of Nalgo* (*National Association of Local Government Officers*).

neither foreigners nor Dominioners will be willing to import bulked foods as interest upon loans that no longer exist? Still less will they pay for manufactured goods that their own industries already make for themselves and can make in the future by using war-plant for peace purposes. Nevertheless, the cry went up for feeding the cockpit of "international trade" without the nation noticing that it had turned from a creditor into a debtor nation; still the wiseacres shook their heads over our cornfields and demanded the future imports of those cheap foods that had ruined so many millions acres of foreign soils.[1] Our own nation's health suffered with them, nearly half of it, by Sir John Orr's figures, being half-starved from malnutrition.[2] Thus, the policy of "international trade" profoundly affects the condition of the soil from which we receive our daily bread. Nobody who reads the evidence can doubt for a moment that the modern economic system is in process of converting the earth into a desert.[3]

But so far from combating this giant of all our evils, the tendency and pressure of the times are to increase its stature and magnify its ravages. The frantic power-farming of all the belligerents in the present war, together with such deliberate devastation as "scorched earth," the breaking of dams and the occupation of good land by military and industrial works, these, partly necessary, partly not, have yet further depleted the limited resources of the soil. The programmes of post-war policy pay scant heed to such warnings. The "backward" countries are to be improved and industrialized, while the progressive ones are to become still further parasitic by the organized reception of their produce and commodities. Vast areas of the earth's surface are to be set aside for specialised crop-production, the very factor that made a wilderness

[1] "In California the desert has advanced forty miles in a single year, destroying 2,500 farms. . . . The gravity of the problem of erosion is one that cannot be exaggerated, and it is one that is almost entirely neglected in all our fiscal controversies. Yet it does give the final answer to the doctrinaire free traders. . . . Most people know in their heart of hearts to-day that they are living on capital, but they conceal the truth from themselves, because they do not really mind, so long as things can last out their day. And such a mentality is inevitable . . . so long as you have a secularist generation that does not see any divine purpose in the scheme of things. 'The fear of the Lord is the beginning of wisdom.' "—Death of a Gentleman: The Letters of Robert Fossett. Ed. by Christopher Hollis (1943).

[2] It should be needless to point out that our export town-criers do not mean exports in exchange for oranges, tea, coffee, and other commodities we are unable to grow for ourselves.

[3] The book that is now a classic—Jacks' and Whyte's Rape of the Earth (1939)—is by no means the only authority to which I am referring.

of 250 million acres of the American Middle West. Mechanisation is to be speeded up; the combines are to be developed in the name of international trade and finance; airway systems to ramify hugely; mechanical transport to carry exports from ultima Thule to the Antipodes; fluid labour forces to be rushed from one Tower of Babel to another and the Golden Calf to be the standard for all.[1]

If this Faustian dream should be fulfilled, it will assuredly enjoy as brief a power and suffer as fearful a nemesis as that of the totalitarian nations whose downfall appears to have conveyed so easily scouted a warning. That downfall is a Cautionary Tale so plain that we heed it not. So we regard the prophecy of Nostradamus in the 16th century that our century would see " the greatest famine that has ever been" as mere magic-mongering. The nemesis of this export dream will be the sterility of the earth.[2] Some might call it the final punishment of the Creator for man's final disfigurement of the world. Not upon us perhaps but upon our children who reap what we have sown.

The dream may be put in the form of a fable. When Farmer Bull listened some five years ago to the fervent vows of marital fidelity his flighty town-wife gave him on her knees (" Oh, John, never, never again will I be unfaithful to you!"), his heart misgave him that her rich lover was hidden all the time in the cupboard. For that had been the trouble with John; the extravagances of his wife had made him a poor man, and that lover of hers, the wealthy merchant, could shower upon her the riches of the Indies, the Africas, the Americas. His wife had left him for twenty years to go gallivanting with this sparkish adventurer, left him in debt and desperation how to keep the wolf from the door. When she came running back to him, he could not help connecting all her protestations of undying truth with certain disastrous consequences that had befallen the commercial enterprises of her speculating

---

[1] The twisting of the Government pledge at the end of 1943 on the question of prices to cover costs of production and labour in farming is an ominous indication that the war-economy of self-support may once more, as in 1921, be abandoned.

[2] "Get every Chinese peasant using machinery to the same extent as the Middle West of America and you will have the result Colonel Elliot foresees." (From an article by Peter Cromwell in the August (1943) number of *Horizon*). What Colonel Elliot foresees "is the greatest exodus from the country into the towns that has ever been seen." This is regarded by the writer (who has evidently never heard of the Dust Bowl of the Middle West) as an ideal to be worked for. How then can one speak otherwise of the post-war super-power-policy than as an evil dream, an unholy enchantment ?

paramour. She was willing enough to be supported by her husband
in adversity (he could not help remembering the old saying about
when the devil was sick), but what was likely to happen if this
partner of hers managed to extricate himself from his embarrass-
ments? Nor had Honest John much reason to feel comfortable
in his mind and free from anxiety about the way things were
going after his wife had returned to him, even though he was
once more making a good living, not for himself but for her. She
had become very high-handed and exacting, not to mention im-
perious and shrewish; she interfered in his business and made
out that she could run it a great deal better than he could. The
poor man ceased to have any say at all in his own affairs. Worse,
from time to time he heard ominous rumours of what the merchant
was up to. Instead of cutting his cloth to suit his coat, learning
prudence from catastrophe and sobriety from the wreck of his
former fortunes, John heard that he was once again indulging
schemes and ambitions of economic cosmopolitan and international
trade on the vastest possible scale. Farmer Bull knew very well
what that would mean and how that would end. His wife would
once more be captivated by dreams of wealth and high living
and all his skill and industry would have gone for nothing. His
house yet again would be left empty and desolate. Worse still,
he knew that all these high-flying schemes were foredoomed to a
far more ruinous failure than before. He and his wife and the
merchant would all be involved in irretrievable calamity.

This tale does not end like one of Hogarth's—on the gallows—
but on the query—what will she do? There are many ominous
symptoms of a resuscitation of the pre-war spirit which A. G. Street
has described in *Hitler's Whistle* (1943): "There is one thing that
neither reformer nor politician will face—a home farming that pays
during peace. I have suggested it several times in certain places
where such people have been gathered together and every time there
was a sort of shocked silence and I felt as though I had made a rude
noise in church."

Meanwhile, I have another tale to tell which is not moral fiction
but actuality. I cannot bring the issue of health, nutrition and soil-
conservation in its relation to self-sufficiency better *home* to the
reader than by relating an experience that befell me in the Spring
of 1943. I took my wife to lunch at a London hotel-restaurant which
has always been regarded as one of the Fortunate Isles, the Tir Na

Nog, of metropolitans. We had three courses and, exclusive of tips but inclusive of coffee, a pint of lager for me and a cocktail for my wife, the bill was £1 5s. 6d. We began with some languorous, not to say drooping, *hors d'œuvres*, and I made a special point of the spring onions for which I have a relish. The odd thing about these onions was that I could only just taste them and what I have always valued spring onions for is the pungency of their flavour. So I let them lie and passed on to minced chicken with mashed potatoes and Brussels sprouts. But what really interested me were the sprouts, and what interested me about them was that I could not eat them. I left them on my plate. Now I really do know something about sprouts (and indeed potatoes) because I grow them. For the whole winter and early spring of this episode I had been eating them out of the garden, having just reached the stage when I leave the sprouts for the toppings. The reason I could not eat the sprouts in this metro-politan Mecca was because, like the onions and for the matter of that the potatoes, I could not taste them. They might have been anything but they were so large that my eye could not have deceived me that, though they seemed some kind of water-weed, sprouts they were. I am as certain as may be that, apart from the indifferent cooking and the distance they had travelled, they were raised on artificials, as were the onions. How else explain the enormous disparity between these expensive vegetables and my own? It was a difference as between chalk and cheese. The rest of the meal (apple flan and rice pudding) was a difference not so much in the food as the cooking. All I can say is that the cooking I get in my cottage-home from my own apples made this dish taste very small beer.

I looked round at my fellow-lunchers. What were their reactions? So far as I could gather, they were the reverse of mine. They were all people to whom food was no butterfly business, a flitting from dish to dish. They looked and they ate like good trenchermen. And yet they were clearly contented with the food they were eating. Indeed, many looked as though they had spent their whole lives with one goal and ambition before them—to amass the wherewithal to lunch or dine at this place. Poor things, they were much more frustrated than I felt at spending 26 shillings on food that was not intrinsically worth 26 pence.

I did not really grudge that £1 5s. 6d., since it enabled me to make a discovery of moment. That is not only that food grown on a healthy soil organically manured on the principle of the Indore Process is worth its weight in gold for nourishment as for enjoyment. I knew that already. It is more than that. Our de-countrified civilization is a material one; its science believes or believed in a mechanical universe; its "glittering prizes" are largely for the money-makers; it does not mind about ugliness and it has no culture worth speaking of. For a century it has been a civilization of £ s.d., the rest being trimmings. In my young days, the cartoonist, Will Dyson, used to personify this urban pseudo-culture as a gross person with a large belly. And this was the kind of food, obtained at a house of the highest status and *réclame*, that it put into that belly. What is the point of making a fortune if you can't be sure of a good meal? Thus, this urban civilization has defeated its own ends, which are material welfare, and surely good food is part of material welfare? Therefore, it is right to think that the cause of good food is spiritual as well as material. To become a self-supporting nation once more, growing our own food by the true husbandry that alone secures its goodness, would be a spiritual achievement. From the enormous wastage it would save it would be a highly economic one. But it is also the only way of getting food which is really fit to eat. Having lunched expensively as I did in this palace, I now realise that I, the country cottager, know more about the values of good food than those moneyed ones who think nothing of spending anything up to a pound note on their lunches. For I prefer fresh and good food that costs next to nothing to "cheap" imported or transported food that costs a small fortune.

I will not then be shy of thinking of a small garden in a large way as a makeweight against thinking in terms of large-scale industrial mass-production of cash-crops and of planting an astronomical number of cabbages in the shortest possible time. By the strange vicissitudes of our unstable modern world, a garden-plot has become a patriotic widow's mite. It should also be thought of in terms of a larger patriotism and a more fundamental security.

"How can the arts flourish," wrote Herder, "when the culture of the fields is neglected?" And again, "Agriculture is the basis of all higher life and culture." One out of many meanings of this is surely that to regard a garden as a balanced whole of many parts is in itself an art based upon nature; the gardener is taking nature one creative stage further. Thus to remake England as a garden is to "solve" the "problems" of nutrition, of economics, of work and of freedom all in one.

But it cannot be achieved until the weight of predatory self-interest is lifted from the small producer and the weight of arbitrary urban government is lifted from the country. The denial of self-management both for the individual holding and the country at large has resulted in the mismanagement of his affairs, of all country affairs, by a bureaucracy eager for power but incapable of wielding it. This is a bitter jest in every countryman's mouth. The blackcoat rules the fields of corn and grabs the goodness out of them, compelling the men of the land to work them his, not their, way, as he himself is compelled by his own fears. And he is farming out our fields.[1] The official nowadays *is* the farmer, the farmer proper his executant, and the farmer who has lost the free will to manage his own farm is a bad farmer.

Specimens of the idiom he uses in doing it: Here is an order of the Ministry of Food:—

"Compound means, (a) any cake, meal or mixture (other than a concentrate) which contains not less than four of the Feeding Stuffs specified in Part A of the First Schedule to this Order in proportion of not less than 5 per cent. each and which contains not less than $2\frac{1}{2}$ per cent of oil and 12 per cent of crude protein; provided that a different variety or quality or a different product or by-product (of whatever variety or quality) of the same Feeding Stuff so specified shall not for the purposes of this definition constitute another feeding stuff."

Or:—

"Where the oil content is more than 4%, the basic price shall be that applicable on a sale of meal the oil content of which is 3% to 4% less 5/- per ton for each 1% or part of 1% in excess of 4%."[2]

These are the people who annually pollute the rivers with millions upon millions of nitrogen, potash and phosphates in town-tips

[1] Or, as Mr. Street puts it in the book referred to above: "By 1944 there will be a vast acreage of almost bankrupt soil."

[2] A friend of mine, a County Court Judge, asked a witness his profession. "An averminizer." Having elucidated what this meant, he asked the witness what type of vermin-killing. "Deratization" said the rat-catcher.

which, if composted, might restore to the fields the fertility of which they are robbed wholesale.

One day, I received a striking example of the consequences of this bureaucratic-commercial domination of the country by the town, when carried to the extremity of nationalisation. An Australian farmer had come over to see the garden, and he told me that he had had a citrus fruit farm in a part of Victoria where the temperature reached 120 degrees in the shade, though shade there was next to none. Consequently, the irrigation of the fields had to be (1) according to the incidence of arid or humid conditions—five days of the former being more than enough to cause distress in some years, and (2)—the partial irrigation of certain parts of the farm according to the needs of the crop grown, some requiring more and some less water than other crops, and also to enable the livestock to be moved from the irrigated to the dry areas of the farm. The government, however, ordained that irrigation should take place once a fortnight, drought or flood, and that the whole of the land should be irrigated at one time. Thus, after rain, the irrigating waters would sour certain crops, while the cattle had to be hoisted up by belly-bands from the roofs of the cowsheds. The only way of circumventing this Laputan situation was simply by bribing the channel guard appointed to carry out the government orders to turn a blind eye when any farm needed to turn the water into the channels. The only way that government-owned land could be farmed at all was by breaking government law. He also gave me some details of soil-erosion in Australia from the removal of the original sward. He had seen fences between farm and farm completely hidden by the wind-blown earth-dust piled up on them.

Here is another example of the effects of this domination—this time by way of a contrast. I took a journey right across Hertfordshire to the Essex border at Bishop's Stortford. Having to give a lecture I was obliged to take what I deemed to be the quickest route from my home by way of the main road from Aylesbury and Tring through Berkhamsted, Hemel Hempstead, St. Albans, Hertford and Ware. Even with a knowledge of history no more comprehensive than "1066 and all that," one has but to mention these towns to realise that each of them possessed its own historic personality emanating from its topographical and architectural ones. Yet, had I not been aware of these schoolboy data and had I not caught rare glimpses of buildings that had clearly not been born yesterday, I should hardly have known that this string of towns had existed before 1850. A fair sprinkling of noble buildings remains, such as the red-brick tower of St. Albans' Cathedral. But they have become like an archipelago of islets in a stormy sea. What is more, I should hardly have known that each one had a name at all, so obliterated has been all distinction between one and another. The only one that had any identity left was Hertford: the glorious pargeting on the town hall and the charity figures in the niches and on the gate-piers of the old Bluecoat School had nothing to do with the age of progress. For the rest, the whole journey was an almost continuous stain of Cobbett's big and little wens (and Cobbett made this self-same journey in 1823), partly Victorian, partly suburban and partly industrial, without a single redeeming feature among the lot. The identities of all these famous places had been blotted out. I might as well have been in hell as Hertfordshire for all I knew where I was. What is the point of a place if you don't know where you are? Why Hertfordshire? Why not X20ZB51? Why not call all our modern towns by figures and numerals instead of names, as we do our chemicals and arterial roads?

Yet Hertfordshire is a real county, "happy, homely Hertfordshire," as once she was called. I proved it on the way back. Lanes and byways took me through a county called Hertfordshire. Here in hideling Hertfordshire was yeoman Hertfordshire. Half at least as once she was. You cannot mistake where the yeoman has been; his freehold character is stamped on every brick, flint, beam, stone and tile of his wheaten Hertfordshire home. But you do not detect it by uniformity. In fact, you have only to look at the cottages, bartons and farmsteads to know what the rock is under the road and that this part of Hertfordshire is near Essex and that part near the Chilterns. Exquisitely these farm-buildings and hamlets register whether they are in the Valley of the Gade, of the Lea or of the Ash. Strong and warm are their individualities from the very act of loyalty and deference to the materials of their own particular region. As the landscape changes, so they change. The great silvery towers of Totternhoe stone and the thin timber panels of the brick-cum-flint cottages belong to the west as idiomatically as the needle spires and white weatherboarding belong to the east.

There are many noble manors in Hertfordshire. But it is preeminently the country of the small man and the yeoman in history was always the leader of the small man. The very landscape of little hills and little valleys seems shaped by God for the independent, liberty-loving, small propertied craftsman and husbandman. Once the backbone of England. This is why Hertfordshire looks more like a *garden* than any other county. The difference between the Hertfordshire towns and the Hertfordshire countryside is the difference between a co-operative social organism under the Christian law that brought out the best in man and a lawless competitive social organization that has brought out the worst. The one is built on the sand, the other was built on the rock. So the one will go and the other will return.

What could have caused this violent disruption from a seemly and diverse local architecture to an unseemly and imported one ? Obviously, the invasion and suppression of self-sufficiency. Now the whole meaning of self-sufficiency, whether in a town or a village, or in a voluntary hospital as opposed to a regimented public one, or on a farm or in a garden lies in the exercise of individual choice and responsibility on the part of persons or community. It seems, then, that once this self-acting organism is mutilated or destroyed, beauty, variety and initiative disappear.

A very good example of what I believe to be a self-evident truth occurs in the up-to-date issue of the building of agricultural labourers' cottages.[1] Why is it that I have never yet seen a modern cottage in the country which does not insult its natural surroundings, except on a private estate where it is nearly always built of local materials? Why are the official designs for such cottages almost invariably wrong in spacing and proportion? The reason is the affront to self-sufficiency. Nobody, that is to say, has ever dreamed of consulting the one person who might be presumed to know best what sort of a cottage he wants, namely the agricultural labourer for whom the cottages are built. We have got so far away from self-sufficiency that it never occurs to us how astonishing it is that something so fundamental as a house should be built without any reference at all to the wishes or occupation of the person who is to live in it.

Not only so, but when those wishes are interpreted, they are

[1] Another is forestry which, as a State Department instead of the business of farmer and landowner, consists mainly of blocks of regimented spruces encroaching on hill sheep-farming.

contrary to what has been or is being or is proposed to be done. Is there any labourer in the land who likes to live on concrete floors? If then houses are so built, it is to please the commercial interests in concrete, not him. And what do labourers want with flat roofs? To grow begonias and pelargoniums in boxes and have cocktail parties on warm summer evenings? If there is one thing quite certain that he does want, it is an "outshut" or annexe or some kind of roomy accommodation for the storage of tools, vegetables, fruit, boot-wear and a dozen other necessities and conveniences of the outdoor life and of his wife who does her own services. One has only to take a glance at any average village to see that the traditional cottage very rarely fails to do so. Again, the modern idea of building in the country is to bring the outside into the inside of the house instead of keeping it outside. Hence the green-house effect, the sun-traps, the skylights and all the dodges for pre-tending you are outside when you are really inside. But, unlike the townsman who never gets even his feet wet, the labourer spends his whole workaday life out of doors. So he likes his home to be indoors; he likes warmth, snugness, draughtlessness and solid walls to keep wind and weather out. How often does he get them? Thus it is not only beauty that breaks down when self-sufficiency with its concomitants of personal choice and functional fitness are abandoned.

There are other things that happen. One is the needless compli-cation and over-elaboration of essentially simple issues. If a Rural Council proposes to build a cottage, it must consult the assistant land commissioner, the district valuer, the senior regional officer, the allocation officer and the W.A.E.C., each through a spate of form-filling. Six ministries must each have a finger in the pie. Yet the needs of housing for workers on the land are as plain as daylight: a reasonable rent paid for out of adequate wages, the provision of garden space enough to enable the labourer to grow his own vegetables, some fruit and flowers to make the environment pleasant, a house that will satisfy his particular requirements with-out paining the sight of an outsider with reasonable taste. Yet a government arrogating to itself more and more autocratic and totalitarian powers cannot and does not fulfil any of these primary conditions. Imagine the outcry if it were proposed to revive the Elizabethan law that every labourer's cottage should have four acres of land! Apart from the problems of wages and rents not being fairly solved, the whole affair of labourers' cottages has been tangled up in miles of red tape, beset by fantastic and elephantine regulations, burdened with the chaotic clash of authorities and departments, vitiated by the intrusion of commercial interests. The houses actually built have been at a preposterous cost (£900, for instance) and even the men who knew how to build them (the small country builder's men) have been either removed to the big firms or transferred to other jobs. The squires hardly ever build truly regional cottages nowadays because urban policy has been, and is, to render them too poor to do so. The only fruitful sugges-tion in all this waste of time, money, debate and action was that made by a well-known farmer. Being constructive, it brought the issue halfway back to self-sufficiency. It was that, instead of building 10,000 new cottages, 100,000 old ones should be reconditioned. But this would not do at all, because such cottages have always been considered the prerogative of the townsman.

The fact that he has so monopolised them is sufficient evidence that the labourer would in a reconditioned cottage obtain a real house with certain convenient additions and improvements to it. Quite apart from this partial solution, it is a truism that no cottages worthy both of English country and the English land-worker can be built until the natural materials the region provides are once more utilised. They will not be so built partly because to do so would imply a measure of decentralization and partly because too many interests stand in the way.[1]

Since this wrong relation between town and country has been carried to such extremity, it is hard indeed for the modern age to see that the way of truth and social health is its reverse. Still more difficult is it to overthrow the idea, peculiar to an urban civilization, that a culture based on the fields (regarded as a garden, not as a factory-plant) is necessarily barbarous, static and what Dr. Johnson would call "unidea'd." There is a passage in Christopher Dawson's *Progress and Religion* which is richly pertinent to this illusion. The greater the artist, the more does he project himself

---

[1] A letter in *The Times* of August 20th, 1943, described the building of a cottage of chalk-cob and wetted wheat-straw. The gravel, sand, flints (for the plinth) and the crushed chalk for the walls "were all quarried on the site within a few paces of the house." The cost was 4s. 6d. a yard as compared with 12s. 3d. at the current cost of brick. The cottage has already stood for 23 years without any repairs: "it is warm in winter, cool in summer and charming in appearance." Lastly, none of the builders had had any previous experience in the use of chalk. Yet the watchwords of the modern economics that deny self-sufficiency are "cheapness" and "efficiency."

into his material "and the more completely does his work conform itself to the qualities of the medium in which it is embodied." So with cultures: the richer their development, the more intimate the co-operation between man and nature.

> "Indeed, in the higher cultures, the factor of regional differentiation often asserts itself more fully than in the lower ones. . . . For though the domestication of plants and animals renders man in a sense more independent of nature, it also establishes a new bond of union between them."

He illustrates the olive as the nurse of the Hellenic culture, the date palm of Babylonia, the wine and olive of the Mediterranean, the rice and mulberry of China, the coco-nut and taro of the Pacific Islands, and the maize and tobacco of Central America. The mediæval cathedrals (I may add) were built up on the peasant-craftsman complex. Shakespeare and the whole brilliant inflorescence of the 17th century up to the Puritan Revolution were rooted in the virility, the independence and the freehold cultivation of the yeoman.

This penetrating mind carries the issue yet further:—

> "The strength of the Hellenic culture rested on a regional and agrarian basis. . . . The typical Greek who fought at Marathon was not the sophist not the Levantine trader but . . . the rough Acharnian peasant or the no less rural Dorian noble."

But the Greeks ceased to be an agricultural people, the country was depopulated, the land was cultivated by slave labour (corresponding with our machines) and

> "the vivid and highly differentiated life of the regional city-state based on the land passed away into a formless cosmopolitan society with no roots in the past and no contact with a particular region."

The writer might be describing modern civilization, rather than the prime cause for the downfall of Hellas. If we regard excess urbanism as inevitable and needing only the organising of "social services" to correct its abuses, if we cherish the illusion that the machinery of modern industry and economics only needs patching up and speeding up and improving, if again the only controversy is to be whether after the war the land shall go to the devil or the factory go to the land, it seems that the fate of Hellas and the fate of Rome will be ours also. Therefore I hold fast to the garden philosophy and garden practice I have tried to outline. It maintains in however rudimentary form our English tradition against all the storms that beat upon it. But it is also a guide and prophecy, when their violence shall have subsided, of what is to be.

CHAPTER NINE

NO PLACE LIKE HOME

" As the manufacturing nations of West Europe are meeting with steadily growing difficulties in selling their manufactured goods abroad, and getting food in exchange, they will be compelled to grow their food at home, they will be forced to rely on home consumers for their manufactures, and on home producers for their food. And the sooner they do so the better."

KROPOTKIN, *Fields, Factories and Workshops* (1899).

"Desperate to relieve her unemployment, Holland put thousands of men to work planting wheat on lands reclaimed from the Zuyder Zee. But when these new fields began to bear, more wheat was harvested than the market could absorb. What to do? Devote the surplus to the poor and let them turn it into bread? No, that would wreck the current price of wheat. So instead the surplus was dumped in Denmark, where there was a demand for cheap hog-fodder. But no sooner was that done than a new problem arose. The Danish pigs, having no respect for economics, took advantage of their improved diet to grow inordinately fat and fecund. Before long Denmark found herself with more pigs on her lands than could possibly be sold at a profit? What to do? Bring the price of pigs so low that even the poorest might have bacon for breakfast? Certainly not! That would ruin the established market. So instead the pork was turned into fertilizer to spread on the new wheat-fields that had been reclaimed in the Zuyder Zee."

LEWIS BROWNE, *Something Went Wrong* (1943).

THROUGHOUT this book I have in spirit never for a single moment left my own garden. How comes it then that for many pages it is not so much as mentioned? For the good reason that the many things that have preoccupied me and ostensibly lie outside its boundaries are one and all implied in it. Whither they lead I have no alternative but to follow. The smaller the garden, the greater the issues involved in it. The two most important of these issues have taken shape in the beauty-use and work-play principles. That in its turn is seen to depend on the principle of self-sufficiency. In this chapter, I shall carry the latter a little further by illustrating some of its possibilities from my own oblique experience. With these will appear their contrasts so that both may be seen in clear opposition to one another.

In my county, I know personally but one other man who has
the same interest as I have in what are called bygones, or makes
use of them as I do, namely by bringing them up to date. He is
the agent or manager of the Verney Estate, and he has furnished his
whole cottage with them. Everything in his house has been procured by looking for it himself, mostly at farm-sales in Lincolnshire. When I visit him, I see fine 17th and 18th century yew arm-
chairs, a Regency chest-of-drawers of fruit-wood with bronze
instead of brass handles and poker-work between them and on the
cornice for which he paid 7/6, an Empire sofa for which he paid
2/6, a great elm-bowl in which he keeps his quinces and not dissimilar from my oaken one, apple bowls, Worcester china, Windsor
chairs for which he paid 1/6 the set and recaned himself. Every
stick of furniture, his bedspread, the pictures on the wall, all are
bygones. The link between us is yet closer, for his carved butter-
stamp, a vertical wheel ornamented with corn-sheaves and attached
to a two-pronged wooden handle, is now one of *my* bygones. The
very clothes on his back are home-made. The linen was woven
from his own flax and the tweed from his own sheep. The overcoat
he had worn for thirty years looked as good as new. He made one
reflect that the modern system of supplying massed populations
with cheap devitalised foods, cheap synthetic medicines and cheap
clothing as ephemeral as the houses they live in is more expensive
and impractical than any the world has ever seen.

The relation of this man to his environment was the most
ecological [1] I had ever encountered. His lath-and-plaster cottage in
a village mentioned in Domesday Book was as perfectly adapted
to its natural setting as the furniture to the house and he, the apex
of the pyramid, to all. Nowhere was there an alien note. This wholeness was carried through into the very meals he ate and thoughts
he spoke. I linger in memory over those meals I have partaken
with him. For teas we sometimes had sugar-beet-chutney sand-
wiches with compost-grown celery. Every mouthful had a double
value, its own and that of the beautiful stuffs and ware, integral
with the fields outside the window, round which and from which
we ate it. For lunch we would always eat off the estate, straight
from the flat Swedish cooking stove. I became acquainted with
some of the varieties of cottage dishes from home-bred pig with
home-grown vegetables as described by Walter Rose in *Good Neigh-*

[1] Ecology is the organic relation of living things to their environment.

bours. In summer we would finish a large bowl of strawberries inundated with cream from the Guernseys; in winter, a quince tart, the pastry made from the home-cured lard of the home-pig or from a mixture of home-cultivated wheat, oats and barley. The quinces from the cottage garden in chunks of a mahogany brown tasted like the finest preserves. What with the cream and all, I would after these princely-peasant meals gently resist his intention of taking me a tour of the estate. We have got out of the way of taking cream. When it is poured out on one's plate out of a full pint-pot (with more to follow), the afternoon should be devoted to rest.

The health and variety of the fruit and vegetables growing in his garden and the feats accomplished with cuttings were a constant wonder to me. It all seemed the work of a magician. In summer, it was as clean as a new pin; in autumn, covered with weeds—for green manuring. The cuttings were of every variety of fruit-tree, bush and shrub, the fruit-bushes bearing when only some inches high. Apples clustered like onions round a stick on apple-saplings without any lateral branches. He told me he always used to make these new gardens out of old or derelict ones wherever he had lived and usually left them to take up a new job just when they began to reward his loving husbandry. But he never minded about that. After all, he said, look what our forefathers have left us!

After one of these meals, we would, instead of seeing self-sufficiency in action outside the house, discuss it inside. The first time I took one of these rare traditional meals off his kitchen table, I remember noticing a hand-mill with a great wheel screwed to another table. For this agent is not to be caught napping by the gods of big business. Let them get on with their games, is his idea, but let me get on with the job of running the estate as it should be run. Yes, said I, "but what about when they interfere with you?" "That's why I fixed up the hand-mill," he said. My host is a very simple man—that is the point about him. He is not impressed with a thing because it is big, and covers vast distances. Nor because its dividend percentages run into two or three figures. He is so simple that he believes an ounce of quality to be more than worth a pound of quantity.

Sitting round his log-fire in winter or in his cottage garden in summer, we would talk business. After the hand-mill, we naturally began with bread, that burning question, what Isaiah called "the stay and the staff, the whole stay of bread," but what nowadays might be called a broken reed. My host had to sell the wheat off the estate at 14/- a cwt. It then goes off to the big roller mills at Hull, Cardiff, Liverpool, or other "wen." By extremely devious ways (devious not only in the sense of travel but what is done with it), it returns where it came from as flour and is bought back as flour at 2/2 per 7 lbs. Possibly, if bought by the cwt., it might be got at 28/-, that is to say, at exactly double the price it was sold. Now if this corn off the estate had been ground by a mill *on* the estate or in the neighbourhood, it would have cost 16/6, 14/- for the corn and 2/6 for grinding, while the whole of the costs of transport would have been saved.

But that is by no means the whole of the story. The corn returns as flour not only at double the price but half the value. The simple reason is that, between leaving and returning, it has been deprived of the wheat-germ, containing ten vitamins. In war-time it has had 25% foreign wheat added to it (so that the risk and expense of ocean transport has to be super-added); it has had milk powder mixed with it and calcium naturally present in vegetables artificially added to it. Its weight has been increased by something like 10% of water. Lastly, the foreign wheat in it is reaped out of exploited soils whose low yield has been yearly forced by heavy druggings of artificial manures. Yet this shadow of the substance of the bread of life is a better thing than pre-war bread, even though the flour goes bad unless baked at once. This was nothing more than chemically bleached starch or, as it has been called, "blotting-paper bread," and was, probably enough, one of the causes for the decline of the birth-rate.

Not only is this peculiar system called economics but it is even regarded as "inevitable." It is part of "the march of progress," as though the stars had ordained that modern Englishmen should eat bread with the life taken out of it or the wheat from the fields was lost in the bread on the plate by the workings of natural law. Moreover, those who work out these simple sums are regarded as romantics, cranks, laudators of past times and interferers with the clock. They are even called the dangerous fomenters of "economic aggression." But perhaps these derogatory terms are applied because, if this kind of simple arithmetic were to become at all prevalent, it would interfere with something else beside clocks. Twenty six thousand country mills have not been put out of action for nothing.

I told my host about the Californian experiment in Paul de Kuif's *Why Keep them Alive?* Two groups of children were divided into Alphas, fed on wheat-germ flour and Betas, fed on "white bread" for a period of three months. As might have been predicted, the Alphas gained so heavily in weight over the Betas that the story might have lacked edge. But the contestants had duplicated the experiment by each group keeping white rats on the same dietetic principles as their own. The results upon the Beta rats proved so acid a parable to the Beta children that they refused to continue as control patients any longer. The two groups amalgamated under the sign of what might be called Alpha of the Plough.[1]

The agent capped this with an incident that had occurred while he was managing an estate near Guildford. Some children rejected from school for anaemia and general debility were sent him. When he saw them, he feared they would die on his hands. A year later, the children having been fed on home-grown food in the meantime, he took them a week's pilgrimage along the Harroway and by other green roads to Glastonbury. They took no luggage except what would go into their pockets and a spare shirt. From the time of setting forth to their arrival, they walked 35 miles a day and on the last day wanted to explore the Glastonbury country after the daily quota was done. I would not have believed this tallish story but for my own experience by diligent searchings out of the incredible feats of endurance and hardship performed by the old countrymen who lived on innocent foods.

How had the rot set in? Nothing but an examination of the whole modern system of economic parasitism can reveal that. But I communicated to my host what I had gleaned of the actual process of disintegration from a letter about a region in Ireland. There was a water-mill every three miles in which wheat and barley were ground and oats crushed. The loaves were baked in the farm-kitchens, some of the mills removing the coarser bran. Then the millers began making white flour in the bigger towns. It was less trouble to buy a sack of flour than to cart the corn to the

[1] He told me of a local baker who had a prosperous family business from the excellence of his bread baked in a brick oven. Both his sons were taken from him and he was forced to sell his business to the "Co-op." The new business selling a bread very differently baked had no difficulty at all in finding labour for distribution.

mill. So the farmers ceased to grow wheat, since the millers only bought local grain when the price was low. The bakers in the towns sent white loaves into the country and the farmers bought them now and again, then more, then exclusively. As no bread-baking was done, no buttermilk was needed; all the milk went to the creamery and household butter was bought. As the creameries worked only in summer, the farmers adopted summer dairying and grew fewer oats and roots for winter keep. Less tillage meant fewer horses. The journey to the creamery was for bringing imported maize to feed stock, while the barley, no longer ground, was sold to the brewer. The brewers' demands fell and less barley was grown. Meanwhile, the country mills had ceased to function and fell to ruin. When bread and butter-making ceased, the household milking was done by a hired worker and the girls in the family went to jobs in the town. Only Mary was left and when it did not pay to keep her only to look after the chickens, Mary went and then the chickens. At the beginning of the war, farming there was keeping a number of cows for summer milking and raising young stock on grass. The population that should have been producing food and consuming farm products had emigrated. This was what I meant when I said in Chapter Five that, when the country millers were forced out of business by the combine underselling them, the linch-pin fell out of the rural structure. It can be restored by cultivating the principles underlying and overlying the cultivation of a garden and by no other way.

We gourmets had many such post-prandial talks. Gourmets we are, since made-up delicacies with high sauces and fillips to the palate are but the decadence of food. When you eat real food, you are taking in not only the food but the landscape out of the window and the sun that ripened it and the rain that invigorated it and the air it living breathed and the husbandry that fostered it and the creative power of the earth that developed its vitality. My host had lived up all his life to his ideas of going straight to the heart of things, more than I have ever been able to do. Consequently, there was something about him which made you believe in him. A strange, long-faced, bearded man of austerity and realism, a man who followed what he called the "golden rule." Nor do I idealise him; he is the French peasant-leader rather than the English, and once farmed his strips in a French commune. Perhaps that is why his attitude to birds is repugnant to me; it overcomes his profoundly religious sense and short-circuits, I think, the comprehensiveness of his husbandry. But as the gardener who farms or the farmer who gardens, he is a prince among men, the prince of the peasants. Since the future of England depends not upon her industrial super-structure which is "the primrose path to the everlasting bonfire," but on her agricultural foundations, he is a man of consequence.

In the very midst of the great depression between the twenties and forties, he ran a farm of 120 acres in Monmouthshire. It not only was wholly self-supporting in feeding stuffs for the cattle and in food for 30 people, but actually exported its surpluses. It made 160 lbs of butter every week. The community made about 50 per cent. of its own clothes, spinning and weaving being done on its home-farm and the wool coming from its flocks. It consisted of half a dozen different nationalities, and one of the families was that of a Russian landowner who gave his lands to the peasants and, under my friend, did his own farming. During this same period he also kept an old inn near Tattershall Castle in Lincoln-shire. It was derelict when he bought it and a free house. The object of a tied house is simply to sell drink of a particular brand. He reconditioned the house, filled it with good furniture and made it into a kind of guest-house that became celebrated all over the county. He set up an exhibition of bygones and a private theatre with acoustics that would carry a whisper from one end to another. As a farmer, he was accustomed to train his pigs and bulls by simple association of devices, so that, when he moved them, they would come to his whistle and follow him. Just before the present war he was about to become manager of one of the hotels of the Trans-atlantique Co. in Algeria. These hotels were built in the oases of traditional local materials in an enlargement of the regional style and became entirely self-supporting.

He once told me of his discovery of the Golden Age—a valley of the Dordogne near Sarlat. The châteaux, none of which post-date the 14th century and are built of the local limestone, are mostly empty because the seigneurs could never get any of the local popula-tion to work for them. Why should they? There was no economic urge to do so. They lived in an Eden-like land where the temperate met the sub-tropical zones and the walnut met the vine. The people were almost wholly self-supporting. They imported only coffee and sugar and grew the best tobacco in Europe. You would see

among these small farmers some 14 or 15 in one small field, each
ploughing his ox-team. Why so many? Out of neighbourliness.
A solitary ploughman would be lonely, and so they made the
business of ploughing a communal pleasure. Communal loaves
were made from a common bake-oven on the village green. There
were three *vins du pays*, and the people made their own brandy. It
was, of course, the great goose country and the meals were cooked
in goose fat, than which no other could be richer. The loathly
practice of fattening the livers of geese for *paté de foie gras* produced the only exportable article. The serpent of commercialism
had crawled even into this dateless demi-Eden, or, as it should be
called, Lotus Land. So, in our own country, the tradition of the
barnyard fowl ambling and foraging about the yards, was bas-
tardised by modern economics into the heartless captivity of the
battery system. Our ancestors were often cruel, but they rarely
made a business of cruelty for profit.

So responsive the earth, so kindly its fruits, so traditionally
and faithfully performed the rule of the return of all wastes to the
land, that the community supported itself with little toil. The only
trafficking was conducted once a year in a small market town.
Thither a man would take one bullock to sell. The affair was settled
just before déjeuner, and the afternoon was whiled away by bar-
gaining for the halter. The day's work-amusement over, he returned
to his fields. So these peasants have lived for six centuries, un-
changed, undisturbed, unheeded, "the world forgetting, by the
world forgot."

Indeed, they grew soft with the very abundance a self-sufficient
husbandry had brought. It is hard to eat a daily meal in which all
would partake of three kinds of wine followed by brandy (I remember to this day my own lunch at Les Eyzies for two francs
thirty years ago) without a certain drowiness of spirit and laxness
of body. Thus they fleeted the time carelessly as they did in the
golden world, caring nothing for the glittering prizes of the external
world and knowing better how to live than the most luxurious
of millionaires. This peasant community ransacked no world-
resources but gently husbanded its own. One of the greatest villainies
of the most villainous of all modern governments has been to
transfer the "man-power" of the French peasants to its own industrial hells. This Satanic application of the "fluidity of labour"
will make the name of Germany execrated for centuries, and justly

so. For these peasants were a living witness to the truth of Cobbett's words:—

> "Agriculture when it is thrown into a number of hands becomes the life of industry, the source of plenty and the fountain of riches to a country; but if grasped into a few hands, it must dishearten the bulk of mankind, who are reduced to labour for others instead of themselves, must lessen the produce and greatly tend to general poverty."

The reply of the Basques to the revolutionaries is forgotten to-day: "*Ici, tous les gens sont propriétaires.*"

He told me too of a farming family in Sweden where the house and every single object in it except the books—furniture, silver, table-ware, carpets, picture-frames, glass, china—had been built and made by the large family that lived in it. He spoke of the summer shielings in Sweden when the milkmaids take the cows up the mountains and at evening summon them with great conches across the upland miles. I in turn told him of those in the Western Isles, now in ruins. I spoke of those heroes, Sir Alexander MacEwen, Dr. Fraser Darling, Compton Mackenzie and J. L. Campbell, Laird of Canna, who have fought for the restoration of co-operative self-government for the crofters. Of the old man, Seonardh Coinbeul, who could neither read nor write and carried 4500 lines of his own bardic composition in his head, together with all manner of songs and stories. Of the "clearances" there and John McCulloch, a utilitarian doctrinaire, who brought them about and (to quote Mr. Mackenzie) "could not see a community of peasant cultivators without thinking how much more profit could be got out of the land if their holdings were thrown together and given over to a single farmer." Of the misery and degradation he and his like were responsible for in evictions, rural depopulation, slums and the destruction of all values that found themselves in the way of commercial enterprise.

Progress, that ambiguous term, likes to think of such bad old days as obsolete. What if, in polite and modern terms, it magnifies them? I told him of the new Act for the electrification of the Highlands. Precisely the same mentality has been at work on this Act as transformed the small property-owners of the Isle of Barra into a landless proletariat,[1] and drove this McCulloch with his

[1] See *The Book of Barra* by J. L. Campbell and Compton Mackenzie.

demonic energy to lay waste large tracts of the Western Isles. There were two alternatives considered by the Committee. According to one,

> "any attempt to introduce modern industries and industrial methods was foredoomed to failure, for the Highlander could not and should not be separated from his croft or his boat, however meagre the existence which they were capable of yielding. The limited constructive proposal was that, while the Highlander must be left to his croft, an effort might be made to ameliorate that lot by cheap electricity for lighting and heating crofts, attracting summer visitors and assisting in the working of light home industries and crafts."

This proposition was as obviously reasonable, desirable and capable of fulfilment as any simple measure for helping honest and worthy cultivators to help themselves. When the crofters of Lewis were confronted with Lord Leverhulme's schemes, they replied:—

> "No, better houses may mean higher rates, and higher rates would mean we could not afford to work the croft and the boat which support us now, and we would have to work in the factory and obey the call of a whistle every morning. We prefer our way of life."

That way of life would have been alleviated without being dislocated by the first alternative for the Highland crofters.

It was rejected by the Committee as "quite impracticable." The Committee favoured the other alternative that "the one acid test of the validity of any electrical project was the promise it held out of attracting new industries." These were set out as 12 major industries of electro-chemical and electro-metallurgical enterprise, together with the construction of dams and reservoirs and power-stations to employ 10,000 men and roads, transport and housing estates to employ 10,000 more. If any land in any part of North Scotland is coveted by the Board, the owner is given 28 days' notice to quit. A poor little squeaking brat called the "Amenity Committee" was only permitted to raise a puling cry after a particular site had been selected for these enormous works. The Central Electricity Board, the Electricity Commissioners and the Secretary for Scotland would then combine to sit on its head. For to shift the site would involve the loss of 10% extra cost, and what is 90% in the cost to the beauty of the countryside compared with that?

The Act for the industrialisation of the Highlands can and will have no other effect than that of pushing new Birminghams into the one piece of extensive wildness, the land of the croft and the clan, still left in Britain. McCulloch's "clearances" in the Western Isles will but take a new form. For once the modern attitude to the land and its people became urban and predatory, repudiation of it could mark the only change. Lacking such change, industrialism could but become excess industrialism. It will end, as unreality must, in catastrophic failure. But in the meantime the noble Highlands will be ravaged. The cardinal error of modern industrialism is that it has proved incapable of understanding the nature of man. The Christian idea of him as sinful and imperfect because "fallen" but capable of redemption, sensible of eternal values and creative because the child of God, fits the facts of history and individual life. Under its governance, the pointless progress of modern industrialism would have been impossible.

What can exorcise the spirit of McCulloch from hag-riding the world of the immediate future? Only the tragic consequences of its efforts to distort the true nature of man from its twin polarities, heaven and earth. Man now drifts like a feather in the void between them. Thus, no plans for the post-war world can but lead to chaos until industrialism is subordinated to agriculture, machinery to craftsmanship, and money to things.

I ponder these things as I go my morning round over the garden in the winter of the year. Just as a world of life is hidden beneath the dark and unrevealing sod, so a world of implications touching the destiny of nations lies behind the Voltairean maxim of cultivating a garden. All my journeys, my experiences, my conversations with the estate agent appear to lead back to it. I am never more in my garden than when I am away from it.

Because he is himself a kind of peasant-leader, my friend has the peasant attitude to the land. In many ways he is more French than English. We once had a discussion as to how far a nation's economy should be regional and how far national. His view was that roads, drainage, electric and water supply and wayside trees were a national concern. He told me how he had once tried and failed to induce the Government to plant fruit-trees—cherry, walnut,

pear, plum and apple—along the highways of Britain. Trees of
quadruple purpose, for their fruit, for their beauty, for their wood
in furniture-making and other craftsmanly trades and for firewood.
Apple-wood, for instance, was once used for making the teeth of
the windmill wheel and the very hard pear-wood had the share
attached to it in the old wooden ploughs. Compared with other
countries, our own is uncommonly poor in fruit-tress.[1]   But the
authorities would have none of it on the plea that the fruit would
be stolen. Thereby they insinuated that in contradistinction with,
say, France, we are a nation of thieves, at any rate in all counties
except Kent, where nobody steals the strawberries that run up to
the sides of the roads.

    This proposal of his, which he spent three years in maturing,
reveals his French propensities. Yet to me his stewardship of the
Verney Estate demonstrates a reknitting of the continuity between
the old England and the new. In 1653, 21 cows were kept by 11
families in one small hamlet on the estate. To-day, not a single
cottager there keeps one. Sir Ralph Verney had a personal knowledge of all the farmers and their families; he knew the qualities
of all his "wain-men"; he wrote a memorandum on "How to
relieve Claydon Poor," pensioned them and instructed his steward,
John Roaden, to find them work. He paid apprenticeship fees and
formed a co-operative cow-club. The cows were bought by subscription and remained its property, the numbers being increased
as the funds of the club allowed. He carefully planted his park
and orchard—"cherry stock will be two shillings by the hundred,
gathered out of the woods; but any better and bigger ones from
the gardens will be from three pens to twelve pens a pece.   The
holly setts price are eighteen pens the hundred." He was sent
grafts of good apples for cider, 800 abeles were sent from Flanders,
together with limes or "lindeboomes," and some of these are still
standing. There was a nursery of young trees on the estate whose
seeds were carefully saved. Alders were planted in the wet places
of the woods. In July, the new trees were constantly watered,
"especially the Lime trees in the Garden, and those in the whitening
yard, and lett a loade of water be conveyed to the Wallnutt trees in
Barley yard." The brickyard was kept busy in this stoneless region
and the "Brick pavements" were fetched with a team of six oxen,
500 to a load. The brickmaker was paid 6/- a thousand for making

    [1] In the thirties, 10,000 walnut trees were wantonly felled.

and burning bricks, 1/- a quarter for burning lime and 5/- a
hundred for making and burning "pavements." He sent young
trees—mountain ash, called "Quickenbury"—from the nursery to
Charles II., who had them planted in Greenwich Park.

But Sir Ralph Verney, though a loving husband to his estate,
was not going against the stream of his times, like this modern
agent of the Verney family. 17th century Memoirs of the county
gentry are full of such self-sufficient husbandry. The intimate
connection between house and garden, still-room and herbarium
is seen in Robert Graves's *Wife to Mr. Milton,* which faithfully
delineates the manners and customs of a country estate. It produced its own essences, liqueurs, cosmetics, syllabubs, possets, conserves, cordials and medicines. It brewed its own home-made
wines, mead, metheglin and spiced frumenty. The smaller Jacobean
or Carolean manor house, rich in bartons and more farm-like than
manorial, reflected the husbandry of self-maintenance. Capability
Brown substituted the "sham natural" for the sham ruins and
architectural ornament of the generation immediately preceding
his own, and Kent made the old gardens of the Jacobean and Stuart
manors, like that of Sir William Temple at Moor Park, seem "barbarous." But the formal parterre, the bowling green and pleached
alley, the turfed walk and clipped hedge of the 17th century never
interfered with the husbandry of self-support realistically applied
to the garden-estate as a whole. How deeply this first principle
was implanted may be gathered from Evelyn's recommendation
that young Englishwomen should grow mulberry trees to cut
out the silkworm imports from France and the East. The Georgian-
Palladian mansion definitely broke with this tradition and so
looks like an imported government building. It does not
look in the least like a farm that belongs to its own neighbourhood.

From this alienation was born the system which compelled a
farmer-friend of mine to grow potatoes on land unsuited to them,
forbad him to sell them to the aerodrome near by, ordered him to
transport them to a town ten miles away and then had them returned
to this farmer's village to be sold to the aerodrome. I am not
drawing a long bow, therefore, in binding together the Highland
Development Act with the peasants of the Dordogne, Sir Ralph
Verney in 1653 with the Verney Agent in 1943 and one and all
with my own garden. For these things

"near and far
Hiddenly
To each other linkèd are."

Indeed it is the dearest ambition of my friend, the agent, to rebuild the Verney Estate as a post-war self-sufficiency community. Thus, it would not be helplessly dependent on Wales for roofs, Bradford for cloth, Liverpool for bread, Nottingham for leather, Burton for beer, the Argentine for meat, Canada for apples, Czecho-Slovakia for shoes, Denmark for bacon, Peterborough for bricks and Imperial Chemicals for manures. It would produce, manufacture, fashion, process, grow, cultivate and prepare all these things for itself at half the cost and double the quality. For the division between a distributed autonomy and a propertyless parasitism is incomparably more real and profound than that between Socialism and Capitalism. This division has ceased to be anything more than a camouflage to conceal an almost identity of interests. That is why my friend cannot get the sanction of authority to build even a single cottage for his houseless land-workers out of the materials on the estate and at no cost of transport or manufacture. Authority is for interests, not needs.

Part Three

CHAPTER TEN

THE WAY HOME

"A limited liability company has no conscience. . . . The urge of enlightened selfishness begat plutocracy, plutocracy begat the monstrous materialistic and pagan tyrannies we are now fighting to destroy. It was England that at first unconsciously led the world into this morass. It is England—wisest and greatest of the nations—that has to discover the way out."

ARTHUR BRYANT, *English Saga*.

THERE has necessarily been a tragic element in the pages preceding this chapter. But is not our period, now given over wholly to destruction, one of the most tragic in the history of the world, more tragic even than that of the fall of the Roman Empire? But from that fall, a new light rose upon the shattered world; new growths seeking the sun of a new day sprang up from the ruin and litter of the old world. Are any such to be discovered in the darkness of our own age? They are not to be so discovered as in the fourth and fifth centuries A.D. because they are scattered and there is no puissant new Faith to unite them. The new realistic spirit in the Forces and a re-interpretation of that Faith, stressing its Doctrine of Creation, are not my business here. I can only give a few of such intimations from my own experience and so far as they are related to this garden book. But I find them full of promise.

In my Hermitage hangs up a great yew bow which is the frame of a Windsor armchair. Within it is a "strick" of dressed flax, the self-same material from which the woodman's wife made his smock. It is seldom nowadays that the opportunity presents itself of re-visiting those parts of my native land that have more fragrant memories for me than others. When this manna does drop at my feet from the empty skies of circumstance, I make the most of it. Not so much for the sake of dwelling in the memorial spirit upon the old familiar faces of hill and vale but by contrasting this recovery of old loves with what I feel now. My former explorations of the Wiltshire Downs were partly archæological, partly topographical, partly architectural and partly in search of stray evidences of our lost rural culture. There was therefore a strong nostalgic and historical element in them. But when I once more set my eyes on the round barrows of Overton Hill and looked across the rich Pewsey Vale to the long sweep of the scarp of Salisbury Plain from the summit of Oare Hill, I realised that the old self had given place to a new self.

But I was happy to know that the continuity between them had not been broken. Rather I felt that the old preoccupations had been fused and distilled into a new perspective. It was more generalised and less concerned with the complexities of detail than with a few broad principles both of man's relation to the earth and that something more than the earth which the mediæval philosophers called the natural law. These principles can more or less be boiled down to one—the principle of beauty-in-use and use-in-beauty. I venture to think that these can be still further reduced to a single term, that of quality. For quality, as I have needfully repeated several times throughout this work, is an attribute both of beauty and use, the true bridge that unites them. Before it was broken down, all the native cultures which left their imprint on the Wiltshire Downs obeyed this tripartite principle. Fashions, periods, ideas, economies, attitudes changed, but this trinity no more than the Downs themselves. It had behind it the eternal validity of the natural law and, so long as man did obey it, he was always in harmonious relation with his natural environment.

So, in revisiting those Downs, I no longer bothered to distinguish one age or civilization from another. I saw them all as different aspects of this triple binding force. I had forgotten a good deal of what I knew in the old days, but I had this trinity firmly embedded in my consciousness. Its incarnations, variations and interpretations are endless both on the face of Wiltshire nature and in the works of Wiltshire man. But three examples of its application, as being more definite and direct, fixed themselves upon my mind. One was an old red-brick wall built in a succession of inward and outward curves round a kitchen-garden at Market Lavington. The design, I gathered, was to prevent fruit-trees trained along the bastion-like projections from touching the wall and so being accessible to insects. The flowing curves that gave the wall such individuality and beauty of line were only incidentally for beauty's sake; their purpose was to protect the garden from exposure and the fruit-trees from the

.predator. The second example was the celebrated Market Hall at Malmesbury. This most lovely and sumptuous monument of an integrated art and religion was nothing more nor less than a local stock exchange, so long as the word "stock" be relieved of its modern debasement.

The third example was the High Street of Marlborough, that generous street of a small town whose spaciousness is so companionable with its downland setting. Smitten with the consciousness of Victorian chaos, our inferiority complex is loud with planning programmes. But Marlborough, built by men who had never heard of planning on paper and punctuated by a church at each end of its noble high street, is a perfect example of the planned market-town. The roomy residences, workshops and public buildings of the old russet-red town are, a great many of them, hung with fish-tail tiling, a local character much commoner in southeastern England than at the axle-tree of the Marlborough Downs. By thus drawing upon the gault in its neighbourhood, the sturdy little chalk town adds to the comfortable utility of its houses the touch of grace that transforms it.

I have maintained in the earlier pages of the book that this beauty-and-use principle is closely bound up with self-sufficiency and self-sufficiency comes from belonging to the land. Nearly a thousand years ago, King Athelstan granted small holdings to the citizens of Malmesbury in perpetuity. He was a wise king; he understood that the way to make people love the place where they lived was to attach them to it. It is when you look at Wiltshire from this angle of belongingness that you notice things that never appear in the guide books. I have, for instance, never read a single word in any Wiltshire book about the variations in the style and materials used in those five chalk valleys whose rivers converge on Salisbury. This, of course, is the true meaning of Salisbury; it is the meeting place of the waters and this is what gives the great spire its peculiar significance. It is not only an arm lifted to heaven but holding the reins of those five rivers. The cottages and farmsteads built along the sides of these valleys adapt themselves both to their contours and their rocks, each cluster of villages in each valley according to its own particular interpretation. Their natural diversity is thus exquisitely caught up and translated into terms of building. Yet these variations are in degree not in kind and there is considerable overlapping. This is because each river valley belongs

to Salisbury Plain and Salisbury Spire draws them together into one
transcendant unity.

There is an abundance, for instance, of thatched and tiled walls
in the Upper Avon Valley as far as Upavon and Rushall; in the
Wylie Valley they are few, but there is an extraordinary proliferation
in reed-thatching. I have never read a single mention of this local
reed-thatching, though, combined with chequer-work of freestone
panels and "flush-work" flint ones, it is the identification mark of
the whole valley. These soft mole-coloured thatches, whose material
the river supplies a few yards away, add a crown of beauty to the
natural loveliness of the valley. Each valley, in fact, where it has
not been ruined by the sprawl of modern standardisation, is the most
delicate register of its own special geology. Use, beauty and self-
sufficiency are inseparable.

Thus, if the modern age is the same everywhere, it is because it
belongs nowhere. Only in acknowledging our attachment to earth
and accepting the limitations gently imposed by it, can variety and
independence flourish and create beauty. Only thus can the variety
of man respond to the variety of nature, as Wiltshiremen once
responded to Wiltshire. In abandoning this sense of place, the
modern age has lost itself. Homelessness is what has happened to
us, and so we think in terms of mere size and mere distance.

I did not go into Wiltshire for a sentimental journey but to find
out something about the flax industry recovered[1] since the war. One
of its stations, employing 200 workers and processing the crops of
from 2000 to 3000 acres scattered over a wide area, is in North
Wiltshire. First of all, the fields of flax had themselves to be seen
and of these, thanks to the good offices of the Director, my friend
the great farmer and husbandman who has filled other pages in this
book, I saw many. It would have meant little to me if I had seen
the mill without the fields or, for the matter of that, the fields
without the mill *in their neighbourhood*. It is only in and through
their organic inter-relation that use and beauty can find their union.

Flax is the most aristocratic of all our home-grown crops. This
applies alike to its manifold utility and to its special qualities as to

[1] The growing of flax in England was as early as her Neolithic colonization in 2000
B.C. The fibre was spun with bone spindle-whorls and carded with bone or wood weaving
combs. In Tudor times, small acreages of flax and hemp were grown everywhere and spun
and woven in the farmhouses during the winter evenings. The "stamping bill" was used
for beating out the flax-seed to make linseed and oil.

its highly decorative appearances in the field, in stook and in stack (especially when the stem of the stack is well-sprung), in the various stages of the processing and finally in bale. It is the best of nursery crops for a seeds mixture and is only three months in the field. And one of these special qualities is shared by no other plant of which I have knowledge. The fibre, being cellulose (compounded, that is to say, of hydrogen, oxygen and carbon) obtains its substance entirely from the air, the sun and the moisture in the ground. It thus takes no minerals nor plant-foods from the soil. Even the soil-druggists give it only potash. Linen, as the Director said to me, is nothing but "converted air," so that flax can be indefinitely cropped without "mining" the soil. When burned, the straw leaves no ash. Only the seed borrows from the soil and that is partly oil, also formed from the air. In the double meaning of goodness linseed is to cattle exactly what butter is to us. The seeds, being fed to cattle, return to the soil what they have taken from it—unless all the milk is sent to London and so the potash and phosphates are through modern sanitation lost in the sea.

The utilities and qualities of flax are faithfully reflected in what it looks like. Flax is a supreme example of beauty in use and use in beauty. It is entirely without the bluey sheen of oats, and I was baffled in conveying any impression of its subtle and softly toned colouring. But I suddenly remembered a line of Coleridge describing a certain effect of sunset which Byron scoffed at as fanciful. Yet Coleridge in the line "And its peculiar tint of yellow-green" was accurately recording an uncommon but recurring colour-type of sunset. This is seen in English landscape only in the field of flax just before flowering. It is a colour of soft pastel refinement and delicacy. The yellow-green light is subdued and the texture so silky, when the crop is growing evenly from the proper distribution of moisture after harrowing, that only by borrowing from the skies can it be described at all. The grace of line in the bent heads, a little fuller than that of the fritillary and absent from garden flax, contributes to a flawless memory of tone-value like none other in our England of the water-colourists. Later, other glories appear when the field is of a fragile elusive blue and in the Baling Room where the bundles or "pockets" are piled to be sent to Belfast for the spinning. The colour then might be called old gold but it is too soft for any mental. Or it might be compared with certain effects of Van Gogh, but they again are too hard. The glow and lustre the bales give out are a kind of life-colour, and indeed this "life" is a definite indication for testing the quality of the fibre. I wondered no more in seeing it that such a fibre could make such linen as that of my smock. The "gold" colour also appears in the field when, after 100 days between seeding and pulling, the crop is ripe for the harvest. The seed bolls are then the colour of old tiles.

Is there another crop of English earth which in the final count has such a multiplicity of uses? Uses from the finest cambric handkerchief of the long weft flax which takes fifty miles to the lb. of fibre to the rich oil that fats the cattle. I dwell upon this aristocratic quality of the field of flax for a reason the very reverse of "picturesque." Its singular beauty and the elect nature of the plant have consequences in the string of elaborate processes as practical as they well could be. Its virtue not only communicates itself to the workers in all stages of its preparation from field to yarn, but actually compels upon them a high standard of workmanship. Except at the cost of the fabric, this can never be evaded by mere mechanization. Wholly mechanize the flax industry and that virtue is withdrawn. There is an accumulation of tow, poor fibre-production and enormous wastage. The quality of the plant conditions a responsive craftsmanship in its handling and conversion by the worker. These extend in a long chain from harvesting to the bundles of dressed flax made ready for the spinner. The crop is first pulled (not cut) by hand or machine, hand-pulling being the much superior method. It is then loosely put up into sheaves, carried after drying, stacked and deseeded. The seed either for re-sowing or cattle-feed is separated from the chaff which is itself a fodder. After that, it is tank-, dam- or dew-retted and "gaited," "chapelled," "coned" or "steepled" in the field to be dried by the winds and bleached by the sun, ending its field-adventures by being hand-tied into closer sheaves. The factory processing begins by deseeding and, after the handling to which I shall refer later, is broken or scutched into the green or retted flax, the "shive" or skin being burned or, as should be, returned to the land.

At this mill, the "shive" is used as a top-dressing in the little gardens under the mill-walls. The tomato plants grown in it were of superlative excellence and productivity. I discovered they were so at another mill where the shives were the only dressing. Yet laboratory analysis declares the shive to be of no nutritive value for plants. Is nature wrong or science ? Has science, with its formula of nitrogen, potash, phosphates, fitted a pair of blinkers on itself that prevents it looking to the right hand or the left ?

Besides the green flax there is the tow or short flax, either green or retted (the same word as rotted), and this is used for various fabrics. After the scutching, the sheaf of flax becomes a "strick" that can easily be held in the palm of the hand where it is dressed and evened by the fingers of the other hand. After dressing, it is sorted, twisted and piled into "pockets" or "kindles" or bundles which are taken to the flax store for final grading. Here weathered or damaged flax is removed and the finer separated from the coarser fibres. This requires a very sensitive touch and keenness of eye. Lastly, the processed flax is baled for transport into Ireland or Scotland for spinning, the markings on the bales indicating the grades and types. The green flax or flax scutched from the green straw as opposed to retted flax is mainly used for parachute harness. It has nothing like the exquisite texture, buoyancy and creamy-gold colour of the dressed and retted flax. Beside this Brunhild's hair would have seemed coarse.

There is a primary factor to be noticed about this series of chapters which begins and closes the development of crop into bale. The first is the integration between field and workshop. It is enforced by the curious similarity in handling and motion between the hand-chapelling or steepling out in the fields and the hand-dressing in the mill. Of old, of course, all was done by hand, as it used to be up to quite recently in Belgium and Ireland. A buyer of the best quality flax all over Europe, whom I met on one of my subsequent visits, told me that Belgian flax was incomparably finer fifty years ago than what it is now. This he attributed partly to the mechanization of the industry, partly to the neglect in returning all wastes to the fields. This buyer, a very astute, experienced man of business, with an unrivalled knowledge of flax both in the United Kingdom and on the Continent, was uncompromisingly in favour of hand-work in all the processes of growing and manipulating flax.

But I am speaking of the mass-production of flax for war-needs and in mechanical conditions. Not even in the most machine-made Utopia of the modern planner can flax ever be victimized to the automatism that has already been the fate of its sister, wheat. Only a limited mechanization can be applied to it. Only up to a point can the crop from the field be severed from all association between field and factory. The officials have, of course, tried to do it ; but they have failed. In all the other flax-mills over which my friend has no control (he has three in all), conveyor belts have now been installed between deseeding and dressing and grading the crop. These include "opening up the beats" ("beat" is an East Anglian term for the flax-sheaf), levelling up the straws into parallel lines and evening the butts, before passing through the breakers and entering the scutching machine where the "shive" is removed. They all require skilled hand-manipulation, as I have seen for myself. The conveyor belt does these jobs so cursorily and maladroitly that there is enormous wastage. But in the mill on the North Wiltshire Downs, there is no conveyor belt. Under the guidance of my friend, the Director, I paid many memorable visits to it.

It was certainly the oddest kind of factory; the people in it moved in a leisurely fashion; they conversed as at a social gathering; they remained individuals; there was nothing automatic in their actions; no hurry; no regimentation and no clock. The whole place seemed rather a number of workshops blended into one than that modern Church of Industry whose altar is the assembly line. One of the reasons for this is doubtless because the workers are nearly all local men and women from the neighbouring villages. But it is not the only reason. The key to the whole was the Scutching Room. Here, at the end of the scutching machines, ran a line of Belgian hand-scutching timber wheels—Belgium being the country where peasant flax-craftsmanship produced fibre of the highest possible quality before the recent introduction of turbine scutching machines. With this difference, that a small motor had been attached at the end of the line to set the wheels in motion and a small electric power-plant to carry off up a shaft the dust which impairs the health and chokes the nostrils of the hand-workers in Belgium and Ireland.

I regard these two very modest and unobtrusive mechanical appliances as of the utmost importance. In the first place, they did not encroach to the smallest extent upon the free display of the hand-skills—and scutching by hand is a highly skilled operation. On the contrary, they may be said to have furthered them. They relieved the workers of the toil of setting the wheels in motion and of the discomfort of breathing in the fine dust. Secondly, the electric motor was noiseless, the petrol one almost so, while the electricity was generated from local resources. Lastly, there have been analogies to this local use of electric power elsewhere. The one working mill left on the stream at Belbroughton, where scythes are still made (see my *Men of Earth*), generates electricity to this day, though the water is hardly more than a trickle. A friend tells me that the miller of Church Minshull in Derbyshire used one wheel for grinding and the other for generating power *for the village*, and exactly the same device was adopted by the mill on the Kennet at Kintbury near Hungerford. This supplied both meal and current to the whole village. This true economy and proper adaptation of modern knowledge to human needs were killed by the grid system, and the villagers now pay just double what they did when the miller generated their electricity.

My friend wisely suggests that both local charcoal and wood shavings could be used for small gas engines where water power was not available. When the Bill for the electrification of the Highlands was being drafted (see pp. 233-5), an alternative proposal was submitted to the Committee which reported on the Bill. It suggested the use of local power for local needs as proved so successful and economical at Church Minshull and Kintbury and is so in the Devizes Flax Mill. It was turned down as "impracticable," that is to say, as displeasing to the industrialists. All private generating stations operated by water power with a rating exceeding 50 kilowatts were forbidden to be established.

But I have no doubt at all that the problem of mastering and adapting modern machinery to the service of mankind in general and to the purpose of fostering the revival of local communities in particular could be entirely solved by exploring and developing this principle of the small machine operating, where possible, by local power. Otherwise, the machine exercises a dangerous and deleterious influence both upon human health and psychology. The most obvious example of the first are the highly elaborate steel roller mills at the big ports. Their cunning and ingenuity are directed towards one end, the separation of the wheat-germ and the "offals" from the grain. A supremely delicate mechanism of man's inventive genius operates to effect a national malnutrition. The example of Denmark demonstrates a reverse effect. During the blockade of 1914-1918, the meatless Danes enforced the use of the whole of the wheat grain in their bread. The death-rate as a result was lowered from 12.5 per 1000 to 10.4. Here is the clearest possible evidence of a complex machinery operating to the detriment of human need and vitality.

The adverse effect of the machine upon human psychology is seen at its most obvious in its frustration of the normal human skill-interest and pleasure-interest in work no longer done by man but the machine. This directly encourages the violent outbreaks characteristic of our times. It encourages a depreciation of character, will and hard work, as exemplified in the following quotation from Sir John Russell which bristles with fallacies: "It is no longer sound policy to do work by hand that can more speedily be done by machine. . . . The young people of the countryside do not want it and they generally prefer getting a tractor and letting the machine do the work, rather than doing it themselves." It also stimulates all manner of acquisitive cravings. Take, for instance, a wholly mechanized farm. The tendency of such a farm is always towards monoculture and larger units, and one reason for this is that a machine is "uneconomic" unless it is always kept running. It can only be kept continuously running by covering greater and greater areas of ground. So the tenant or owner of a farm of 150 acres will want 200, and will never be content with his own but that he must have more than his own. This is utterly contrary to the spirit of garden or holding cultivated by manual labour. Here the tendency is exactly the reverse, to make the most of the holding as it is rather than extend it into a larger one. Mechanization has thus come to mean the antithesis of content.

But encouragement of the acquisitive itch is not perhaps the most momentous effect of mechanization. In the *Times Literary Supplement* of August 21, 1943, this sentence occurred in an article about prisoners of war: "He is delivered from the disgraceful sin of being bored, and begins to cultivate his garden." I heard of a yeoman-farmer the other day who at the age of 81 was still doing eight hours a day on his farm and spending his leisure in bicycling off to see the local craftsmen on farm business. Sodden harvest fields, carrying corn not worth the trouble because the home-market was in ruins—these were all in the day's work for this yeoman during those years of hopelessness and the invasion of the thistle between the two Great Wars. But what he could not stand was taking a holiday. His work was his pleasure but leisure with no work was his purgatory. Through every adversity artificially imposed by the urban dictatorship and with only a week's holiday in seven years, he had delivered himself "from the disgraceful sin of being bored" and had found his salvation in cultivating his farm as a garden.

I have yet to meet a bored countryman. Worried, yes, anxious,

continually persecuted by ignorant officials, overworked, even
despairing, bitterly cynical about the future, even resolved to leave
the land because of bad conditions if he is a labourer, of insecurity
if he is a farmer, of crushing taxation if he is a good squire. But
boredom is not a word that can be found in the true countryman's
dictionary. Why? Because except on the most highly mechanized
farms all countrymen follow ill or well Voltaire's maxim of cultivating their gardens. They take, that is to say, pleasure in and exert
skill on their jobs. But when, say, 90 per cent of modern workers
have been deprived by the machine of skill and interest and pleasure
in their daily work, they are suffering from the disgraceful sin of
being bored. This explains at once why, when they are released
from the boredom of their daily work, they depend upon the
mechanical hedonism of being amused by others. But it does not
release them from the disgraceful sin of being bored. This is the
nemesis of modern urban civilization which has all but killed rural
England: it is delivered over to the disgraceful sin of being bored.

From this digression I return to the hand-wheels. I saw the girls
scutching the flax upon them and noticed something which gave me
the clue not only to what kind of factory this was but to the
philosophy of life underlying its operations. This was nothing more
than a peculiar swing and curve of the arm when the strick of flax
was applied to the ends of the wooden lathes attached to the wheels.
Some of the girls were doing their scutching better than others and
one was doing it superbly. I could not but link this in my mind's
eye with two things I had already seen—the curve of the flax-heads
in the field and a magnificent round stack in the factory yard,
beautifully sprung[1] and crowned with a finial at its apex. Actually,
this was the work of one of the best thatchers in Wiltshire whom
the Director had procured. Even in spreading the flax to feed the
scutching machine a craftsmanly grace and dexterity are necessary.

But the culmination of this strange and beautiful affinity between
the way the flax grew in the fields and the way the girls were
handling it was when I saw two girls dressing the flax. One of them
was the champion at the hand-scutching. I do not pretend to be
able to give an impression of this carding of the tresses of the flax
between the fingers. The looser gossamer-like strands are teased out,
and there is a peculiar turn of the wrist and toss of the arm when
they rejoin the cascade of lustrous flax fibre flowing from the other

[1] A well-sprung rick has a base shorter than the eaves and sloping walls.

hand. The levelling and evening are done by a caressing motion of the fingers. All I can say is that the action or series of actions was like a figure on a Greek vase. *Noblesse oblige:* the flax itself ordained this art and the genius of the Director had transformed the factory to a gallery where girls made gestures as in a sculpture or painting, and quality and skill were the final arbiters. The essence of machine-work is that each motion is the same and invariably repetitive. But in the hand-scutching and dressing there is a hierarchy of skill and the greater the skill, the finer the grace. The machine was but the base of the pyramid and the workers who prepared the fibre were conditioned by the nature of the material in which they worked. "The art itself is nature." This is the actuality of every artistic process, whether the example be Michael Angelo working his stone or these girls working the flax. It is almost superfluous to add that this factory has turned out some of the finest flax in England.

The seal was set upon this remarkable experience of a factory in process of redemption, the "Deformed Transformed," by what I witnessed the next day. This was the gaited, steepled or chapelled (from the French *capellier*) flax being turned to dry and bleach by the factory girls up on the high downs whither it is taken from the retting tanks. For the wise Director, being a husbandman himself, is fully aware of the organic need for the correlation between field and workshop. He gets the workers out into the fields as often as he can, not only for their *health* but the *wholeness* (the same word) of this essentially country industry.[1] The steepled flax is set up in parallel lines of sheaves or "beats" (see p. 246), exactly as in the cornfields with the difference of the superior elegance of each steeple. The stem or column is very slender and is maintained in its upright position by the butt being spread out fanwise in a wide skirting. The object of this is to "cure" the flax with sun and air, exactly as a side of bacon is cured in the smoke of the hearth. The chapelling takes a couple of days and then, after tying, the beats or sheaves are "barted" or stooked for a fortnight, if the weather is favourable, to complete the curing. The "barts" are made twenty feet long and hollow both in latitude and longitude. Both barting and steepling are works of art. Never does this superior plant ever fail to look the aristocrat it is. When the beats are seen in long aisles of parallel piers resting on these circular plinths of its own straw on the summit of windy downs that look from the great bluffs of Oare and Martinsell

[1] He is also trying to get the horses back.

north-west to the purple oolite ranges between Chippenham and Malmesbury and south again to the dim cloudy escarpment of Salisbury Plain, it would seem that our English earth has nothing to show more fair.

But something more there is. That is the girls moving between the aisles in bright tops and dungarees and turning each steeple so that wind and sun can reach the straw. The action has all the elements of ritualism and must be performed *just so*. Their foreman (like the "leader" or "lord" of the old sicklemen or scythemen) achieved this inevitableness with the casual easy command of the true craftsman. The steeple is bent over the knee, the skirting shaken out and deftly turned and a stem twisted round the top of the steeple before he passes on to the next. So little more there was to do—a slight formalising of the scene, a closer pattern—and I might have been looking at a complete Calvert picture, like "The Cider Feast" and "Sheep Shearing." In these the workers are celebrants and the task is a form of worship. I could not have believed that I should in this age have ever witnessed a canvas of timeless social husbandry like this. For true husbandry is immemorial by its very nature, because it is a fulfilment of the natural law. To trample on it, to deride it as we have done is but an invitation to catastrophe.

What the Director of this flax-mill is doing is nothing less than bridging the great gap in the continuity between past and present. He has begun to restore that pattern and interplay between man and the earth which are indispensable to the vitality and indeed the survival of the social organism. To apply the ideas and methods of industrialism to farming and the industries that are interlinked with it is necessarily destructive of all pattern and rhythm and so of quality. The magnitude of what is being achieved in the flax-industry of North Wiltshire may be partly measured from the fact that this mill is as bound to mass-production as any other. The urgent demand for the fabrics of flax to meet the insatiable requisites of war prevent the development of a true organic local industry that might well be a variant in modern terms of the mediæval and Tudor weaving industries in the cathedral and market towns of a self-sufficient past. He has in addition to cope with the ignorance which the violent break with our rural past effected by the Industrial Revolution entails. Nor is that ignorance by any means dispelled by the fact that all agricultural and rural operations are controlled and managed by the urban bureaucracy.

These impediments have been accepted and are being moulded, so far as circumstances will allow, to something much more far-sighted than the temporary expedient of mass-production. He has been able to avoid the conveyor belt because his concentration on quality has saved the wastage it causes and so increased the *quantity* over and above that of the mechanized mills. With the conviction that all genuine husbandry and craftsmanship are an art like any other, the Director is using the means to his hand, the very machines themselves, to build up a hierarchy of function of which mechanical work shall be the basis and the hand-skills the ultimate purpose. He regards the machinery as a scaffolding to this exalted end, a scaffolding that he may one day be able to cut down to its minimum.

This is surely the beginning of man's mastery over the machine, without which no civilization can or deserves to survive. It means putting the machine in its right place[1] as the servant both of humanity and craftsmanship. To attempt to abolish the machine (even if it were desirable) is as Utopian as the paper-paradises of the mechanists. In the present condition of society, in which mass-production, cheapness and profit have submerged the older principle of use-and-beauty, the true task of the future is the conquest, not of nature, which is impossible in the goal and disastrous in the attempt, but of the machine which has been used as the instrument of that conquest. The Director of the Flax Mill has perceived that the flax-plant itself is a means to this end, because it insists upon quality in its growing and cultivation and quality in its manipulation through the workshop.

The function of the machine is to be ancillary to craftsmanship, just as the best of the Lincolnshire farmers use the tractor as supplementary to horses. Captain Wilson of the celebrated Surfleet Estate in Lincolnshire has recorded the improvement of crops from horse ploughing. On the other hand, the strain on horses of pulling farm machines is much heavier than it used to be when mowing and reaping were done by hand, and machinery needs to be available at certain times to enable the small man to master his multiple culti-

---

[1] The following event illustrates to what lengths of absurdity standardisation is carried by the bureaucracy. A Flax By-Products Department was established and one of these was numbered "weed-seeds." A mill was ordered to send a sample; it proved to be charlock. Arrangements were made to dispose of it to a merchant. All the mills (there are 17) were then ordered to send in their weed-seeds by the ton. They proved, of course, to be all different, according to the region whence they came. The result was chaos, since the Department had expected nothing but charlock. Thus ended the attempt to standardise the diversity of English soils.

vations. Again, Mr. F. Sykes's invention of a mechanical Muck-Shifting Grab (made by Ransomes and Rapier) for handling compost and farmyard manure, is a first-rate example of the machine conferring benefit and saving drudgery. Thus, the machine needs to be used in the right place, at the right time and in the right way.[1] It is when the machine encroaches upon the domain of the craftsman that its social and industrial repercussions become hostile to human welfare. It is when the purely quantitative assessment is broken down and the machine subserves the higher functions of a recovered pattern of life and work that the age of cheapness will be superseded by the age of quality. In so doing, the Mill on the Downs has achieved the quantity denied to the others. Aiming at quantity alone, they have missed not only what they did not seek but what they did.

The idealists of the nineteenth century applauded the introduction of the machine into industry as a means of eliminating drudgery. Our own century, made wiser by experience, has come to see, at any rate in glimpses, that uncontrolled mechanization imposes a drudgery of its own worse than the most toilsome of former hand-labours. That is because it frustrates the natural skill-hunger of the normal worker. But in this sense these earlier idealists were right. It is the proper business of the machine to reduce the element of drudgery in all work. But drudgery ceases to be so when skill and so interest enter into the work. They were unable to foresee that the actual effect of the machine would be to destroy the skill and interest-value, not the drudgery.

That this is true has been unconsciously recognized by the workers themselves in this flax-mill. They have come to choose and aim at the hand-skill over the automatic labour. With such wholeheartedness that they actually preferred to come and listen to me talking to them on a Saturday evening about the marriage between work and play to the cinema, the wireless, or the week-end party. Something of what I have been writing in this book I told to them, and the welcome it received from staff and workers alike was richly indicative. That ready reception of ideas foreign enough to those in modern industrial currency proved to me that the ground was ready for the seed. For this mill is rather a large family than a

[1] A perfect example of man's control of the machine and of its adjustment to husbandry is the mechanical hand-plough, "Trusty," used by Dr. Frazer Darling on the Isle of Tanera, as described in *Island Farm*, that absorbing account of the fusion between man of science and peasant.

small factory. The spirit in it, inspired by the Director and his staff, is one of happy co-operation for a common purpose. Each worker feels it to be his or her purpose, because he and she take pleasure in their work, exert skill upon it and control a material that will allow no liberties to be taken with it. And the girls sing at their work; there is no wireless to deprive them of their own voices and vulgarise the songs. The Mill is, in fact, a living witness to the truth that, when a system is in tune with the social and craftsmanly faculties of the normal human being, it produces good people no less than good workmanship.

If this principle of skilled workmanship were applied to all industries connected with agriculture, and the economic one of the fair price was to be firmly established, it would not be long before the flow of the tide from the workshop to the factory and from the country to the town would be reversed. Here is a life-work worthy the noblest traditions of our country—to harness the machine in the interests of a rural culture of the future in which quality will reunite use with beauty.

In what I saw of the flax-fields and the flax-mill, this goal of a self-supporting regional ruralism, duly adapted to its natural environment, is already in the making. It is possible to see the end in the means adopted to reach it. To what extent a local peasantry can be rebuilt by part-time work in the mill; how far there could be a local distribution of the products and a local spinning industry to take the dressed flax;[1] whether or no the workers themselves could ultimately have a stake not only in the land but the mill—these possibilities lie in the future, perhaps very far off in it. But the foundations of these great matters are being laid and continuity with the past is being recovered by deflecting modern means to that end. The future is with "autarky," to use the modern jargon for self-sufficiency, plan the economists and financiers what they will. Development upon these or similar lines is the only way to achieve it.

Thus was the continuity between my own former journeys into Wiltshire preserved by my latest journey into a new world. In my own past I was wholly preoccupied with the evidences of past cultures. Now I was concerning myself with what is building on the worn surface of her ancient Downs. So too, when I see the flax

---

[1] There is one flax-farm-mill in Northern Ireland where linen dresses of the first quality are made on the spot. My friend, the Director, is resolved to do the same when the occasion offers. When I last left Wiltshire he was already planning a weaving workshop. May the joy be mine of being present at its inauguration!

hanging from the yew bow in my Hermitage, memory of the past and hope for what is to come are made one. They are enhanced by the thought that in an infinitesimal way I have contributed to the great experiment in Wiltshire. On two of my visits to the Mill, I gave addresses to the mill-workers. A sentence I used—"Take care of the quality and the quantity will take care of itself"—has now been inscribed in the Baling Room. It has been literally fulfilled. Both in quality *and* quantity, this mill has, I repeat, beaten all the others, but only because it has put the first first. "His present," as Hardy said of the old countryman, "is futurity."

CHAPTER ELEVEN

FOUNDATIONS OF THE FUTURE

"For the few hours of Life alloted me
Give me Great God but Bread and Libertie."
ABRAHAM COWLEY, *On Libertie.*

IN this chapter, I shall relate other of my experiences which seem to me to point towards a happier and more stable future and come within the scope of my interpretation of a garden. These experiences may be considered as corollary to the story of the Mill on the Downs.

Among my more recent and memorial bygones is a basket from Langport. I mention it partly because it has only just become a bygone and partly because it brings to me a message not of melancholy but of hope.

Langport was once a port indeed when the barges loaded with merchandise came up the Parrett from Bridgwater Bay. It was up to yesterday the centre of the basket-making industry whose withies were extensively grown and still are on the great fen of Sedgemoor at the feet of the little town. But for the basket-makers, Sedgemoor might well be Beddoes's "fern (far away and long ago) wilderness forlorn." The eye becomes aware of yet another distinction possessed by this ancient village-town; an historical-religious one. Langport lies nearly half-way between Athelney and Muchelney Abbey. Glastonbury Tor can in some weathers be picked out on the northern horizon from the high ground whence the main street descends in a thin wavering line to sink into the fen at its base. On the summit of the steep hill where the town so felicitously begins at an archway supporting the "hanging chapel," stands all along this plateau a cluster of the celebrated high towers of Somerset. Langport Tower is one, Huish Episcopi a quarter of a mile away another, Long Sutton a mile or two, further east a third. Still further, the landscape is studded with yet others of these celestial towers—Kingsbury Episcopi, Muchelney, South Petherton and Martock. These towers, with their likes at Evercreech, Bruton and elsewhere, are all of the fifteenth century and all of one noble family. Each might well have been built by the same guild of Somerset masons and, whatever their diversity of form, they have certain characteristics in common. They are lofty, richly decorated, perfect in proportion, very solid and yet of an aerial grace and poise that even the great towers of Northants and the eastern Fens cannot rival. One other beauty they share. The local genius of their building is matched by the brilliant precision of their siting. Huish besides is sumptuously ornamented with quatrefoils, string courses, canopies, pinnacles and supporting crocketed spirelets. How great, then, the honour of Langport that its portals should be a pair of these towers! Here we walk in the Holy Land of Somerset.

The little town is not unworthy of the honour. It is graciously sited itself. As it drops down the steep in elastic curves to the marshes where the Parrett joins the Yeo, stone alleyways and court-yards are lateral twigs to the main stem. They are paved and some-time have flights of steps, one such side-pocket being dominated when I saw it by a single giant sunflower. The main street itself is full of local mannerisms and individualities—stone walls with copings of thin slabs, many hipped roofs, house-walls of rosy brick, a local white stone and the terra-cotta stone of the Upper Lias. There are windows each with a miniature keystone, minute shops of the saddler, the basket-maker and others, long low brick buildings where the withies were copper-boiled, dried and bundled. From the neat churchyard on the crest or cliff, the great scarp of the Upper Lias across the Parrett extends in a generous horseshoe from the rich wheat-lands of South Petherton (reputed the most fertile land in England), by way of Yeovil, Wincanton and Castle Cary to Bruton; from the Street of the Basket-Makers at the foot of the hill I looked back to see the twin fretted towers ghostly white against black breakers of clouds riven by livid lightning. Langport is a town of strong personal identity, homely and friendly and yet a little foreign-looking, as befitted its once traffic with the Bristol Channel. So its country. What more individual waterland than Sedgemoor[1] and its rhines, while on the high land to the east there is a special thatching technique for the ricks, the ridge-pole being rolled and gracefully projecting at the gable-ends.

Yet Langport is dead, because the continuity between the grower and the maker has been broken, and the dealer who only sells the withies has come between them. I bought one of the last of the

[1] One of the most notorious robberies of a Private Enclosure Act was engineered in 1775 by George Selwyn, St. John, Lord Webster and Lord Stavardale as a means for quitting Stavardale of his gambling debts. It was Sedgemoor.

T.P.E.   R

Sedgemoor baskets for my garden; it cost me 14s. 11d. A few years ago it would have been at most a quarter of that sum. All the basket-makers I have known in the past have been growers *and* makers. In Langport to-day, the withies are still grown but exported to London—like milk. And the large-scale drainage schemes are lowering the water-level of the fen, as they have done along the River Witham (ten feet), at Romney Marsh and the Isle of Axholme, and so lowering the fertility by too quickly carrying off the flood-silt. In the same way, the felling of woods on Cranborne Chase has led to the lowering of the water-table and the level of the springs. I have come to the conclusion that urbanly controlled dealings with the land, however good the intentions, always do and always must do the wrong things in the wrong way at the wrong time. They are so because they are the opposite of the methods and punctuations of husbandry.

But there is hope for Langport. My friend, that husbandman and flax-man who has occupied my thoughts many times in these pages, is establishing a small industry there of growing a very great variety of seeds, of testing, selecting and drying them. He hopes one day to revive the traditional basket-making by way of this business. He has already begun to grow the traditional teazle which is superior to any mechanical device in working up the pile of woollen fabrics.[1] So Langport may yet live again through the vision of this man and save its beauty not through the urban idea of a museum piece but by becoming self-supporting once more on its own work, its own skill and the riches of its own land.

But my Hermitage has something more positive than a piece of country art of which I can only say that it "may live again." For my personal use I have a woven scarf and in the Hermitage no fewer than twenty-seven wools dyed in the fleece. They are evidence of a country industry not reported dead nor a prisoner of war in the hands of big business nor in hospital but actually born into this naughty world. The dyes are all vegetable ones and cover a very wide range, principally native from gorse-flowers, onion skins, ling, bedstraw, elder-berries, sloes, damsons, walnut husks, tormentil root, dandelion root, ivy berries, privet berries, acorns, nettles, lichens, bracken tips. madder. The only foreign dyes are experi-

---

[1] Lord Portsmouth in *Alternative to Death* (Faber; 1943) has written:—"I have seen extremely good coarse cloth made from the peelings of withies used for making baskets. Here is a chance for a new industry to grow side by side with the old one, and, above all, an industry that saves waste."

mental but most are from traditional recipes, while the young craftswomen keep lists of all the dye plants that require mordanted wool with alum, tin, chrome and iron and of those that will dye without a mordant. Now with the growth of confidence, the only mordant used is alum. I can only say that these dyed wools, so soft, pleasing and various, confirm me in my previously held opinion that the old country vegetable dyes beat the modern aniline and chemical dyes every time.

Who are these craftswomen celebrating a birth in the churchyard of rural industries? They are the pupils of the Beaumonts' Senior High School at St. Albans. And where do they get their wool from? The answer is from the hedgerows. This is a sufficiently amazing achievement when you consider that it is not every bush that catches a sheep in passing and that there are precious few sheep to be caught. But the gatherings have been swelled when the girls go away for their holidays and spread the glad news that a new craft is born. Farmers give them bags of wool; aunts and uncles go gathering themselves or send parcels from what few sheep-lands are left. Even New Zealand, Australia and South America have heard the good tidings, this time not to kill a native industry as was their rôle in the past but to act as midwives for its rebirth. The pleasant wool-horde, much of which is extremely dirty, is then very gently washed in plenty of slightly soapy water, rinsed and washed again and then again in the open air, where it is dried. Carding is the next process after the dyeing. This is done entirely by hand, the finished product being far more satisfactory thus than in mechanical carding. This tends to break the wool, especially the long stapled wool of the Shetlands, into short pieces, and there is far less strength in the yarn than when it is hand-carded. Mr. Charles Hills writes me: "I saw a Shetland woman take two pieces of yarn, one hand-carded and hand-spun, the other mill-carded and mill-spun, and break them. The hand-made stuff seemed to stretch interminably and then just come apart. The mill-made stuff stretched a very little and then just snapped like a piece of string."

Carding is heavy work even for adult hands, but the difficulty is overcome by a multiplicity of them. For, while the whole of modern civilization, whether in peace or war, is earnestly occupied with eliminating skill and getting metal hands to do the jobs of human ones, this School is engaged in the very reverse. Its object is more labour not less and the more hands to the work the better for both.

At the Beaumonts' Senior Girls' School, the economics of output per person, which means how much work can be done by how few people in an age when no Government can solve the problem of unemployment except by war, are not considered at all. Even the waste wool is not burned, as modern farming burns its straw, but carefully preserved and used as down for cushions. The spinning is done upon hand-spindles which the children make for themselves with cotton reels and crotchet hooks and even with rubber plugs and wooden skewers. They start from the beginning, and at the end the spun wool is woven into scarves, pochettes, cushion covers and the like. The only mechanics in any of the processing is the machine-spun wool of the warp and this is confined to the first attempts. My scarf, which the mistress who trained these girls has sent me, was the first thing the School made. I shall wear it with pride for its quality and colour, with comfort for its utility.

It shall also be an emblem to me of the England to be. It will come to the conclusion, a mere heresy to-day, that the million years' evolution of the human hand was not for nothing. Whole libraries have been devoted to speculations upon the nature, customs, environment, cranium, society and manner of life of palæolithic man. But there is one thing about him which admits of no controversy. He was distinguished from all animals by the possession of an opposable thumb. With it in the long run he built everything human that exists in the world. Up to the Industrial Revolution and the century that has followed it. The object of that Revolution was to abolish the opposable thumb. But children recall the habits of their ancestors; all honour to the School of St. Albans that it makes good use of what made man into man.

In February, 1943, I paid a visit to an estate in Hampshire. The manor was a mediæval house built of flint and stood several hundred feet up on a swell of the Hampshire Highlands. It took its present shape in 1731 and had a new wing added to it before the war, the flint being collected from the adjacent fields. The knapped and squared flint was empanelled within a Portland freestone casing, the south façade having eighteenth century "Gothick" windows with arched stone frames and keystones. The centre, a semi-hexagon, is entirely of Portland stone, while the long lower windows have straight stone-beards. They resemble the gold face-masks of the dead in the Mycenaean rock-cut tombs. All is bare of ornament except for the heraldic goats rampant and the family coat of arms.

It is thus a Dower House of uncompromising austerity. This is enhanced by a walled kitchen garden flanking the east wing, a mere strip of lawn severed from the countryside only by a ha-ha hedge and by the downs-fashion groves of beech, holly and yew coming up to where banks and borders of flowers might be expected to stand. For an ornamental water there is a frank dewpond. Such a house, fully exposed to wind and weather, is the nurseling and consummate flower of the Downs, built of their very bones. The very ball-finals to the wings are a miniature rendering in stone of the beech clumps. The deep voices of the very fires that draw up from the open hearths within are like the moan of the wind in the beechen tops. I did not know which I liked best, the house from the Downs or the Downs from the house. They are wedded, the Downs to the house being as the foliage to the flower. There was as intimate a relation between them as the stone circle or monolith to heath or hill. I doubt if I have ever seen a house, certainly an eighteenth century one with a modern wing, that had so completely caught the megalithic contact with nature. It was the temple of nature. Like the Cotswold houses, it fitted the rotundities of wold and downland landscape by its very rectangularity. The only departure from the grey monotone of the compact pile were the colours of the squared flints, pink, pinkish grey, white or whiteish, black, purple, buff, buffish pink and pale reddish. Grey it was under the clouds but in the sunlight it sparkled like a great diamond.

The flint-work of the new or restored wing was remarkable. It was just as good, perhaps even a little better, than that of the older building. No finer is the best flint-work of a Roman wall or mediæval church or seventeenth century barn or, except for its plainness, the ornamental flush-work in Norwich, on the Norfolk Heights and along the Broads, where it is exuberant. It was entirely done by a local flint-knapper who took two years at the job. He worked as a foreman under a local builder whose reputation for good workmanship is so firm that he did not even submit a tender. This was yet one more demonstration among the hundreds of examples I have met of a traditional craft being independent of time. Erroneously regarded by the progressive as embedded in the past, it actually is a guarantee of escape from the time-sequence to which the theory of automatic progress is irrevocably committed.

This flint wing was neither new nor old; its bond was with the land, with its own place, not to time. It affords a perfect analogy with my yew armchair, built in the Chippendale style and design by a local chairmaker of my own Downs. But it is sufficiently different to live in its own right and not as an imitation. In both instances you did not imitate a good thing; you went on creating the good thing because you were bred up in the tradition. Just as in a self-supporting garden you inevitably follow nature and yet discipline and direct her thrusting life, so the fields through the intermediacy of the craftsman had built this flint house. This is one of the secrets of a timeless beauty, as it is of a true economics.

So close was man to nature here that I could see from the house the mating gambols of a pair of hares, chasing one another turn by turn. They doubled, they swerved, they turned hair-pin bends, they twisted like eels. Pausing for breath, they sat up and then the hunter became the hunted. So, like the vegetation of that premature spring, the March became the February hare.

From the window at the back of the house could be seen a herd of Ayrshires and a flock of black St. Kilda sheep. The dappled whites of the straight-horned cows and the coal-black or smoky grey of the sheep on the green down were as ornamental as they well could be. Some of these goat-like sheep had four horns, not volutes as on the Horned Western of my own neighbourhood but very irregular, some goatish, others recurved and often at different angles to the forehead. They are agile and light-stepping, alert and tense, as befits natives of the wild. The legs are very thin, the long wool wiry, the face agreeably satanic. But they were not there merely to be looked at. Only the curse of centralization and the money-power prevent these sheep forming the staple of a self-supporting local industry. They are easily crossed with Hampshire Downs and make excellent mutton, while their wool is good for strong rugs or overcoats.

These and many other designs of a kindred self-sufficiency have been the fruitful ambition and life-work of my host. We discussed them. A retired tailor might teach the village to weave cloth from the sheep; a village clinic might be established; home-brew might be encouraged from what was once a barley country; a communal orchard might be planted. It would not be owned communally so that what was the business of all became the business of none. Each shareholder would pay a small rent for a few trees, with an apple-warden in charge. As we discussed these dreams of reality, we were sitting in a library very noble in agricultural and other volumes. It used to be the underground kitchen of the mediæval house. I was drinking mead, brewed in 1935, and I had on my knee two duodecimo seventeenth century books, both with Izaak Walton's signature in them, one being the poems of Charles Cotton who fished the Test with him. Upon them lay open a first edition of Cobbett's caustic "Legacy for Parsons" which I had been reading prior to this conversation, and Cobbett's Uphusband, where he stayed with his friend, Blount, borders another part of the estate.

Here there is a chalk-pit which already employs a few men in chalk-crushing and lime-making and can employ fifteen; here there are osier-beds by the stream which my friend hopes to reclaim for basket-making; here is a little saw-mill that preserves, not destroys, the many stands of fine timber; here are new houses built of the local materials and so in concord with the old. Thus, everything was a single harmony composed of a number of diverse themes like a river enriched by the offerings of many streams or a garden growing many fruits and flowers. As I sipped the mead and felt the calf of the volumes beneath my hand, I was touching and tasting a complex and multiform life gathered into a single moment of time. Past, present and future were harvested into one moment and one place. Nature and man stood in heraldic opposition and communion as God so intended them to be. An epitome and condensation like this in which I enjoyed all while possessing none is surely a greatness of life.

Fortunate the man who owns this house like a jewel on the long finger of the Downs, but more than fortunate in that he has had a great living craftsman to help build it. Fortunate who possesses this vault-like library of old folios, of Columella and Vitruvius, of Vergil's Georgics and the seventeenth century husbandmen, of Izaak Walton and Cobbett, but more than so who has the will to put Cobbett's vision into living practice. Fortunate who can call a piece of that great range with Inkpen on one side and Butser on the other as its bastions his own, the snowdrop-stippled hangers, the alder-fringed stream that Walton fished, the seeded-down fields as green as in May, the whiskered barley and the tasselled oats. But more than so who desires to build from it all and has begun to build a happy community of free, responsible and craftsmanly men to husband it and live by it and make it fairer than it is already. Could it be other than medicinal and benedictive for one's native land to stand on her own feet, self-reliant but not proud, sufficient unto herself but sharing with other lands? In being true to herself she would in the very act be owning obligations to others. Small wonder that the England who has become the very reverse of this England has lost the way of peace. She can be redeemed only by craftsmanship and self-sufficiency, depending upon the eternal values of the eternal God. When they are reunited, all becomes significant, from the flint nugget to the landscape whence it came. In 1175, Robert Grosstête, the son of a Suffolk peasant and Bishop of Lincoln, wrote "Rules" for Margaret, widow of the Earl of Lincoln, "so that he who observes them will be able to live on his means and keep himself and those belonging to him." How much corn, the Rules ask, should there be in any given region for bread, for brewing, for alms, "so that no corn be sold without need"? Self-sufficiency, once a commonplace, a truism of man's daily life, has become a rarity like a choice piece in a museum. The owner of the house of flint on the Downs, who models his estate on the "Rules" of Bishop Grosstête, will be honoured—by posterity. At present, Government penalises the good landlord (as in the Uthwatt Report), not the bad.

The story of Clifton Park is another of these hopeful signs and as convincing a rebuttal as it well could be, and from the technical point of view alone, of the urban and industrial way with the land. What Robert H. Elliot[1] did (he died in 1914) was to convert derelict and exhausted hillside land into that of the highest productivity. His method was to lay it down to four-year leys of deep-rooting grasses and legumes like cocksfoot, lucerne, burnet, chicory, kidney vetch and others. These plants performed a similar function for farming land as double digging does for the garden. In his first season he took two tons of hay per acre off his fields so planted and an aftermath as well. By means of these leys he afterwards established a regular rotation of superfine corn and root crops alternately without using a single ounce of artificial manures. The land (grazed off by sheep) became so exceedingly fertile through the penetrating, aerating and humus-forming qualities of these deep-rooting plants that this typical yeoman was able to discard even the phosphates he had first used on his roots. In his own words:

[1] Elliot's book describing the experiment of Clifton Park was reissued in 1943 with an Introduction by Sir George Stapledon.

"With the aid of liming and a freer and freer use of artificial manures, the decadence thus caused is steadily continuing. And the farmer expects that foreign competition may be met by ever augmenting bills for purchased fertilizers, which will cause the soil still further to decline in fertility, while the agricultural chemist, aided by the manure merchant, is emptying his pockets, and at the same time enabling the farmer to run out the remaining fertility of the soil."

The triumphant success of the Clifton Park experiment in Roxburghshire as a modern adaptation of the peasant principle of self-sufficiency was accomplished with the aim of *cheapness*. But it was not the cheapness of modern economics that wastes the resources of the whole world and yet leaves the people in squalor and penury. The story is all the more remarkable from the fact that Elliot had not discovered the extraordinary benefits of wild white clover. But since the breaking of the subsoil by deep-rooting plants to tap plant-foods from it uses up those foods when farm-products are exported from the farm, it is vitally necessary to couple such wise and pioneer methods with a policy of self-support. Soil-fertility is inseparable from it.

In respect of the use of artificials, the Clifton Park experiment is almost exactly paralleled by a story my estate agent told me in the course of our many conversations. He bought a field of white sand for £3 an acre in Hampshire and nothing would grow on it except the little dwarf geranium. First, he limed it, then sowed it with rye, oats and tares (vetches), and went the whole NPK hog with his doses of artificials. The first year he cut this for hay and sowed it with turnips not for the root but the leaf. This he ploughed in in the autumn, and gave half the dose of artificials once more. Next year he ploughed in the turnips and sowed with mustard. He again ploughed in the autumn and gave a quarter of the artificials. He then sowed again with oats and tares. The following year he sowed with King Edward potatoes without any artificials, took a bumper crop and, being offered another farm, sold the field at £50 the acre. The fact that he did not graze this field nor sow deep-rooting plants to pulverize the subsoil almost proves that he could have made this stupendous revolution in the condition of the soil by using only half or even a quarter of the artificials he actually did use, and quite possibly discarded them the sooner. On the estate he now manages (a large one), he uses no artificials whatever, in spite of the efforts of the County Committee to force sulphate of ammonia and muriate of potash upon him. Yet the land has become so fertile that the officials have desisted.

Both these examples perfectly illustrate the legitimate use of artificials, as the Wiltshire Flax Mill illustrates the legitimate use of machinery. They are a tonic, not a food, and tonics are handy as a stimulus. To live on tonics, as our land is now doing, is, as Elliot called it, the decadence of agriculture, while to the healthy man and the healthy land a tonic is a superfluity. If modern science could disembarrass itself from the limitless use of artificials and return to the only reason for its existence, the search for truth, the authentic husbandry of the garden could survive the modern age. The true gardener neither tames nor exploits nature; he learns her fundamental laws and with love and understanding converts them to that use whose concomitant is always beauty.

It is almost universally held that self-sufficient peasant-gardeners are backward. They need to have their countries industrialized and their farms to be specialized and mechanized. But must they be driven with the whip of artificials and engrossed into larger farms? And has an industrialized and unpropertied society with its millions upon millions of eroded acres, its wage-servitude and un-employment, its ugliness and joylessness, its destitution and mal-nutrition, been so successful that it can afford to preach at peasants? The "Survey of Rural Poverty in America," issued in 1942, gives what I feel to be a convincing answer. The economic typhoon which has beggared so many of the rural areas of the United States makes dreary enough reading. All of a sudden occurs a bright patch which stands apart from the havoc that factory-farming has caused. The golden exception to the tale of economic pillage and economic poverty is the pueblo of Taos near the Rio del Norte in the semi-arid country of New Mexico. It is a village of 800 Indians whose pattern of husbandry (in spite of the natural poverty of the soil) has been in existence without any change, except for extortions and encroachments by the United States and the State of New Mexico, for four centuries. During these centuries it has been and still is a self-supporting farming community whose soil, in spite of its natural disadvantages, has been brought into a high condition of productivity. This has been accomplished, not by experts, agronomes, subsidies, agricultural colleges, bags of sulphate of ammonia and "efficiency," but by the integrated social system and agricultural economy of the people themselves. It is worth while, then, pausing at this antiquated village which manages to take such good care of its own lands and its own affairs.

The community has a communal organization which does not exclude individual possession and responsibility. The reservation covers six square miles. 2000 acres crop grain and alfalfa (lucerne, one of Elliot's deep-rooters) for cattle-feed, 15,000 acres of pasture support 600 horses and mules and 600 dairy cattle, and the rest is devoted to garden-farms of from 2 to 6 acres. These are fenced enclosures growing orchard fruit, vegetables, including melons and sweet potatoes, a small plot of maize and cane sorghum for molasses and stock feed. These plots, together with the woodland, ranch country and arable fields, are owned by the village as a whole and managed by its chosen representatives without any external assistance whatever.

The pasture and arable are the collective concern of the community. But each separate plot or close or toft (as traditional England would call it) belongs to an individual family or household on the sole condition that it should be properly cultivated. It is, in fact, as though, instead of opening my garden annually for the Nurses' Fund, I arranged with my village or Parish Council for an annual inspection of it purely on the grounds of good cultivation. I should also have a voice in the selection and husbandry of the crops I can see from my terrace. The Parish Council of this New Mexican village, elected by ballot or common consent, is a governor, sheriff, alcalde (a magistrate), a war chief and the Council. The Council superintends the rotation of crops, the conservation of the grass and timber for fuel, building, corrals, fencing, etc., and the equipment of the cottagers and husbandmen with tools, rakes, horse-ploughs, harrows, wagons and harness. A tractor, a modern grain harvester and a grist-mill are owned by the village collectively. The springs at the base of a mountain in the parish boundaries are carefully channelled by means of seepage ditches and irrigation courses with wooden lock-gates. Only surpluses are sold as money-crops. The produce, milk, butter and cheese, go first to the villagers themselves, while the money from sales goes to a common fund of which the Council is trustee. The individual farmer also sells his surplus as he chooses, reserving the best yields for his own family. In actual figures, the village produces 90% of its own food, 100% of its fuel,

50% of its own clothing, and 95% of its own recreations, "amenities" and occupations. Since these are based on its agriculture, they are all inter-related and inter-dependent. Taos, that is to say, is an "island of example" of wholeness in the pattern of living.

But what has this remote pocket of life in New Mexico to do with our civilization? Nothing and everything. Nothing because our entire economy is based on the reversal of that of Taos. It has far closer points of analogy with our own open field system whose sole survivor is the village of Laxton in Nottinghamshire and with the peasant farming of the French communes of which my friend the agent has told me much. Everything, because the verdict of the Report is as follows: "As an agrarian institution Taos is definitely more advanced than most of rural America," and again, "The pueblo of Taos contrasts very favourably indeed with general conditions among American farmers during the past couple of decades." Taos, that is to say, is both primitive and "advanced." How can this be so? Because the cardinal prerequisites of all human society in every age—namely, the family, co-operation, individual responsibility, local self-government and contact with the earth—are fulfilled in the social economy and methods of husbandry practised by this Indian village. It exists among the sands of New Mexico, but it is built upon the rock. And I know that my own husbandry in my own garden, however amateurish, is nearer to that of this village ten thousand miles away than it is to the urbanly controlled and expediency farming of the fields I can see from my terrace.

In previous pages,[1] I gave indication of a change of mind and so method in the attitude of the United States to their own land. If nature is regarded as a mechanism only and the coupling of use with beauty a sentimentality, nothing can stop the predatory speeding-up of soil erosion; if a creation as a garden is, the conservation of earth will be man's first thought for himself and his descendants. The self-sufficient mixed farm is the only unit that can stop it, and this kind of farm is conducted on the same organic principles as the cultivation of a garden and on the same self-acting principles as are practised by the Taos village-community.

Of late years this has become so self-evident a truth that even publicized Conferences have come partially to recognize it. The United Nations Conference on Food and Agriculture at Hot Springs in 1943, for instance, had, in spite of the absence from the Board of

[1] See pages 56 and 113.

any of the farming community, sufficient grasp of reality to utter these words:

> "Soil-erosion has in the past destroyed or severely limited the utility of vast areas of land and will in the future, unless checked, constitute the greatest physical danger to the world's food production."

It even went one step further by recommending "balanced mixed rotational farming" as the proper means for preventing the whole earth from slipping away under the feet of humanity. It then proceeded to undo and render void this promising approach to facing world-facts by reverting to the old and seemingly incorrigible habit of modern civilization in putting first things last and last things first. It not merely accepted but welcomed, that is to say, a post-war industrial expansion and large-scale international trade which were the prime cause of the soil-erosion with which the delegates were so "gravely" concerned. So long as the debt system is maintained, (viz.: the payment of interest on loans or investments by way of cheap food), soil-erosion must inevitably be the consequence, and that system accompanies economic expansion and international trade. So long as industrialism is expanded, soil-area must be diminished and soil-productivity exploited. As Jacks and Whyte wrote in *The Rape of the Earth*, "The unprecedented economic expansion during the nineteenth century has been followed by a world-wide biological deterioration of the land." What the Conference gave with one hand they took away with the other, the right hand not knowing what the left hand was doing. It is this fatality of thought rather than the determination to pursue self-interest at any cost which vitiates all land-policy emanating from urban quarters. It is the supreme reason why nothing can be done to save world soil-erosion without a complete change of mind and purpose.[1] In the Hot Springs Conference, that change, even though cancelled by reversion to the old ways of thought, is beginning to take place.

Now for an example of a self-sufficient farm in my own country. Horace is an agricultural labourer who fell off the rick he was thatching and broke his ankle. During his convalescence in the

[1] The only article I have seen which grasped the true meaning of the Hot Springs Conference was one by Mr. Jorian Jenks in the *New English Weekly* of August 26, 1943.

early year, he used to pay me a weekly visit when we would talk over old times together. He is a man of slow deliberate speech and solid country wisdom. Everything he has to say is weighed before it is spoken. He draws his recollections from what seems a bottomless well of variegated experience. His way of seeing life is as a network of associations between man and man, man and beast, beast and land, crop and soil, past and present. The authentic countryman is in a sense the eternal child. His store of memories and his maturity and variety of labours, his sagacity and method of looking at a thing by circling all round it cannot crust over nor bury this essential childlikeness. Horace's round face and blue eyes, even his unhurried, rhythmic and rolling gait of the ploughman, make me think not incongruously of the child in Hans Andersen's *The Emperor's New Clothes*. He would not understand Wordsworth's lament of the loss of the child in the man. It is with the eyes of the child as well as of the seasoned husbandman that he looks steadfastly at the contemporary scene. Nor is he overawed, still less seduced, by its hugeness and noisiness and global complexity, his roots firm in his native soil. In a few simple words, he will penetrate the fallacies and illusions of mass-mentality behind its sky-scraping façade. He holds fast to the matured truths by whose compass he steers his life and his own perception of reality, if circumscribed, is just and searching.

On his first visit, I took him down to my Hermitage. He had not seen it for some years. There was nothing he saw and handled, the horse-gear, the thatching tools, the harvesting tackle, the basketry, the sheep-bells, the utensils of dairy and kitchen, the shepherding apparatus, which failed to be evocative of narrative, reminiscence or technical exposition. They welled up either from his own experience or that of older men he had known or heard about. He brought every exhibit to life again with a touch of his hand or some graphic concrete turn of phrase. This dramatization is of the very essence of the countryman's mind and in direct continuity with the realistic and illustrative speech of the Gospels, which is peasant literature. Men like Horace never leave the fields; they have absorbed them into their innermost beings. So the Christ of the Parables absorbed the country life of Galilee, threading the heavenly and the universal through the needle's eye of the homely particular. Poetry is a by-product of such men's talk, as beauty is a by-product of the craftsman's work. It is not deliberate but an emanation.

How restful to talk to such men! One enters an inner circle of quiet and stability in the midst of our heathenish turmoil, as a man finds refuge from the desert sun under the shade of a tree. They are indeed tree-like. Its many branches are their variety of skills; its roots are their durability and earth-wisdom; its trunk is their solidity and poise. This inner world of daily husbandry, of ploughing and sowing, of growth and harvest and renewal, is remote as the stars from the outside one of war and the industrialism which inevitably leads to it and has brought to pass the fear and prophecy of Shakespeare that men would tear each other "like monsters of the deep." While the foundations of the third World War are being well and truly laid, Horace looks forward to sowing the spring barley.

He was fond of giving me glimpses of a self-sufficient farm of twenty years ago where he had been a cowman. The sheer tenacity and self-sacrifice of its owner had saved this small yeoman's farm from the dereliction of pre-war farming England and the drive towards mechanical cow-keeping or "large-scale economic units" of specialized money-crops. It is not clearly understood that these small yeoman farms suffered almost as heavily under the Enclosures as did the peasantry which was virtually wiped out by them. Now these farms are themselves in danger of extinction from a further extension of the Enclosures, with business men and economists of the Left in place of landlords as the aggressors.

It was, of course, a mixed farm and entirely self-supporting. The cattle and ewes were fed on trifolium, on sown mixtures of peas, beans and oats cut for hay just after flowering and when the legumes were podding. In Horace's view, there was no milk-producer like this crop, better than all the cheap feeding stuffs and foreign concentrates that contained you knew not what but probably the germs of cattle-diseases. Another crop his farmer used to grow was "a land of green thatches." "Land," he used in the old meaning and "thatches" were a cultivated form of the trailing everlasting pea mown by the scythe or, when lodged, by the "thrower-out." This "land," which came in handy before the early bite of spring grass, was always dressed by the water that washed down the cows, mixed with their urine by means of the chain wheel-pump. According to Horace, there was no fertiliser like it. Nothing was used on the farm except this and the muck-cart. There were also clover leys and seeds mixtures, together with roots. For the sheep the beans were threshed out with the "frail" (flail) which always left a few beans in the "kids" (pods), and the ewes fed it from the sheep-racks, mixed with the haulm. Everything had some use, nothing was wasted. The oat and bean-straw went through the chaff-cutter, the roots were pulped, the peas and beans ground and mixed with meal. The cattle were given a "bait" of a layer of chaff, a layer of corn and a layer of pulped roots, wheat being used sparingly, a bucket to a sack of beans. The owner of this "obsolete" farm would not have been impressed by the advanced farming that has taken its place and can think of nothing better to do with its straw than burn it.

Not a single beast was lost from disease. This is a sufficient contrast from to-day when mastites, Johne's disease, tuberculosis, contagious abortion and sterility, whose ravages science with all its serums and prophylactics is powerless to prevent, have become the nightmare of the farmstead. Nor was the stamina of the dairy-cow undermined over a long period by forcing for milk-yields. The cowmen of those days, like the shepherds, were their own vets.[1] The mishaps of sheep, cows and horses were righted not by book but empirical knowledge born of close and unremitting observation of their habits. Clover-blown sheep, for instance, were cured, not by Gabriel Oak's method in Far from the Maddening Crowd, but by an ounce of pepper in a pint of cold water. If a cow's milk was rancid, he would guess that it had been eating mayweed. Another thing I noted about Horace's farm was its unwritten law about mixed stock on the leys and pastures. The big teeth of the horses, the little teeth of the sheep, the tongues of the cows, all grazed and so manured the sward in a different way and performed different functions. This untutored knowledge was in unconscious accord with the expert analysis of the benefits conferred by mixed grazing in Michael Graham's Soil and Sense.

The earth-scholarship of this yeoman and his men was encyclo-pædic. Its practice was an unformulated and illiterate application of the famous Howard scientific formula—healthy soil means healthy plants, healthy plants mean healthy animals and healthy both mean healthy men. He constantly referred to my own criterion for testing the quality of food, namely by taste. One can but imagine (in these days) what the milk tasted like when it was so thick that a penny could be laid on its surface without sinking. If agricultural science had not taken the wrong turning and deserted field-observa-

[1] Fifty years ago, the cattle cured themselves or were cured of foot-and-mouth disease. Now they are killed for it.

tion, it might have developed an articulate and reasoned development of this traditional husbandry of self-support.

Perhaps the most significant thing in Horace's narrative of this yeoman farm, kept in fertility by organic methods only, were its yields. The average yield of oats was 9 quarters per acre and of wheat 7 or 8, while the same for hay was 30 cwts. With all the machinery and bags of chemicals, all the accumulated fertility of arable tumbled down to grass between 1920 and 1939, all the natural richness of the heavy wheat and bean land of my region, the average yield of cereals is only 4 to 5 quarters per acre, often less, while a ton of hay is considered a good crop and 15 cwts. a fair one. So steep a drop entirely confirms the comparative figures I gave on p. 204 as to the superiority in quantity of yield per acre of husbandry or peasant farming over modern urbanly controlled mechanized farming with a scattering of key men and gangs of unskilled labourers at the peak seasons.[1]

From yields we passed on to cultivations. On this yeoman farm the single-furrow plough four times was used. It took longer to cover a field than the multiple plough, but set up a sharp ridge from which the soil trickles into the furrow to make a tilth. So the spade-digger in the garden sets up his spits so that the weather can get all round them, and the frosts pulverize them. The multiple plough, used once or twice, sets up a flat and so tilthless ridge. In harrowing, the practice of making good use of few resources in contradistinction from making bad use of generous ones was exemplified by laying a sheep-hurdle on the ground and interweaving blackthorn bushes between the bars with a stout gate-post tied in on top. Horace maintained that the old bush-harrow was far better for scouring pastures and removing moss after a wet

[1] In respect of modern yields of cereal crops per acre, it is interesting that the five farms of the Mackaness family who have farmed Northamptonshire land for 250 years, cropped in 1943 between eight and nine quarters of wheat per acre, ten of oats and eight and a half of barley. The reasons for such high yields that about or nearly equal those of Horace's yeoman farm and are considerably higher than the average yields of modern mechanised farms are as follows:—(1) a fair supply of labour: the farms of 1500 acres in all employ 70 men, women and boys. This works out at just less than 1 person per 21 acres as compared with 1 man per 33 acres for the whole kingdom. (2) Variety of crops: the three cereals together with beans, peas, potatoes, roots, greenstuffs, fruit and seeds mixtures. (3) The yarding of 300 store cattle and the heavy use of farmyard manure for which farmyard manure spreaders, previously unknown to this country, are used. (4) Frequent cultivations and (5) As much self-sufficiency as modern centralisation allows. Thus the market produce is distributed to local towns, and the farms maintain their own hedger, carpenter, blacksmith, repair and other workshops. All this is traditional farming adapted to modern conditions. The famous Surfleet Estate of Captain Wilson is, of course, a somewhat similar example.

T.P.E. S

winter than the modern link-harrow. But of course the values of
this self-supporting craft-husbandry went far beyond technique. It
regarded the land as a garden. It was an outlet both for a natural
self-esteem and an intuitive art-sense. The art-forms of peasant
self-expression only degenerated when the intimate relationship with
nature was submerged under the scientific-commercial concept of
"the conquest of nature." Modernization should have meant the
conscious development of this craft-husbandry.

When my rose-walk was blown down by the hurricanes of early
1943, I went up to the crest of the hill for some whitethorn poles.
There a gigantic thorn-hedge, nearly twenty feet high, was being
"plushed" by a couple of land-girls and the manor gardener in
charge. The job was being creditably done because the man was a
gardener, but only as a temporary expedient to keep the shade off
the corn. The conversion of pasture into arable has thus made great
demands on the hedger. Why not then make provision for the few
hedgers left to train apprentices? But we have been accustomed for
a century now to look out of the window, as Cobbett said, for other
people to bring us our food and drink, and it occurred to nobody
to put this obvious measure into action. What was done was to
employ this gardener and his girls to plush this one hedge and to
give the foreman of a ditching gang the task of instructing pupils
in the craft of hedging. After all, ditch and hedge are usually next
to one another. Meanwhile, the professional hedgers were sent into
the coal-mines.

This is the modern "efficiency," but it was not Horace's. He
always used the tough and durable whitethorn for staking his sheep-
folds on turnips. The sheep Horace penned or let into the spring
corn to feed down winter-proud crops and feed up the soil on which
they grew and to consolidate the lighter lands with the "golden
hoof." They were Oxford Downs, our local sheep, sturdy and mus-
cular and "almost as big as a donkey." They are good sheep for
roots because, as Horace said, "they aren't afraid of getting their
noses dirty." But the arable sheep have been driven off the land
because the price they fetch is not worth the keep. "There is no great
future for arable sheep," said the Ministry, when approached by the
National Sheep-Breeders' Association. And no great future for the
fields they no longer feed on. The sheep on arable one very rarely
does see are grass-sheep which don't like getting their noses dirty,
eat only half the turnip and are often succeeded by wireworm. The

Oxfords (black-faced like Suffolks but, unlike them, with wool round their faces) ate down the roots. Only a two-tined turnip-pecker, such as I have in my Hermitage, was needed to fork out the fragments, while the roots left in the ground by grass-sheep are wasted. These Oxfords, now almost extinct in my region, threw a fleece of 10 lbs., 2 or 3 lbs. heavier than average since a tod (28 lb.) was the usual reckoning for four fleeces. On the ground of cheapness, our wool was then imported from Australia, the usual rake-off for all imports being taken by the shipping company and the dealing and distributing interests. With our own undersold arable sheep went the shepherds. The grass-sheep fed to roots were in charge of farmers who had other things to do than look after them, even if they knew how to. So, just as Darwin connected cats with clover, Horace connected ovine foot-rot with modern economics.

Thus, a true self-sufficiency can only come from resettlement of the land under equitable economic conditions. The land cries out for at least, at very least, a million and a half more men, not to come and go but to stay. It has been calculated that the conversion of farmyard manure and wastes into humus would alone permanently employ 300,000 men. To flit is expediency farming; to stay garden-husbandry, and this is the choice that confronts the futures of all nations, and most particularly our own. Only thus can the enormous facilities of transport and distribution play a due and ordered part in a true economy. Namely, by the swift exchange of surpluses conducted under a monetary system in ratio to productive power and rescued from misuse for profit in being issued by the Banks. The abstractions of the economists are pitted against the realities of the fields. To put the Beveridge Report before a decision like this is not for Moses to lead the children of Israel out of bondage but for Esau to lose his inheritance for a mess of potage.

In February, an official speaker turned up at our village to form a Produce Association, and he proposed that a Committee should be formed with chairman, vice-chairman, secretary and treasurer, the treasure consisting in half a crown subscription. To what end? To revive the Parish Council? To reanimate the defunct village industries? To encourage apprenticeship for thatching and other necessary industries? To advise the villagers to grow buckwheat and maize on their allotments for chicken feed? To persuade them to plant fruit-trees along the lanes and byroads of the parish for parish consumption and with a small parish rate for upkeep? To propose the rebuilding or reconditioning of the village windmill, so that the farmers of the parish might grind their corn at it and not only save the cost of transport and the expenditure of petrol but improve out of all comparison the quality of the village dietary? Or to encourage the gardeners and allotment-holders to make compost heaps or to suggest an arrangement with the neighbouring market town to receive its waste for the local fields?

None of these things. What this paternal official was anxious to impress upon his audience was the desirability of growing its own vegetables—which they had done since the village was mentioned in Domesday Book—and the advantage of the half-crown subscription for purchasing artificial manures at 16/- instead of 20/- a cwt. Since my neighbourhood is one mainly of small farmers who keep cows, the more serious gardeners and allotment-holders already receive all the farmyard manure they want. Could the speaker suggest some arrangement for disposing of the surplus of the vegetables and fruit that were already grown? This completely nonplussed him, and the meeting broke up in mutual bewilderment. He did not understand Cato's maxim that "a good husbandman should be a seller rather than a buyer." For myself, the meeting was a tragi-comic revelation of the great gulf fixed between our urban civilization and the rural community it despotically rules. Yet it is upon self-sufficiency that the future of our nation depends. There is no alternative to it but the struggle for foreign markets whose final consequences are the world-wars—which make it a matter of life and death for the nations waging them to be self-supporting. The story of this abortive Produce Association[1] is, in fact, paralleled by that of the Hot Springs Conference. In both, there is the illogic of an imperfect grasp of reality but in both there is a recognition of that reality.

It is for those few who are not blinded to this reality and still believe in free will to avoid the fatalism whether of optimism or despair. Travelling in my neighbourhood one day, I saw a sight that would have rejoiced the heart of Cobbett. It was a Cattle Pound of baled straw with a neat coping of thatch two feet above the six-foot walls and very similar in technique and appearance to the thatching of the traditional wichert walls, highly characteristic of my region. The break in the continuity was only in the material

[1] I believe that this Association under more local direction has of late greatly improved its ideas and methods.

used. There were two entrances with the end-walls gabled and the enclosed square covered perhaps half an acre of meadow. It stood there on the flat plain like the Bronze Age Cattle Pound outside Llewelyn Powys's cottage on the Dorset Downs between White Nose and Chaldon Herring. But if that cattle-pen of earth was hard to decipher in its history and purposes, not so this cattle-pen of straw. In the agricultural depression between 1920 and 1939, one by one the cattle-yards fell into disuse and the muck-treading bullocks became "uneconomic." This straw-yard was a substitute for them, with the same end in view—to fertilize the fields. It was the sign of a return to husbandry and self-sufficiency. It confessed the failure of artificial manures to do without natural manures. It was a novelty that was very old and in it the cattle would once more tread the straw.

The garden may be looked upon as the cell or embryo of all these converging lines of reality. When a man goes into his garden and forks up his leeks to carry into the house to be cooked, he is a Ministry of Health in himself; he is making a stand against that absolute and totalitarian State to which nation after nation has surrendered, and the destruction of which is our only spiritual stand-by in the war. He is making an implicit protest against that industrialism whose only end *can* be the totalitarian State, as we by imitating it more and more are logically demonstrating. He is asserting the principles of traditional English liberty. He is cutting himself loose by the plunge of his fork and the stride of his foot from the whole complex of world-transported cheap imported foods at the cost of the soil, the farmer, his own country, the country he exports to and the value of the food. He is making his comment upon the pre-war arrangements whereby Durham miners were extracting coal exported to Denmark for which Denmark paid in butter, eggs and bacon which could and should have been produced in Durham. He is expressing a shattering opinion upon a situation which, to take milk alone, was before the war importing each year 67,000,000 gallons of machine-skimmed condensed milk and 32,000,000 gallons of skimmed milk powder into the finest dairy-country in the world and bringing to the hapless consumers what has been called "partial starvation." This partial starvation was hardly alleviated by the deliberate destruction (to keep the price up) of 570,000 wagons of grain, 420,000 wagons of grain used as fuel,

140,000 wagons of rice, 267,000 sacks of coffee and 56,000,000 lbs. of meat in 1933 alone.

If he is lifting onions, he is bringing the attack still closer home. Of all the onions eaten by this nation before the war, only 2% were home-grown. No matter what he grows for his own table, he is swinging an axe at the root of that system which only yesterday was importing 82% of our wheat flour, 90% of our butter, 70% of our cheese, and 75% of our fruit.[1] All of them we could have grown with incomparably superior results ourselves. But perhaps the most remarkable thing of all he is doing is to reassert the principle and reaffirm the significance of what religion and economics have in the past asserted and affirmed to be the greatest human reality on earth. This is Home. Socialists, States, combines and finance have been united in despising and undermining it. But it remains true that there is no place like home.

[1] Into a country where hundreds of thousands of acres were poisoned by rabbits, were imported before the war 100,000 cwts of fresh and 200,000 cwts. of frozen rabbits per annum. In 1900, half a million gallons of cider were imported from U.S.A., while our apples rotted on the trees. In 1938, we imported 12 million tons of fresh fruit, all of which we could and ought to have grown ourselves. Even during the war we imported (in 1943) 275,000 turkeys from Ireland, while the home-breeders were forbidden enough food for them.

CHAPTER TWELVE

THE GARDEN OF ENGLAND

"The whole material universe is an expression and incarnation of the creative energy of God, as a book or a picture is a material expression of the creative soul of the artist. For that reason, all good and creative handling of the material universe is holy and beautiful, and all abuse of the material universe is a crucifixion of the body of Christ. The whole question of the right use to be made of art, of the intellect and of the material resources of the world is bound up in this. Because of this, the exploitation of man or of matter for commercial uses stands condemned, together with all debasement of the arts and perversions of the intellect. If matter and the physical nature of man are evil, if they are of no importance except as they serve an economic system, then there is nothing to restrain us from abusing them as we choose—nothing, except the absolute certainty that any such abuse will eventually come up against the unalterable law and issue in judgment and destruction."

DOROTHY SAYERS.

A GARDEN is many things, a piece of man but also of nature, a text-book of economics, a stronghold of liberty, a means of safe-guarding the principle of person, a vent for craftsmanship, a nurse of character, a condition of health and physical maintenance, a poem and a prayer : in brief, a way of keeping body and soul together.

Through my smatterings of knowledge I perceive these things. So I venture to write a garden book, though every book I have read about gardens, even the more elementary, knows a great deal more than I do. But I cannot regard a garden as utilitarian only or merely a pleasance. My idea of it thus takes in the family farmer, in so far as he obeys the principle of use and beauty in his cultivation, and indeed all farms both great and small which so do. So regarded, the farm or garden is, I have been led to see, a miniature of the whole Creation, as the earth itself is. For the combination of these two principles of use and beauty is part, at any rate, of what Miss Sayers calls "the unalterable law" of the mysterious being in ourselves and the universe.

This conception of the garden or farm is now considered as

out of date.[1] But there are still many gardeners to keep soil and person intact against the corruption of the modern world. That corruption has gone so deep that it is hard to see how it can recover; the more imperative is it for the gardener to cultivate his garden. He is the base of the society of to-morrow. For he and his like obey the primary laws of nature and within himself. His private ownership has the sanction of millennia and the voice of the wise men. His responsibility is the first condition of man's moral and his usefulness of man's physical being, while the beauty he creates is part of the whole visible universe.

It is often said that we are a nation of gardeners and as such easily overtop all other nations. But it is seldom asked why this is so. I have no doubt myself that this passion for gardening is a legacy from our pre-industrial past. Then we were a self-supporting nation based on peasants, yeomen and squires with our roots deep in our native soil. But we have in us also that streak of mercantilism which, since the eighteenth century, has gone to extreme and unbalanced lengths and developed into an intricate and all-powerful usury. It has landed us in a succession of major wars and now bids fair to crush our culture by means of our civilization. Some of the more pregnant words written by Sir George Stapledon in *Disraeli and the New Age* (1943) were: "If every country of the world were as nearly as possible self-supporting . . . then one of the chief causes of war would have been eliminated." Our culture has grown out of our rural traditions; our civilization is a top-heavy superstructure which is antagonistic to it. Unless we check it, it will be our ruin. And it is from these rural and country town traditions, surviving to-day only in our garden sense, the small farmer and small business class, now persecuted by big business and bureaucracy, a handful of writers and thinkers and the dumb uneasiness of a very large number of Englishmen, that we derive our love of personal liberty, regional independence and constitutional government. We derive from them, too, a power of craftsmanship and skilled labour that was once second to none in the world-records of the arts and crafts. Inseparable from these was a predilection for variety, and indeed eccentricity. Of these self-

[1] The expansive post-war economic policy outlined by Mr. Cromwell in the August (1943) number of *Horizon* discusses among other stirring themes the industrialisation of the "backward" peoples. One of them is the Arabs—"One factor militating against economic advance is that the Koran forbids the lending out of money on interest." Progress must also reckon with Christianity, which is, or was, just as reactionary.

sufficiency is the necessary framework and quality the necessary outcome. With these endowments and their seed-bed in a bountiful nature, we did indeed make England a garden. In the reinterpretation of the individual garden I have attempted, I am thus reaffirming the values of those rural traditions which for years have been at the point of death from the hands of that excess mercantilism whose issue has been the "great wens."

How then can our England be remoulded into a garden in tune with those rural traditions that are our life-blood? I can only lay down here a few practical suggestions in broad outline. The foundation of this real England is self-sufficiency. Can it be accomplished? In spite of a shortage of labour serious enough in view of war-needs but made artificially extravagant by official incompetence and ignorance of agriculture, we are producing 65 per cent of our own food. We are doing so in spite of the official encouragement given to the distributing interests which hamper the producer at every turn, in spite of the waste of time in compelling farmers to do unnecessary clerical work, in spite of excess taxation on their produce and in spite of the farmers' lack of any confidence in Government pledges. At the same time, our yields under excess mechanization and the inevitable fall of fertility it causes, have declined and are declining from what they used to be. If in such circumstances and under such handicaps we can raise two-thirds of our own food, what could we not do under a system of intense cultivation that conserved the high natural richness of our soils, with abundant labour, under the equitable economic condition of standard prices for produce and a family farming fostered by Government and protected from financial exploitation? China with her poorer soils but by a traditional composting maintained for forty centuries has been able to feed three persons per acre. She was able to support 1783 people per square mile in comparison with North America's 61. Could we not feed our whole population from our greatly superior soils at the rate of one person per three-quarters of an acre by extending our composting from garden to farm and organizing town-tips, wastes and refuse for distribution upon the fields instead of as now wasting millions of tons of potential humus by discharging them down the rivers into the sea? The answer is perfectly clear: we could and with a comfortable margin.[1] If we do not, it

[1] Mr. F. Sykes, to whom I referred on p. 113, has said—and he speaks from experience of what can be done on his own farm: "When the whole of the farms of England are

is only because finance comes before the health and prosperity of our people. It is only because we prefer making money to gardens.

But England cannot thus become self-supporting without reforming her economic system. The nation, therefore, must recover the issue of credit from private monopoly and according to the productive capacity of her people. But the State, as Germany has proved, can be an even greater monster than the private interest. Thus, the State, after regaining its former control over the issue of money, should delegate powers to provincial credit-bodies empowered to issue money free of usury but not necessarily of a small interest for the all-important task of financing agricultural and industrial works, each in its own region. It is the business of the State to establish fair prices and to control imports in such a way that they do not overbear the home market. It should distinguish between national and provincial undertakings in all its operations. Matters like the regulation of markets, sewage disposal, the checking of food-adulteration and the like, the maintenance of security for the cultivator, reclamation, highways, land-purchase and other national concerns, these are for State supervision.[1] Its main function is in fact the guardianship of individual and regional responsibility and to use its powers for penalizing irresponsibility. It is needless to point out that the modern State, of which Germany is the most notorious example, misuses its powers by depriving individuals and communities of their liberties, their properties and their responsibilities. England cannot become a garden once more until all three are seen to be integral parts of one thing.

But how is industrialism, that inveterate enemy of a gardened England, to be controlled? First, by finding its best customer in the home market. The exchange of surpluses on the lease-lend principle is its only true business abroad and the only method of avoiding international friction culminating in world-wars. Secondly, by decentralization. This means rebuilding industries in proper relation to agriculture instead of accepting an industrialism detached from the land as inevitable and in improper relation to finance. Because of the variety of our soils, vegetation and weather, this infers a natural division into regions managed by self-government.

farmed with compost . . . there is not the slightest doubt that we can grow enough food here . . . to sustain a population more than twice that in Britain to-day." Colonel Pollitt in *Britain Can Feed Herself* is equally sure of our powers of supporting ourselves.

[1] Mr. Boothby in *The New Economy* suggests 3 post-war State controls: (1) the State issue of money; (2) control of capital for export; and (3) control of imports.

A prosperous agriculture demands a large and varied number of industries *dependent upon it*, and these can be developed in training centres, on estates and central farms. The Danish Folk High Schools have shown the authentic way in education to this end. Facilities must be given for apprenticeship to existing craftsmen, for part-time work on farms, for the acquisition of literary and historical values. Ours are dyed in the rich associations of our own land, far richer than Denmark's and what Denmark did we can do.

I once heard Miss Edith Olivier describe how the individual and integrated life of her little mayoral town, Wilton, fell to pieces when the Wiltonians and the Wylie Valley villagers no longer sent their sons and daughters to be apprenticed at the 300-years-old Felt Mill. Here was a true interdependence between market town and village, a microcosm of the true interdependence between town and country. The market town binds the villages together by receiving their surpluses both in people and things; the regional centre binds the market towns, the capital binds the regions, and as a region is to its capital, so is a nation to the world. This natural adjustment between town and country, where the urban industry both depends upon and feeds it with commodities which it needs, is a formidable check upon the cancer-like growth of industrialism. A third has been put forward by Mr. Walter Elliot in respect of the future of those heavy industries that would still remain. I mention it here because it is highly relevent to all I have written about the contrast between skilled and fluid labour. We have to recreate "the industrial peasant." "The man with a skill is the man with a craft; he is the peasant in overalls." "The industrial peasant's plot" is his fashioning of and control over his material in the factory. Here is the old Guild system reaffirmed, the only urban counter to industrial slavery.

All these possibilities rest upon the fertility of the soil. Our true model here is not the old America of the dust bowl (which we are now imitating) but the new America of soil-conservation. To guarantee that fertility we need to return all wastes, to rotate our crops, to increase our livestock. Sir George Stapledon's "alternate husbandry" of short-and long-term leys is a modern adaptation and development of traditional peasant practice. But it is futile without livestock, especially sheep and without cereals. It is also futile so long as meat, wheat and other products are exported from the farm *without return* for the obvious reason that they take part of the soil-fertility with them. Since this milk, corn and meat ulti-

mately find their way to the sea by our fatal sewage system, we have
(1) to reform that system and (2) restore a measure of fish products
to the soil, as my friend, the husbandman, has suggested. What is
certain is that the issues of fertility and a self-supporting economy
are one. The political nucleus of such local husbandry is the village
and its Parish Council, for the village is "the cradle of the nation."
The economic nucleus is the family farm, not excluding large-scale
farming where the region is more suitable for it, and apprenticeship
both for holdings and crafts.[1] Forestry is as much a part of such
local husbandry as a hedge is part of a farm or garden. It should be
the concern either of the local estate or of the central farm (they are
the natural orbits of a cluster of family farms) or of the Parish
Council. The distribution of small ownership cannot be effective
without some such hub or core *on the spot*, for buying seeds, for
marketing, for the maintenance of proper equipment, for supplying
machinery and for apprenticeship. Each region or division of a
region might well be suited to different forms of local authority.
But all finally depends upon the fertility of the soil, and if the social
structure or the authority or the technical methods pursued impair
that fertility, something is wrong with them. They must be changed
to suit the soil, since all health and all life depend upon the life and
health of the good earth.

This last is by far the most important innovation-return we have
to make for the all-sufficient reason that the life of mankind on
earth will end without making it. The profligacy of modern civilization is not only gambling up the earth's fecundity but its own
resources for recharging it. Only one county (Hampshire) has made
(in 1943) 1000 tons of compost from 3 in. sewage sludge sandwiched
between 18 in. surplus straw. Seven towns now make this compost,
including Southampton, which from spending £10,000 a year getting rid of its sludge now makes 3000 tons of compost with it at a
cost of 10/5d. for delivery on the farm. Only two towns outside
Hampshire (Maidenhead and Leatherhead) have adopted the system
of "activating sewage-sludge" for use on the fields instead of waste
in the sea, and only 1 per cent or less has attempted to convert its

---

[1] Part-time work for industrial workers on a farm, in a garden, or a workshop should
be an essential of education. The Welsh miner, Mr. B. L. Coombes, has, for instance,
made a gallant experiment of clearing a holding on the mountain above the mine, producing his own milk, butter and vegetables. He wants to see all the desecrated land of
the mining area reclaimed by his fellow miners in 12-acre holdings. He is in fact the
pioneer of a saner future.

town-tips and garbage into good compost. In all the others destructors and incinerators are, in the words of the author of *Cleanliness and Godliness*, "burning up the land on which we live." Government has consistently shown itself hostile or indifferent to the tentative efforts of a few local authorities to utilize town-wastes for the renewal of the soil; it would have to face the organized pressure of the chemical combine and the heavy industries that manufacture chemical by-products if it encouraged them. But at least these seven towns have shown the way of redemption. As this titanic issue of soil-fertility becomes more and more urgent, their example is bound to be followed, no matter how ponderous the weight of the Interests against it. Here is the most fruitful of all the returns the town can make for the food and drink the country supplies it.

All these issues are severely realistic. They may be looked at from the angle of nutrition and quality, of social harmony, of the preservation of the person as a responsible agent, of creative activity, of variety as against quantitative standardization, or of freedom and craftsmanship as against machine-minding and the fluidity of gang-labour. All are implicit and involved in the concept of a garden which, as I have tried to expound it, is the concept of home and stability. Perhaps they can all be integrated into one term among them which includes them all, namely quality. In his presidential address to the Fellows of the National Institute of Agricultural Botany in 1943, that wise husbandman to whom I have so often referred in these pages remarked:

"Quality in food is something more than calories, dry matter or starch equivalent. We can evaluate fuel in calories and timber is rich in dry matter, but no one would suggest that they are foods. Nor is starch alone a satisfactory food. We can assess quantities but we are lacking in a standard or standards for a real valuation of all those complex and often subtle characteristics that constitute quality."

But this same quality is something more than a material factor, whether applied to food or soil or work to produce the one from the other. It is ultimately a spiritual element, and so the gardener who works his plot for quality cannot avoid the one side of Miss Sayers's synthesis in dwelling upon the other.

I quote here from a letter I received from a L.C.C. school teacher which I think justifies this contention:

"My experience has shown that children in early childhood have sound instincts. They cling to their parents, brothers and sisters and home. . . . They learn by making and doing . . .; they have a great interest in growing things. I have taught retarded children and gardening has sometimes roused the dullest child. It is always their own bit of land and what they have planted and watered themselves that gives them most joy. . . . Modern life seems always to cater for the exception. There are some bad parents, so build more nursery schools, so that parents become worse through not practising their craft. Some people spoil their own land, their own business and their own craft, so take the land, business and craft from most men who naturally care for what is their own. . . . We are made up of soul and body and have neglected religion for the soul, and the land and crafts for the body and its welfare."

This is one of the best counters to collectivism as the illusory remedy for the ills of our age I have read. For collectivism is as great an enemy to the true gardener as a predatory individualism. Only when a nation of responsible property-owners, large and small but mostly small, cultivates its own land as a garden can it recover its soul from bureaucracy and industrialism.

A wise thing was said by the Austrian rural poet, Adalbert Stifter, who lived in the first half of the nineteenth century:

"The breeze of the air, the gentle flow of water, the growth of corn, the waves of the sea, the vegetation of the earth, the bright sky and the shining stars—all these I consider great. The thunder-storm, the flash of lightning which destroys the homes of men, the volcano, the earthquake, all these manifestations I do not consider greater than those mentioned before. I consider them smaller because they are only the indications of much higher laws. The power that makes the milk boil over in the pot of a poor woman is the same that forces up the lava of the volcano."

He goes on to draw an analogy with the human race. A life of

simplicity and reasonable self-limitation, surrounded by the enjoyment of beauty, is great; the life of violent emotions, revenge,
hatred, revolutionary dynamics, inflammable action, these are
smaller. The comment of the editor is that these reflections express
the serenity of man who accepts a life limited in scope but with
eternity and its creation about him. They could not be more applicable both to the life of the gardener and to that strange story of
the choice of the Lord of the Universe to dwell within the household
of a peasant-craftsman.

A letter I received from my friend, Adrian Bell, illustrates what
the Austrian poet means by his picture of a small estate managed
like a garden :

> "I say, what a fine thing a little country estate is! . . . The 65
> Red Polls winding in procession through the park to the milking;
> the village church just over the wall, its one bell ringing out of
> the old round tower. We shall never see anything so fine in the
> world again, John, so seemly, so civilised, so essentially England.
> And then I think of the industrial politicians ruling all that—
> ruling it all out, I suppose hardly noticing it. The obvious pride
> of the dairy herdsman in his Red Polls was the complete answer
> to them or any blue-print Utopian, if ever they wanted or would
> wait for a human answer."

In an extremely dilapidated village some miles from where I
live there is a plain and beautiful little church with a homely
weatherboarded tower. It contains within it box pews with Tudor
hinges, a thirteenth century nave, a very ornamental crusader's
tomb, with cusped and crocketed ogee canopy surmounted by a
carved finial and exceptionally fine work on the buckles of the
armour, a stately Norman basin-font, a Renaissance tomb of the
richest decoration, a carved three-decker Jacobean pulpit and superb
fragments of stained glass in all the windows and lancets. A church
that is simplicity itself and situated in one of the remotest villages
of a featureless plain has been adorned and enriched with the most
lavish workmanship of six centuries.

Close to the church is a thatched and weatherboarded barn whose
porch has two orders of Early English pointed arches. The intimacy
and interchange between husbandry and religion were here so
unobtrusively profound that it would never have occurred to

twenty-five generations of villagers who lived in this place to separate them. In this wholeness of work with worship, the tillage of the earth was made sacramental, the offices of the church realistic. The church had its feet on the earth, the barn its roof-tree in heaven. Body and spirit accepted one another; they were not parted each at the other's expense. So was accomplished the saying of old John of Salisbury in 1154: "The Prince is the head, the Church is the heart, and Farming is the feet upon which the whole stands and moves." But when I came to the village, the decline of the emptied church had accompanied that of the disused barn for so long a period that both were falling to pieces. The disintegration of rural life had proceeded step by step with the impotence of the church; separation had spelt decomposition to both. Only by their inter-acting recovery can the desperation of our days, foretold in *King Lear*, be removed.

I do not see how they can be reunited except by extending the idea of the individual garden to that of the garden of the world. Whether the testimony be regarded as mythology or the symbolism of reality (as I regard it), it was surely not without meaning that the first news of God upon earth was as walking in a garden and the last news was the same.

THE END